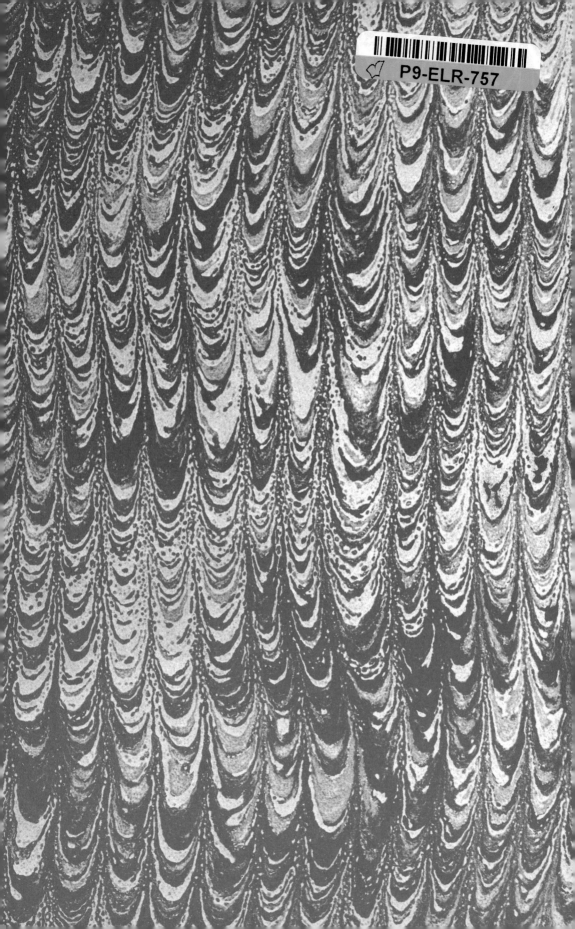

THE

EVENTFUL HISTORY

OF THE

MUTINY AND PIRATICAL SEIZURE

OF H. M. S.

BOUNTY:

ITS CAUSE AND CONSEQUENCES.

———————

ILLUSTRATED BY SIX ETCHINGS FROM ORIGINAL DRAWINGS
BY LIEUT.-COLONEL BATTY.

———————

LONDON:

JOHN MURRAY, ALBEMARLE-STREET.

MDCCCXXXI.

Capn Bligh

Sir John Barrow

The Mutiny of the Bounty

edited by Gavin Kennedy

David R. Godine · Publisher · Boston

First U.S. edition published in 1980 by
DAVID R. GODINE, *Publisher*, Inc.
306 Dartmouth Street
Boston, Massachusetts 02116

Library of Congress Cataloging in Publication Data

Barrow, John, Sir, bart., 1764-1848.
  The mutiny of the Bounty.

  1. Pitcairn Island.   2. Bounty (Ship)
I. Kennedy, Gavin.   II. Title.
DU800.B3   1980   996'.18   80-66459

ISBN 0-87923-343-5

REVERSE OF FRONTISPIECE: Facsimile of title page
from the first edition of *The Eventful History of
the Mutiny and Piratical Seizure of HMS Bounty:
its cause and consequences*, published by John
Murray, London, 1831.

FRONTISPIECE: Portrait of William Bligh by J. Smart.

Printed in the United States of America

Contents

Color Plates

NOTE: *The page numbers given are those opposite the color plates, or, in the case of a double-page spread, those either side of the plate.*

Introduction

Sir John Barrow's *Eventful History of the Mutiny and Piratical Seizure of HMS Bounty: its cause and consequences* was first published anonymously in 1831 by John Murray in his popular Family Library series. It went through several editions in the author's lifetime and has been through many more since. In 1914 Oxford University Press published it in their World Classics series with an introduction by Admiral Sir Cyprian Bridge. For a book to be in print 150 years after it was first published it must have some remarkable qualities.

The mutiny on board HMS *Bounty* at 4.30 am on 28 April, 1789, is one of those tales of the sea which effortlessly captures the imagination. The accidental discovery of the mutineers' final haven at Pitcairn Island by Captain Mayhew Folger in the Boston sealer *Topaz* in 1808 added a new and romantic dimension to an already thrilling and controversial story. The mutiny, the epic boat voyage of Bligh and his companions across the Pacific, the fateful voyage and sinking of HMS *Pandora* sent to Tahiti to arrest the mutineers, the trial of some of them in 1792, the pamphlet 'war', in 1794–95, between Bligh and Fletcher Christian's brother Edward, the tale of the apparent redemption of the last mutineer, John Adams, at Pitcairn Island and the struggles of the little community he left behind, all gave, and continue to give, the *Bounty* story its remarkable fascination.

Of the dozens of books written on the *Bounty*, none stands out like Barrow's. He was uniquely placed by temperament and position to write *the* classic account, which, because of its high literary qualities, comes closer than any other to the real story of what happened – and why.

John Barrow was born in 1764 near Dragleybeck, a little hamlet near Ulverston in Lancashire, in northern England. He went to Ulverston Grammar School until he was thirteen and then used his talents to rise from obscurity to high office in the Admiralty. He became successively: a tutor, a clerk, a landsman on a Greenland whaler and a tutor at The Greenwich Academy. It was through private work to supplement his school salary that Barrow met Sir George Staunton, through whom he was introduced to the Earl of Macartney. When Macartney led a British embassy to the Emperor of China in 1792–94, Barrow went along as part of his suite. The embassy was unsuccessful. The Chinese Emperor disdained to believe that Western 'civilization' had any benefits for his kingdom.

In 1797 Barrow set off again with Macartney to the Cape Colony, taken from the Dutch. He was away for six years, returning to London in 1803. While at the Cape, Barrow gained another patron in the person of General

Francis Dundas, nephew of the powerful Lord Melville. He also got married. Barrow's return coincided with a change at the Admiralty. Lord Melville was appointed First Lord. On a recommendation by Macartney and a favourable impression of Barrow from his nephew, Melville offered him the post of Second Secretary. Barrow accepted and he held that post, except for a minor break, for 41 years. He had arrived. He had come a long way: from his parents' humble cottage in the north of England to the top of the world's most powerful navy. In his official position Barrow established himself as a talented administrator and man of letters, closely associated with many of the most brilliant and influential leaders of his day.

He published twelve books and a prodigious number of essays, including 195 in the *Quarterly Review* and a dozen in the *Encyclopaedia Britannica*. He was elected to the Royal Society in 1806, through the influence of his friend Sir Joseph Banks, and was a founder member of the Royal Geographical Society. He tirelessly promoted geographical exploration, particularly in the Arctic. His first two books – *Travels into the Interior of Southern Africa* (1801) and *Travels in China* (1804) – established his scientific credentials. He wrote once that he could think of no more honourable or useful role for the Royal Navy in times of peace than exploration and hydrographic surveying. (Lloyd, 1970)

When Barrow wrote his *Eventful History . . . of HMS Bounty* he was a long-established senior civil servant at the Admiralty. He was extremely well connected and had lived through the controversies surrounding the causes of the mutiny and its aftermath. Through Banks he probably met Captain Bligh socially, if he had not met him professionally in his early years at the Admiralty. He certainly met with many people who were involved in Bligh's turbulent career. He was an intimate of Heywood's family and, as a result, was able to consult Captain Peter Heywood's papers relating to the mutiny. As a senior official at the Admiralty he had access to the official Logs, letters and accounts of the mutiny and the trial of the mutineers. He was therefore ideally placed to write authoritatively about the whole affair – and sufficiently detached to write with generous impartiality.

Barrow describes himself as, 'the Editor of this little volume' rather than the author. This was more than modesty on his part. To make public his conclusions about the mutiny and what had caused it invited misunderstanding of his purpose. Being so closely identified with the Admiralty – he was widely known as 'Mr Barrow of the Admiralty' – any criticism of a senior officer was bound to be taken as an official rebuke, whereas Barrow's purpose was to draw lessons, 'from which the naval service . . . in all its ranks' would benefit. Hence, Barrow chose the discretion of anonymity.

Barrow used five principal sources: Bligh's *Narrative of the Mutiny on board HMS Bounty* (1790), the *Log of the Bounty* (1787–89), letters and papers of Peter Heywood (1791–92), *Minutes* of the Court Martial of the *Bounty* mutineers (1792) and a manuscript *Journal* of James Morrison (1792).

Bligh was accused, anonymously, in 1831 (many years after his death) of falsifying his *Narrative*. His accuser was Captain W.H. Smyth, a friend of Peter Heywood, who also made the claim that Bligh 'mastheaded' (sent aloft as a punishment) Midshipman Heywood for eight hours while the *Bounty* was battling against a blizzard at Cape Horn. Barrow rightly dismissed this as a nonsense: no boy could have lived through such an ordeal – even the seamen could spend only moments on deck in a blizzard, let alone eight hours aloft. But on Smyth's charge of falsification Barrow partly agrees, though he states he was more guilty of ommission than outright mis-statement. The more serious charge of falsification remains in currency however (McKee, 1962; Du Rietz, 1965, 1979). Bligh's *Narrative* and his Log present his views on the mutiny as he saw it. He was not writing a balanced account of the pros and cons of Christian's conduct. He omits several revealing incidents from his public account which would have placed his subordinates in a bad light because of their general incompetence. He gives opinions in his *Narrative* about the cause of the mutiny and the general disposition of the crew, and these opinions may be controversial; but on the charge of malicious falsification of facts, Bligh had every right to plead not guilty. Smyth replied to Barrow's reservations about Bligh's falsifications with a list of so-called examples, all of which are differences of interpretation of the events by Bligh, not examples of his falsification of facts (Smyth, 1831a, 1831b). What Barrow read in Bligh's Log led him to the conclusion that the *Bounty* officers were of 'a very inferior description'. Cyprian Bridge (1914) went to some length to show that the officers were 'above rather than below the average of their class'. But Barrow was describing their competence not their social class. Bligh's Log, written contemporaneously with the events and therefore not open to post-mutiny doctoring, showed them to be 'inferior' in their posts. Huggan, the surgeon, drank himself to death and caused the death of a seaman, James Valentine. John Fryer, the master, committed numerous gaffes. He allowed the spare sails to rot; the ship's chronometer to wind down; a Tahitian to escape who was suspected of assisting three seamen to desert, and was a contributory cause of the temporary grounding of the *Bounty* in a channel he had personally surveyed. His mistreatment of a Tahitian girl almost caused a breach in relations between the Europeans and the islanders. His behaviour during the open boat voyage was disruptive in an already difficult situation. On the outward voyage he tried to blackmail Bligh but his bluff was called. Two of the midshipmen, Hayward and Hallet, slept on their watches (including the night of the mutiny) and Hayward displayed such little concern at the punishment of a seaman he was responsible for that Bligh lost his temper. The carpenter, Purcell, was insubordinate and troublesome and provoked Bligh to challenge him to a duel with a cutlass when the starving boat party reached an island off Australia. Bligh recorded these and other incidents in his Log, which Barrow read, and in greater detail in his private Log (now in the Mitchell Library, Sydney). In sum these statements give a poignant meaning to Bligh's description of the men left on the *Bounty* (mainly seamen) as the 'most *able* men' in the crew. Christian's own views of the quality of the officers mentioned by Bligh are not in any doubt: he would not let any of them stay with him after the mutiny: they were all sent into the boat with Bligh.

Bligh and Christian quarrelled at the Cape of Good Hope but about what is not known. No letters have yet come to light from Fletcher Christian to his family about the first part of the *Bounty* voyage so we do not know how matters stood between them. We do know that Bligh favoured Christian with promotion to Acting Lieutenant and that this almost guaranteed Christian an Admiralty promotion to this rank on his return to England. Bligh's Log does not mention Christian by name in any of the incidents that caused Bligh to criticise the officers. This is significant, though there are hints that Christian may have been responsible for a couple of incidents, such as the disruption in relations with the Tahitians when someone at the shore camp flouted one of their taboos, and the becalming of the launch during the movement of the *Bounty* to Oparre. But after the *Bounty* left Tahiti, Bligh's relations with Christian become strained beyond Christian's breaking point.

Bligh was probably the most stunned man in the *Bounty* when the mutiny erupted. He was astonished that Fletcher Christian, of all men, could lead a mutiny against him. He never did understand why. He searched his conscience and characteristically absolved himself from any particle of blame for Christian's conduct. He concluded that the mutiny was a long-standing conspiracy linked to the idyllic life awaiting the crew if they returned to Tahiti. He never changed that view. He claimed that he heard shouts of 'Huzza for Otaheiti!' among the mutineers, but Barrow comments that, 'Bligh was the only person who said they did so'. Evidence is available that he heard what he reported. Peter Heywood's private journal, extracts from which are among the papers of Captain Edward Edwards of the *Pandora*, reports a statement of Charles Churchill, one of the leading and most violent of the mutineers, that, 'the Ship was to be taken back to Otaheite and those in her to settle there'. John Adams confirmed that there was some 'huzzaing' for Tahiti during the mutiny in his conversation in 1825 with Captain Beechey at Pitcairn Island. Edward Christian, while denying Bligh's assertion, reported that Midshipman George Stewart was 'dancing for joy' during the mutiny. (This, incidentally, is the same man whom Barrow considered to be innocent of mutiny and whom Heywood in his letter to Beechey, quoted in this book, denies, contrary to the evidence of both Adams and Morrison, was implicated either in Christian's scheme to swim away from the ship or in his later decision to mutiny.) Bligh believed the mutineers desired to return to Tahiti and he did not discriminate between Christian's motives and those of the other mutineers. His failure to appreciate Christian's motivation does not gainsay his interpretation of what motivated the others.

The fictional image of Bligh as a sadistic bully driving a demented and terrorised crew to mutiny by floggings and deprivations is such a nonsense that it is hardly worth debunking. By eighteenth-century standards Bligh was, physically, a soft commander. He was more than ordinarily careful about his crew's health, and in the magnificent desperation of the open boat voyage, proved himself to be a selfless, compassionate and competent commander. Bligh's failings were confined to his unrestrained mode of expression. Even his severest critics praise his seamanship and navigation. But his tongue and temper combined into a fatal flaw. George Mackaness, author of the first major biography of Bligh in 1931, published additional manuscript material between 1949 and 1960. Some of this material throws fresh light on Bligh and his relationships with subordinates. Unfortunately, many of the letters published by Mackaness appeared in limited editions of scholarly works whose restricted circulation explains their general lack of impact on the debate. Among the first to recognise their importance was the bibliographical scholar Rolf du Rietz. He used them effectively in a polemic against the view that Christian's mutiny was totally inexplicable and therefore must have been caused by something else other than Bligh's behaviour, such as the intervention of Midshipman Edward Young, first noted by Barrow to have kept a very low profile during the mutiny. Madge Darby drew attention to Young's possible role in her book in 1965. She also suggested the most recent 'explanation' of the mutiny – that it was the result of a homosexual lovers' quarrel between Bligh and Christian. This theory rests on the letter published by Barrow which Peter Heywood wrote to Captain Beechey in 1830. In the letter there is an enigmatic statement which Darby suggested was a hint of a homosexual relationship. Heywood refers to Christian's farewell speech to him the night he took the *Bounty* away for the last time. Christian, he wrote, 'also communicated to me, for the satisfaction of his relations, other circumstances connected with that unfortunate disaster, which, after their deaths, may or may not be laid before the public. And although they can implicate none but himself, either living or dead, they may extenuate, but will contain not a word of his in defence of the crime he committed against the laws of his country.' What the 'secret' was that Heywood communicated to Christian's relations is unknown, and will remain so until some documentary evidence is discovered either among some 'lost' papers of his own, or among some as yet unfound Christian family papers. Smith (1936) suggested it referred to Christian having venereal disease and Darby opted for homosexuality (a speculation picked up recently by popular authors).

Apart from the evidence of the Bond letters published by Mackaness, it is more likely that the 'secret' does refer to some illness of Christian's which he was ashamed of, such as venereal disease or even mental illness, and that this explains Heywood's reluctance to make a public statement. Whether he left anything in writing is not known, but even if he did it is likely that the papers were burned by his wife after his death. We know that just before his death Heywood went through a family crisis involving his stepdaughter, Diane

Belcher. Diane had married, with Heywood's active encouragement, Captail Belcher, and she contracted VD on her wedding night. She returned to Belcher once more and contracted it again. Heywood was mortified by embarrassment. His wife was near hysterical. Any reference to venereal disease involving Christian was clearly out of the question in the circumstances. Christian alleges that the extenuating circumstances implicated 'none but himself', which presumably excludes homosexuality. He could hardly claim also that one crime (sodomy carried the death penalty) extenuated another. After the *Bounty* mutiny Bligh returned to the Pacific in HMS *Providence* to complete the mission of transplanting the breadfruit to the West Indies. He had as his First Lieutenant, Francis Godolphin Bond, who was a near relative of his. In some of Bond's letters a picture emerges of their relationship, not at all flattering to Bligh, which taken with other evidence confirms the cause of the mutiny on the *Bounty* as Bligh's irascibility, which wore Christian down. Whether impartial judges would find that Bligh went too far, or that Christian was too weak or too distracted, is beside the point on the issue of what *caused* Christian to mutiny. The fact that Bond did not mutiny suggests that he was a stronger man than Christian.

'I assure you that it is no small disappointment to my hopes that I have not gained as much information as expected; – an insurmountable bar has always lain in my way, since my pride will not allow me to receive magisterial tuition, nor bow with servile flattery. Is it the fashion to begin or end a miscellaneous epistle with our grievances? . . . Before this enigma is cleared up, let me enjoin the strictest secersy [sic] and insist on your not acquiring even your good wife, my mother, nor my dear sister with the circumstance. . . . Yes, Tom, our relation had the credit of being a tyrant in his last expedition, where his misfortunes and good fortune have elevated him to a situation he is incapable of supporting with decent modesty. The very high opinion he has of himself makes him hold every one of our profession with contempt, perhaps envy. Nay, the Navy is but a sphere for fops and lubbers to swarm in, without one gem to vie in brilliancy with himself. I don't mean to depreciate his extensive knowledge as a seaman and nautical astronomer, but condemn that went of modesty, in self-estimation. To be less prolix I will inform you that he has treated me (nay, all on board) with the insolence and arrogance of a Jacobs; and not withstanding his passion is partly to be attributed to a nervous fever, with which he has been attacked most of the voyage, the chief part of his conduct must have arisen from the fury of an ungovernable temper. Soon after leaving England I wished to receive instruction from this imperious master, until I found he publically exposed any deficiency on my part in the Nautical Art, &c. A series of this conduct determined me to trust to myself, which I hope will in some measure repay me for the trouble of this disagreeable voyage – in itself pleasant, but made otherwise by being worried at every opportunity. His maxims are of a nature that at once pronounce him an enemy to the lovers of Natural Philosophy; for to make use of his own words, "No person can do the duty of a 1st Lieut., who does more than write the days work in his publick journal!" This is so inimical to the sentiments that I find the utmost difficulty in keeping on to tolerate terms with him. The general orders which have been given are to that purport. – I am constantly to keep on my legs from 8 o'th morning to 12 or noon, altho' I keep the usual watch. The officer of the morning watch attends to the cleaning of the decks; yet I am also to be present, not only to get it done, but be even mentally active on these and all other occasions. He expects me to be acquainted with every transaction on board, notwithstanding he himself will give the necessary orders to the Warrant Officers before I can put it in execution. Every dogma of power and consequence has been taken from the Lieutenants, to establish, as he thinks, his own reputation – what imbecility for a post Captn! The inferior warrants have had orders from the beginning of the expedition, not to issue the least article to a Lieut. without his orders; so that a cleat, fathom of log line, or indeed a hand swab, must have the commander's sanction. One of the last and most beneficent commands was, that the carpenter's crew should not drive a nail for me without I would first ask his permission, – but my heart is filled with the proper material always to disdain this humiliation. . . . My messmates have remarked he never spoke of my possessing one virtue – tho' by the bye he has never dared to say I have none. Every officer who has nautical information, a knowledge of natural history, a taste for drawing, or anything to constitute him proper for circumnavigating, becomes odious; for great as he is in his own good opinion, he must have entertained fears some of his ship's company meant to (submit) a spurious Narrative to the judgement and perusal of the publick. . . . The future will determine whether promotion will be the reward of this voyage. I still flatter myself it will, notwithstanding what I have said. Consistent with self-respect, I still remain tolerably passive; and if nothing takes place very contrary to my feelings, all may end well; but this will totally depend on circumstances, one of which is the secrecy requested of you concerning the tenor of this letter. . . .' (Lieut. F. G. Bond in a letter to his brother, December, 1792: in Mackaness, 1976)

Space prohibits a full discussion of Bond's letters, but enough can be read into the above to suggest that Bligh's manner had irritated Bond in the extreme. Similar statements in Fryer (1790), Morrison (1792), Edward Christian (1794) and evidence at the *Warrior* court martial (1805), and the courts-martial of Short (1807), Kent (1811) and Johnston (1811) fully document Bligh's peculiarity of manner. If we project what we know of Bligh's manner back to the situation on the *Bounty* after it left Tahiti, with Bligh highly sensitive about the proven deficiencies of his officers, it is likely that we can see the tragic clash between him and Christian in its proper light. In a word, Christian crumbled.

Whether Bligh gave Christian a *just* cause to mutiny is still hotly debated. On the *judicial* issues Bligh was absolutely in the right and Christian absolutely in the wrong. This has never been seriously disputed. If Christian had been caught and returned for court martial he would have been hanged, there being no defence to an act of mutiny under the British Navy's Articles of War. To ascribe the cause of the mutiny to Bligh's manner is in no way to justify Christian's mutiny. The consequence of Christian's actions was to shorten the lives of many of his colleagues in the *Bounty*, several dozen islanders at Tubuai, an unknown number at Tahiti, over a hundred of the crew of the *Pandora* and most of the men who went to Pitcairn with him. The behaviour of the mutineers after they set Bligh adrift is relevant in deciding on their characters (Bligh's career is ofter invoked as evidence against him in the *Bounty*) and they can hardly be excused as the innocent victims of tyranny. For example, Fletcher Christian is alleged to have mutinied because Bligh cut him to the quick with an accusation that he had stolen some of the *Bounty*'s coconuts; in Heywood's *Journal* he is reported to have been party to an islander being shot in the back in a dispute over the man's coconuts! The mutineers' record of slaughter, wounding, theft, kidnapping, rape and wanton destruction of islander property ought by now to have removed them from the respectable company of history's victims. Whatever Bligh's personal manner, the mutineers had no justification for the crimes they committed once out of his jurisdiction.

Barrow's famous footnote on the possible return of Christian to England is one of the most tantalising rumours of the whole *Bounty* story. That he even bothered to report this rumour, let alone vouch for its truth, is remarkable. It led to a fascinating book by Wilkinson (1953) purporting to show it happened. If it is true that he was in England in 1808–09 then the Christian family to date have kept their secret well. (I discuss the possibility in my *Bligh*, 1978)

Barrow made one calumny against Bligh. He accused him of being promoted from, 'before the mast', and observed that such men, 'are generally the worst tyrants'. Bligh, however, was precisely what Barrow denied him to be: a young gentleman who spent six years in the midshipmen's cockpit in ships of the Royal Navy. He was related to Cornish gentry, among whom the Lords Darnley were prominent. A portrait of Bligh auctioned recently in London shows him in his midshipman's uniform, about twenty years old, which hardly suggests a life-style of a man promoted from before the mast. He was from solidly middle-class parents and first went to sea aged 15, rated as an A.B., and within six months was rated as a midshipman. This was a common entry for young gentlemen at the time and was the route by which Lord Nelson and, incidently, Fletcher Christian, joined the Royal Navy. Bligh did not, as Cyprian Bridge alleges, spend his early years in the 'lower section of the merchant service'. Like many officers after the American War of Independence (which for Bligh included four years with Captain Cook's last Pacific voyage) he went on to half-pay for the duration of peace. During the peace, while a lieutenant in the Royal Navy, he *captained* merchant ships for his wife's uncle, Duncan Campbell, and acted as his agent in the West Indies. On two of his voyages he took with him Fletcher Christian, still a midshipman. Bligh was a victim here of early Victorian class snobbery, doubly unfortunate in view of Barrow's own origins and the fact that Bligh was a gentleman *and* a foul-mouthed curser, a not uncommon feature of the eighteenth-century navy.

Barrow 'looked over' a manuscript journal of James Morrison, the boat-swain's mate in the *Bounty*, and quotes from it. A close comparison of Barrow's quotations with the original Morrison manuscript in the Mitchell Library, Sydney, shows considerable discrepancy in language and style. He did not use the original manuscript, which at that time was among Peter Heywood's papers, for his quotations but appears to have used the quotations that appear in Peter Heywood's entry in *Marshall's Royal Navy Biography* (1825). This may have been a matter of convenience while writing his book but it may also have been the case that there was another version of Morri-son's manuscript in existence which is now mislaid. There are two manu-scripts in the Mitchell Library, neither used by Barrow. The shorter and earlier manuscript is the *Memorandums and Particulars Respecting the Bounty and her Crew* written in October 1792, and the much longer and later manuscript, the so-called *Journal*, or *Diary*, written from November 1792 to about January 1793. The Marshall quotations may be just careless transcriptions or heavy editing, in which case they are closest to the later *Journal*, and its dating solves one problem raised by Barrow regarding the mystery of how Morrison managed to preserve a manuscript through his ordeals in the *Pandora*. Morrison would have no difficulty preserving some-thing he did not write until after he was returned as a prisoner to England.

Barrow rightly observes that Morrison's account is 'highly coloured' in parts. This does not eliminate his manuscripts as evidence, but some books treat Morrison's accusations as facts when they ought strictly to be treated as opinions, written long after the events they purported to describe. The manuscripts were not published during Morrison's lifetime but they did circulate privately (it was his *Memorandums* which probably got him his pardon as the Admiralty could not afford any more scandal at a time when war was threatening and the establishment, from the King downwards, was trembling at the excesses exhibited by the rampaging mobs of the French Revolution). Bligh certainly saw the *Memorandums* and wrote detailed replies to the accusations in letters to Sir Joseph Banks in 1793. The London Missionary Society saw the main *Journal* and used some extracts from it, including the vocabulary (now lost) of the Tahitian language, in its prepara-tions for its missionaries before they left for Tahiti. Morrison intended to publish the *Journal* in collaboration with the Reverend William Howell but was dissuaded, according to Du Rietz (1966), by an Admiralty promise to re-employ him. Marshall (1825) asserts that 'publication was only prevented by the death of its original owner' Morrison (who died in 1808!).

Barrow gave wide circulation to his views on the incident of the *Bounty*'s cable almost parting at Tahiti. He suggested it was due to its 'chaffing over the rocky bottom', and thought Bligh's belief that it was the work of a seaman 'wholly gratuitous'. In fact Bligh's first assumption – that the islanders were responsible – was correct. The mutineers were told on their return to Tahiti that the cable was cut deliberately in protest at Bligh's punishment of Midshipman Hayward for sleeping on his watch while three seamen deserted. Morrison reported this in his *Journal*, but Barrow apparently ignored the Tahitian confession.

Barrow's book also gave currency to a story about Morrison's schooner, built at Tahiti after the *Bounty* departed under Christian's command. This story alleges that it was purchased by Captain Broughton for surveying and was used to save the lives of 112 men in a shipwreck. Andrew David has established that the two schooners have been confused, and in any case the dimensions of Morrison's boat were far too small for the role it has been credited with : his schooner had a tonnage of about 18 tons while Broughton's was about 87 tons. (David, 1977)

Barrow's summing up of the characters of the principal protagonists of the mutiny drama are probably about as fair as could be expected. That Bligh was responsible for the mutiny cannot be in doubt given the line of command in a naval ship: commanders had to prevent mutinies and piracy of King's ships. Subordinates, especially aspiring commanders such as Fletcher Christian, had to remain under lawful command and carry out their duties no matter what the provocations. If Bligh failed as a commander, Christian failed as a subordinate in the line of command. There are a number of features of Christian's mutiny that remain unexplained and probably always will. We know he was in a state of torment, and that Bligh was a feature of that torment, but we do not know what else, if anything, was tormenting him. He had formed a relationahip with a Tahitian woman ('Isabella') and he would not be the first man to have his head turned by obsessive love. His famous row with Bligh over the coconuts occurred at least sixteen hours before the mutiny – plenty of time for him to cool down or to brood over *all* of his torments originating both in the ship and back in Tahiti. Christian's act of madness was a tragedy. It eventually destroyed him. He was not tough enough to endure under the stresses induced by Bligh (though it should be remembered he had sailed with Bligh before and well knew what sort of commander he was). The road to command imposes many tests upon those who voluntarily embark upon it and the weeding out process is as ruthless as anything devised by men to ensure that only the hardiest reach the top. Christian's weaknesses and failings erupted during a minor botanical mission of marginal importance to his country. As it was he caused the deaths of many of his colleagues and even more innocent islanders. If he had crumbled while in command of a larger ship, at a more crucial time and place, death's shadow would have covered many more of the men who relied on their commander's steadyness and competence for their survival. War is a disagreeable business but it is infinitely more disagreeable (and pointless) when those in command are incompetent.

William Bligh was violent in speech and abrasive in command. The line between irascibility and tyranny is a matter of opinion. The fact remains that the mutiny caught everybody by surprise – nobody expected it. Bligh slept unarmed and unguarded in his open cabin. Christian apparently only thought of the mutiny moments before he took over the watch at 4 am. That so many men went with Bligh in the open boat on what must have looked like a suicide mission, 3,500 miles from the nearest European settlement, indicates their respect for Bligh as a seaman if nothing else. If Bligh was an isolated tyrant then everybody would have been glad to get rid of him. Even Heywood at his court martial spoke up for Bligh's many kindnesses to him. Christian's mutiny was only possible because his party were armed and apparently willing to kill.

Many famous seamen had harsh dispositions. The loneliness of command affected captains in different ways. Contemporary memoirs of seamen of all ranks for 1780 to 1840 show a wide range of behaviour among commanders. The navy did not produce floating democracies led by liberal-minded do-gooders. Cramped ships, poor food and the unending monotony of routine produced floods of whispered grievances, affronts to dignity, unfair and inconvenient decisions by higher authority, injustices and bad feelings. Madness was a major illness in the Royal Navy of the day, among all ranks. Combine all that with the loneliness of command – where authority may be delegated but responsibility can never be, and the wonder is that there were not more mutinies.

The object of a crew's grievances was bound to be the local representative of the system they worked under. In a large ship the crew only dealt with the mates, midshipmen and the lieutenants – the captain was a remote figure, god-like in his loneliness. In a small ship such as the *Bounty*, Bligh was on top of them every day. He was by no means exceptional in his attitudes; he certainly was never brutal. His kindness was apparent to those who treated him politely and with due deference. Insolence and disobedience brought out the worst in him and sent him into paroxysms of rage.

Most of Bligh's subordinates took the peculiarities of his manner in their stride – serving difficult masters is part of the training for command. Bligh never failed to find lifelong friends who would stand by him, such as Sir Joseph Banks. He was no saint but was at his best in circumstances where the saintly would have been overwhelmed. He was a fighter, a survivor, a man of immense personal conviction and considerable courage. His critics claim he was a bully, a tyrant, a coward and a thief. Such extreme views are unjust. Barrow's classic puts Bligh's command and Christian's mutiny into a more balanced perspective.

GAVIN KENNEDY
Edinburgh 1980

Editorial Note

The text for this edition is a shortened version of the account written by Sir John Barrow, Permanent Secretary to the Admiralty, published by John Murray, London, in 1831.

Every effort has been made to remain faithful to Barrow's original text while retaining the flow of the narrative. Minor omissions are therefore not indicated in this text; however, where lengthy passages, not directly related to the mutiny, have been omitted, such omissions are indicated by the *symbol* (. . .), and where lengthy passages have been replaced by brief summaries, such passages are printed in italic type. Elsewhere, italicised words are as in Barrow's original text.

Words which may be unfamiliar to the reader, and particularly place-names which have changed since the late eighteenth century, are given in their original form followed by their modern equivalents in brackets.

Relevant extracts from the extensive footnotes in Barrow's original are here placed within the narrative, enclosed in brackets.

Portrait of Sir John Barrow (1764–1848).
In Barrow's day the Board of Admiralty consisted of seven members, presided over by the First Lord, a member of the Cabinet, assisted by the First and Second Secretaries. The First Secretary dealt largely with political affairs and was closely identified with the government of the day, while the Second Secretary (Barrow's post) concentrated on administration and the voluminous correspondence of the world's most powerful navy. Barrow served under thirteen different administrations between 1804 and 1845 and, with the First Secretary, was in a key position to influence, discreetly, naval promotions and appointments. He was knighted in 1835 'on the grounds of eminence in the pursuit of science and literature'.
It was at Barrow's suggestion that Napoleon was exiled to the island of St. Helena in the South Atlantic 'where all intrigue would be impossible, and being withdrawn so far from the European world, he would very soon be forgotten'.

Preface

The Editor of this little volume (for he presumes not to write *Author*) has been induced to bring into one connected view what has hitherto appeared only in detached fragments, (and some of these not generally accessible) – the historical narrative of an event which deeply interested the public at the time of its occurrence, and from which the naval service in particular, in all its ranks, may still draw instructive and useful lessons.

The story in itself is replete with interest. We are taught by *The Book* of sacred history, that the disobedience of our first parents entailed on our globe of earth a sinful and a suffering race: in our time there has sprung up from the most abandoned of this sinful family – from pirates, mutineers, and murderers – a little society which, under the precepts of that sacred volume, is characterized by religion, morality, and innocence. The discovery of this happy people, as unexpected as it was accidental, and all that regards their condition and history, partake so much of the romantic, as to render the story not ill adapted for an epic poem. Lord Byron, indeed, has partially treated the subject; but by blending two incongruous stories, and leaving both of them imperfect, and by mixing up fact with fiction, has been less felicitous than usual; for, beautiful as many passages in his 'Island' are, in a region where every tree, and flower, and fountain breathe poetry, yet as a whole the poem is feeble and deficient in dramatic effect.

There still remains to us at least one Poet, who, if he could be prevailed on to undertake it, would do justice to the story. To his suggestion the publication of the present narrative owes its appearance. But a higher object at present is engaging his attention, which, when completed, judging from that portion already before the public, will have raised a splendid and lasting monument to the name of William Sotheby, in his translation of the Iliad and Odyssey.

To the kindness of Mrs. Heywood, the relict of the late Captain Peter Heywood, the Editor is indebted for those beautiful and affectionate letters, written by a beloved sister to her unfortunate brother, while a prisoner and under sentence of death; as well as for some occasional poetry, which displays an intensity of feeling, a tenderness of expression, and a high tone of sentiment, that do honour to the head and heart of this amiable and accomplished lady. Those letters also from the brother to his deeply afflicted family will be read with peculiar interest.

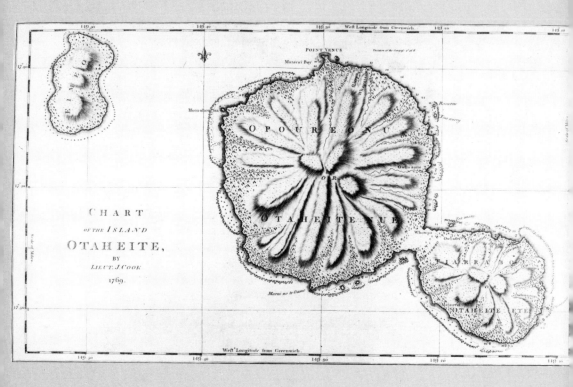

Cook's chart of the Island of Tahiti,
published in Hawkesworth's *Account of the Voyages . . . for Making Discoveries in the Southern Hemisphere.*

Early voyagers heard the islanders call their home *Otaheite*, or O Tahiti, meaning 'It is Tahiti', and it was known by this name until the middle of the nineteenth century. More serious confusion was caused by official acceptance of Hawkesworth's account (1773) of Cook's First Voyage. Hawkesworth had not been to the Pacific and this showed in his verbose rewriting of Cook's plainer and more accurate journals. Cook was mortified when he read the result. In Cook's time Tahiti must have been like paradise, rising steeply through green-clad hills to high volcanic peaks and almost completely ringed by coral reefs. It was a near-perfect place for the two peoples to mix and become acquainted during the first visits by Europeans. The most northerly tip of the island was named Point Venus by Cook because it was at this point, on his First Voyage, that he observed the transit of Venus.

CHAPTER ONE

Otaheite

The reign of George III will be distinguished in history by the great extension and improvement which geographical knowledge received under the immediate auspices of this sovereign. At a very early period, after his accession to the throne of these realms, expeditions of discovery were undertaken, not with a view to the acquisition of treasure, or the extent of dominion, but for the improvement of commerce, and the increase and diffusion of knowledge. ' . . .

These early voyages of discovery had two main objectives. Firstly they were to seek 'lands and islands hitherto unvisited by any European power, within latitudes convenient for navigation, and in climates adapted to the produce of commodities useful in commerce', and secondly they were to discover if possible the Terra Australis incognita – *the great landmass believed to exist somewhere in the high latitudes of the southern hemisphere. It was during the course of one of these expeditions that one Captain Wallis discovered an island which he named* King George's Island *and which subsequently came to be known by its native name of* Otaheite *or* Tahite.

While that expedition was in progress, the Royal Society, in 1768, addressed an application to the king, praying him to appoint a ship of war to go to the South Seas for the purpose of observing the transit of Venus over the sun's disc, which was to happen in the year 1769; and by the king's command, a bark of three hundred and seventy tons was taken up by the Admiralty to perform this service.

The command was conferred on Lieutenant James Cook, an officer of undoubted ability, and well versed in astronomy and the theory and practice of navigation, with whom the Royal Society associated Mr. Charles Green, who had long been assistant to Dr. Bradley, the astronomer royal, to aid him in the observation of the transit. Mr. Banks, a private gentleman of good fortune, who afterwards became President of the Royal Society, and Dr. Solander, a Swedish gentleman of great acquirements, particularly in natural history, accompanied Lieutenant Cook on the voyage. The islands of Marquesas de Mendoza, or those of Rotterdam or Amsterdam, were proposed by the Royal Society as proper places for making the observations. While Cook was fitting out, however, Captain Wallis returned and strongly recommended as suitable for the purpose, Port Royal Harbour on the island of Tahite.

This lovely island is most intimately connected with the mutiny which took place on board the *Bounty*, and with the fate of the mutineers and their innocent offspring. Its many seducing temptations have been urged as one,

Sir Joseph Banks (1743–1820) **and Dr Daniel Carl Solander** (1736–1782) **in Iceland in 1772.**
Joseph Banks accompanied Captain Cook on his First Voyage to the Pacific (1768–1771)
and agreed to participate in the Second Voyage (1772–1775) but a disagreement with the
Admiralty over the working accommodation for himself, Dr Solander (the eminent Swedish
botanist) and ten others, compelled him to withdraw. Instead, Banks took his scientific
party to Iceland. While on the Scottish island of Staffa he complained to his host about the
bed-bugs and was indignantly told that he must have brought the creatures with him.
Banks's great influence easily survived his dispute with the Admiralty and he became a
major influence on government policy throughout the rest of his life. Through Banks,
Bligh received his appointment to the *Bounty* and the two men remained lifelong friends.

if not the main, cause of the mutiny. It may be proper, therefore, as intro-
ductory to the present narrative, to give a general description of the rich
and spontaneous gifts which Nature has lavished on this island, and of the
simple and ingenuous manners of its natives as they existed at the period of
the first intercourse between the Otaheitans and the crews of those ships,
which carried Wallis and Cook to their shores.

The first communication which Wallis had with these people was
unfortunately of a hostile nature. Having approached with his ship close to

the shore, the usual symbol of peace and friendship, a branch of the plantain tree, was held up by a native in one of the numerous canoes that surrounded the ship. . . . *Some time later, however, while the ship's boats were sounding in the bay, Wallis suspected that the islanders were about to attack them and on this suspicion immediately signalled the boats to come aboard and, to deter the natives, fired a nine-pounder over their heads. The danger passed, but subsequently two full-scale attacks were made, during which Wallis' ship the* Dolphin *was surrounded by large numbers of native canoes and subjected to a hail of stones, 'thrown with great force and dexterity, with the help of slings', many of which caused injuries among the crew. 'As to shorten the contest would certainly lessen the mischief, I determined,' says Captain Wallis, 'to make this action decisive, and put an end to hostilities at once.' Accordingly a tremendous fire was opened up on the attackers, who immediately dispersed in terror and confusion.*

Such was the inauspicious commencement of our acquaintance with the natives of Tahite. Their determined hostility and perseverance in an unequal combat could only have arisen from one of two motives – either from an opinion that a ship of such magnitude could only be come to their coast to take their country from them; or an irresistible temptation to endeavour, at all hazards, to possess themselves of so valuable a prize. Be that as it may, the dread inspired by the effects of the cannon, and perhaps a conviction of the truth of what had been explained to them, that the 'strangers wanted only provisions and water,' had the effect of preventing further trouble; for from that day, the most friendly and uninterrupted intercourse was established, and continued to the day of the *Dolphin*'s departure; and provisions of all kinds, hogs, dogs, fruit, and vegetables, were supplied in the greatest abundance, in exchange for pieces of iron, nails, and trinkets. . . .

The ship was visited by persons of both sexes, who by their dress and behaviour appeared to be of a superior rank. Among others was a tall lady about five and forty years of age, of a pleasing countenance and majestic deportment, who conducted herself with that easy freedom which generally distinguishes conscious superiority and habitual command. She accepted some small present which the captain gave her, and having observed that he was weak and suffering from ill health, she pointed to the shore, which he understood to be an invitation, and made signs that he would go thither the next morning. His visit to this lady displays so much character and good feeling, that it will best be described in the captain's own words.

'The next morning,' he writes, 'I went on shore for the first time, and my princess or rather queen, for such by her authority she appeared to be, soon after came to me, followed by many of her attendants. As she perceived that my disorder had left me very weak, she ordered her people to take me in their arms, and carry me not only over the river, but all the way to her house; and observing that some of the people who were with me, particularly the first lieutenant and purser, had also been sick, she caused them also to be carried in the same manner. When we approached near her house, a great number of both sexes came out to meet her; these she presented to me, after having intimated by signs that they were her relations, and taking hold of my hand she made them kiss it.

'We then entered the house, which covered a piece of ground three hundred and twenty-seven feet long, and forty-two feet broad. It consisted of a roof thatched with palm leaves, and raised upon thirty-nine pillars on each side, and fourteen in the middle. The ridge of the thatch, on the inside, was thirty feet high, and the sides of the house, to the edge of the roof, were twelve feet high; all below the roof being open. As soon as we entered the house, she made us sit down, and then calling four young girls, she assisted them to take off my shoes, draw down my stockings, and pull off my coat, and then directed them to smooth down the skin, and gently chafe it with their hands. The same operation was also performed on the first lieutenant and the purser, but upon none of those who appeared to be in health. Having continued for about half an hour, they dressed us again, but in this they were, as may easily be imagined, very awkward; I found great benefit, however, from the chafing, and so did the lieutenant and the purser.

'When we went away, our generous benefactress ordered a very large sow, big with young, to be taken down to the boat, and accompanied us thither herself. She had given directions to her people to carry me, as they had done when I came, but as I chose rather to walk, she took me by the arm, and whenever we came to a plash of water or dirt, she lifted me over with as little trouble as it would have cost me to have lifted over a child, if I had been well.'

The following morning Captain Wallis sent her a present by the gunner, who found her in the midst of an entertainment given to at least a thousand people. The messes were put into shells of cocoa-nuts, and the shells into wooden trays, like those used by our butchers, and she distributed them with her own hands to the guests, who were seated in rows in the open air, round the great house. When this was done, she sat down herself upon a place somewhat elevated above the rest, and two women, placing themselves, one on each side of her, fed her, she opening her mouth as they brought their hands up with the food. From this time, the queen frequently visited the captain on board, and always with a present, but she never condescended to barter, nor would she accept of any return. . . .

This same lady we find in full activity and animation, and equally generous, to Lieut. Cook and his party, under the name of *Oberea*, who, it now appeared, was no queen but whose husband they discovered was uncle to the young king, then a minor. She soon evinced a partiality for Mr. Banks, which appears to have been mutual, until an unlucky discovery took place, that she had, at her command, a stout strong-boned *cavaliere servente*; added to which, a theft, rather of an amusing nature, contributed for a time to create a coolness between them. *It happened that a party consisting of Cook, Banks, Solander and three or four others was forced to spend a night ashore and was prevailed upon to spend it with Oberea and some of her retinue.*

The surrender of Oberea to Captain Wallis, 27 June 1767.
Captain Samuel Wallis discovered Tahiti in 1767, though Barrow, in his 1831 edition,
wrongly insisted on ascribing that honor to Fernandez de Quiros (1606), who is now
known to have sailed much further north than the latitude of Tahiti. After the unfortunate
initial hostilities, the friendship shown by Perea (from O Berea) established the warm
relationship between islanders and Europeans noted by Bligh. Tobias Furneaux, Second
Lieutenant of the *Dolphin*, discovered Adventure Bay in Tasmania while on Cook's
Second Voyage and named the bay after his ship. The bay was again visited by Bligh in
the *Bounty* in 1788.

*Unfortunately, during the night all the Europeans discovered that various
items of their clothing had been stolen – in circumstances giving rise to the
strongest suspicion that Oberea was not only privy to the theft but probably
had some of the stolen property in her possession.*

The Otaheitans, it seems, cannot resist pilfering. 'I must bear my testimony,' says Cook, 'that the people of this country, of all ranks, men and
women, are the arrantest thieves upon the face of the earth; but,' he adds,
'we must not hastily conclude that theft is a testimony of the same depravity
in them that it is in us; an Indian among penny knives and beads, and even
nails and broken glass, is in the same state of mind with the meanest servant

in Europe among unlocked coffers of jewels and gold.' Captain Wallis has illustrated the truth of this position by an experiment he made on some persons, whose dress and behaviour indicated that they were of a superior cast. 'To discover what present,' he says, 'would most gratify them, I laid down before them a Johannes, a guinea, a crown piece, a Spanish dollar, a few shillings, some new halfpence, and two large nails, making signs that they should take what they liked best. The nails were first seized with great eagerness, and then a few of the halfpence, but the silver and gold lay neglected.'

The Otaheitans' thirst after iron was irresistible; Wallis's ship was stripped of all the nails in her by the seamen to purchase the good graces of the women, who assembled in crowds on the shore. The men even drew out of different parts of the ship those nails that fastened the cleats to her side. This commerce established with the women rendered the men, as might readily be expected, less obedient to command, and made it necessary to punish some of them by flogging. The Otaheitans regarded this punishment with horror. One of Cook's men having insulted a chief's wife, he was ordered to be flogged in their presence. The Indians saw him stripped and tied up to the rigging with a fixed attention, waiting in silent suspense for the event; but as soon as the first stroke was given, they interfered with great agitation, earnestly entreating that the rest of the punishment might be remitted; and when they found they were unable to prevail, they gave vent to their pity by tears. . . .

But the sorrows of these simple and artless people are transient. Cook justly observes, that what they feel they have never been taught either to disguise or suppress; and having no habits of thinking, which perpetually recall the past and anticipate the future, they are affected by all the changes of the passing hour, and reflect the colour of the time, however frequently it may vary. They grieve for the death of a relation, and place the body on a stage erected on piles and covered with a roof of thatch, for they never bury the dead, and never approach one of these *morais* without great solemnity; but theirs is no lasting grief. . . . The body being deposited on the stage, the mourners are dismissed to wash themselves in the river to remove the charcoal smeared on the body as a mark of mourning and to resume their customary dresses and their usual gaiety. . . .

The skill and labour which the Otaheitans bestow on their large double boats is not less wonderful than their stone morais, from the felling of the tree and splitting it into plank, to the minutest carved ornaments that decorate the head and the stern. The whole operation is performed without the use of any metallic instrument. 'To fabricate one of their principal vessels with their tools is,' says Cook, 'as great a work as to build a British man of war with ours.' The fighting boats are sometimes more than seventy feet long, but not above three broad; but they are fastened in pairs, side by side, at the distance of about three feet; the head and stern rise in a semi-circular form, the latter to the height of seventeen or eighteen feet. To build

A Canoe of the Sandwich Islands, Rowers Masked.
The great double canoes of Polynesia amazed all visitors to those islands. They were
magnificent in construction and were handled with great skill. The example illustrated here
is the Hawaiian version, which, in comparison with the Tahitian double canoes described
by Cook and others, is of a much simpler and less grand design. The rowers' masks are a
mystery in themselves for nothing appears in contemporary accounts to either describe
them or explain their purpose.

these boats, and the smaller kinds of canoes; – to build their houses, and
finish the slight furniture they contain; – to fell, cleave, carve, and polish
timber for various purposes; – and, in short, for every conversion of wood –
the tools they make use of are the following: an adze of stone; a chisel or
gouge of bone, generally that of a man's arm between the wrist and elbow;
a rasp of coral; and the skin of a sting-ray, with coral sand as a file or polisher.

The persons of the Otaheitan men are in general tall, strong, well-limbed
and finely shaped; equal in size to the largest of Europeans. The women of
superior rank are also above the middle stature of Europeans, but the
inferior class are rather below it. The complexion of the former class is that
which we call a brunette, and the skin is most delicately smooth and soft.
The shape of the face is comely, the cheek bones are not high, neither are the
eyes hollow, nor the brow prominent; the nose is a little, but not much,
flattened; but their eyes, and more particularly those of the women, are full
of expression, sometimes sparkling with fire, and sometimes melting with
softness; their teeth also are, almost without exception, most beautifully
even and white, and their breath perfectly without taint. In their motions
there is at once vigour as well as ease; their walk is graceful, their deportment
liberal, and their behaviour to strangers and to each other, affable and
courteous. In their dispositions they appear to be brave, open, and candid,
without suspicion or treachery, cruelty or revenge.

'The natives of Otaheite,' says Cook, 'both men and women, constantly wash their whole bodies in running water three times every day; once as soon as they rise in the morning, once at noon, and again before they sleep at night, whether the sea or river be near them or at a distance. They wash not only the mouth, but the hands at their meals almost between every morsel; and their clothes, as well as their persons, are kept without spot or stain.' . . .

The greater part of the food of Otaheitans is vegetable. Hogs, dogs, and poultry are their only animals, and all of them serve for food. 'We all agreed,' says Cook, 'that a South-Sea dog was little inferior to an English lamb.' Broiling and baking are the only two modes of applying fire to their cookery. Captain Wallis observes, that having no vessel in which water could be subjected to the action of fire, they had no more idea that it could be made *hot*, than that it could be made *solid*.

One of Oberea's peace-offerings to Mr. Banks, for the robbery of his clothes, was a fine fat dog, and the way in which it was prepared and baked was as follows. Tupei, the high priest, undertook to perform the double office of butcher and cook. He first killed him by holding his hands close over his mouth and nose for the space of a quarter of an hour. A hole was then made in the ground about a foot deep, in which a fire was kindled, and some small stones placed in layers, alternately with the wood, to be heated. The dog was then singed, scraped with a shell, and the hair taken off as clean as if he had been scalded in hot water. He was then cut up with the same instrument, and his entrails carefully washed. When the hole was sufficiently heated, the fire was taken out, and some of the stones, being placed at the bottom, were covered with green leaves. The dog, with the entrails, was then placed upon the leaves, and other leaves being laid upon them, the whole was covered with the rest of the hot stones, and the mouth of the hole close stopped with mould. In somewhat less than four hours, it was again opened, and the dog taken out excellently baked, and the party all agreed that he made a very good dish.

The food of the natives, being chiefly vegetable, consists of the various preparations of the bread-fruit, of cocoa-nuts, bananas, plantains, and a great variety of other fruit, the spontaneous products of a rich soil and genial climate. The bread-fruit, when baked in the same manner as the dog was, is rendered soft, and not unlike a boiled potato. Much of this fruit is gathered before it is ripe, and by a certain process is made to undergo the two states of fermentation, the saccharine and acetous, in the latter of which it is moulded into balls, and called *Mahie*. The natives seldom make a meal without this sour paste. Salt water is the universal sauce, without which no meal is eaten. Their drink in general consists of water, or the juice of the cocoa-nut; the art of producing liquors that intoxicate by fermentation being at this time happily unknown among them; neither did they make use of any narcotic, as the natives of some other countries do opium, beetel-nut, and tobacco. . . .

The Morai at Oparrey, Island of Otahytey . . . Looking towards Matavai.
The Polynesian *morai* was a structure of volcanic or coral stone consisting of a courtyard
with an altar at one end. It could be of very considerable size and was used in religious
and other community activities. Some *morais* had their own priests and were of profound
significance in the Tahitian social system: they were subject to taboos (from the Tahitian
word *tapu*) and were the sites at which sacrifices, human as well as animal, were performed.

There is, however, one plant from the root of which they extract a juice
of an intoxicating quality, called *Ava*, but Cook's party saw nothing of its
effects, probably owing to their considering drunkenness as a disgrace.
This vice of drinking ava is said to be peculiar almost to the chiefs, who vie
with each other in drinking the greatest number of draughts, each draught
being about a pint. They keep this intoxicating juice with great care from
the women. . . .

Captain Cook writes: 'the quantity of food which these people eat at a
meal is prodigious. I have seen one man devour two or three fishes as big as a
perch; three bread-fruits, each bigger than two fists; fourteen or fifteen
plantains or bananas, each of them six or seven inches long, and four or
or five round; and near a quart of the pounded bread-fruit, which is as
substantial as the thickest unbaked custard.'

The women, who, on other occasions, always mix in the amusements of the men, who are particularly fond of their society, are wholly excluded from their meals; even brothers and sisters have each their separate baskets of food, and their provisions are separately prepared.

In this fine climate houses are almost unnecessary. The minimum range of the thermometer is about 63°, the maximum 85°, giving an average of 74°. Their sheds or houses consist generally of a thatched roof raised on posts, the eaves reaching to within three or four feet of the ground; the floor is covered with soft hay, over which are laid mats, so that the whole is one cushion, on which they sit by day and sleep by night. They eat in the open air, under the shade of the nearest tree. In each district there is a house erected for general use, much larger than common, some of them exceeding two hundred feet in length, thirty broad, and twenty high. The dwelling-houses all stand in the woody belt which surrounds the island, between the feet of the central mountains and the sea, each having a very small piece of ground cleared, just enough to keep the dropping of the trees from the thatch. An Otaheitan wood consists chiefly of groves of bread-fruit and cocoa-nuts, without underwood, and intersected in all directions by the paths that lead from one house to another. 'Nothing,' says Cook, 'can be more grateful than this shade, in so warm a climate, nor anything more beautiful than these walks.'

A Dance at Otaheite (*left*)

Captain Cook was lavishly entertained while at Tahiti and Webber, the artist present on
that voyage, captured the dignified formality of these occasions in his drawings of many
of the main events. Tahitian dancing, while designed to 'raise in the spectators the most
libidinous desires,' had nothing of the splendor of the mass dances of the Tonga Isles.
The dancers shown here are 'new and elegant . . . more so than we had met at any of
these islands,' according to Cook's notes.

Chart of the Sandwich Islands and Sketch of Karakakooa Bay.

This chart was publicly credited to Lieutenant Henry Roberts by Lieutenant King, the
official editor of Cook's Third Voyage, and this credit remained unchallenged until 1928,
when a copy of *Voyage to the Pacific Ocean*, with Bligh's own marginal notes, was discovered in the Admiralty Library by Rupert T. Gould. Bligh wrote, under the credits,
'None of the Maps and Charts in this publication are from the original drawings of
Lieutenant **Henry** Roberts; he did no more than copy the original ones of Captain Cook.'
Bligh wrote, with reference to the chart of Hawaii (the Sandwich Islands), 'The opposite
Chart and Plan of Karakakooa Bay are copied from my original Survey, as are all Plans
in this Volume.' Bligh's protests about the lack of credit awarded him by King were
ignored. That Bligh was justified in his complaints is proved by the fact that seven-eighths
of the profits from the sale of the book were divided between the estates of the expedition's
leaders, Cook, King and Clerke. The only other officer to receive anything was Bligh – and
he received one-eighth. It was at Kealakekua Bay (from Karakakooa), Hawaii, that Captain
Cook was killed on 14 February 1779.

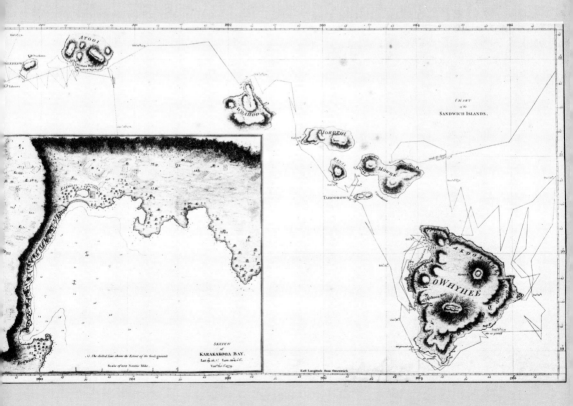

With all the activity they are capable of displaying, and the sprightliness of their disposition, they are fond of indulging in ease and indolence. The trees that produce their food are mostly of spontaneous growth – the bread-fruit, cocoa-nut, bananas of thirteen sorts, besides plantains; a fruit not unlike an apple, which, when ripe, is very pleasant; sweet potatoes, yams, and a species of *arum*; the pandanus, the jambu and the sugar-cane; a variety of plants whose roots are esculent – these, with many others, are produced with so little culture, that, as Cook observes, they seem to be exempted from the first general curse that 'man should eat his bread in the sweat of his brow.' Then for clothing they have the bark of three different trees, the paper mulberry, the bread-fruit tree, and a tree which resembles the wild fig-tree of the West Indies; of these the mulberry only requires to be cultivated.

In preparing the cloth they display a very considerable degree of ingenuity. Red and yellow are the two colours most in use for dyeing their cloth; the red is stated to be exceedingly brilliant and beautiful, approaching nearest to our full scarlet; it is produced by the mixture of the juices of two vegetables, neither of which separately has the least tendency to that hue: one is the *Cordia Sebestina*, the other a species of *Ficus*; of the former the leaves, of the latter the fruits yield the juices. The yellow dye is extracted from the bark of the root of the *Morinda citrifolia*, by scraping and infusing it in water.

Captain James Cook (1728–1779)
James Cook joined the Royal Navy from the merchant service and soon gained promotion because of his exceptional talents in nautical surveying and exploration. He led three major voyages to the Pacific and for his Third Voyage he chose William Bligh, then aged 22, as Master of the *Resolution*, probably in recognition of Bligh's own potential as a navigator and hydrographer. From Cook, Bligh learned a great deal about scientific navigation, seamanship and the command of men. Cook was a stern commander: he flogged delinquents, as was common in his age; he introduced new foods for seamen and flogged any who refused to eat them, and he was driven to chastise many Polynesians for theft – taking hostages, burning their boats, and on one occasion, cutting off the ears of a persistent offender. He had a notorious temper and often exploded into fits of passion which the crew called 'heivas' after a Tahitian dance characterized by the wild gesticulations of the dancers. Bligh certainly had the talents to emulate Cook in navigation, seamanship and exploration, but, as Barrow shows, he did not have the personality to make a truly great commander. Nor, in fairness, due to the parsimony of the Admiralty, did he have the facilities and resources on the *Bounty* mission which Cook had been afforded on his expeditions. The smallness of the *Bounty*, and the lack of either a second ship or a contingent of marines, was a source of lasting bitterness on Bligh's part.

Sitodium altile.

Otaheite

Sydney Parkinson pinxt 1769

Their matting is exceedingly beautiful, particularly that which is made from the bark of the *Hibiscus tiliaceus*, and of a species of *Pandanus*. Others are made of rushes and grass with amazing facility and dispatch. In the same manner their basket and wicker work are most ingeniously made; the former in patterns of a thousand different kinds. Their nets and fishing-lines are strong and neatly made, so are their fish-hooks of pearl-shell; and their clubs are admirable specimens of wood-carving.

A people so lively, sprightly, and good-humoured as the Otaheitans are, must necessarily have their amusements. They are fond of music, such as is derived from a rude flute and a drum; of dancing, wrestling, shooting with the bow, and throwing the lance. They exhibit frequent trials of skill and strength in wrestling.

But these simple-minded people have their vices, and great ones too. Chastity is almost unknown among a certain description of women: there is a detestable society called *Arreoy*, composed, it would seem, of a particular class, who are supposed to be the chief warriors of the island. In this society the men and women live in common; and on the birth of a child it is immediately smothered, that its bringing up may not interfere with the brutal pleasures of either father or mother. Another savage practice is that of immolating human beings at the *Morais*, which serve as temples as well as sepulchres; and yet they entertain a due sense and reverential awe of the Deity. 'With regard to their worship,' Captain Cook does the Otaheitans but justice in saying, 'they reproach many who bear the name of Christians. You see no instances of an Otaheitan drawing near the Eatooa [the god] with carelessness and inattention; he is all devotion; he approaches the place of worship with reverential awe; uncovers when he treads on sacred ground; and prays with a fervour that would do honour to a better profession. None dares dispute the existence of the Deity.' . . .

Such was the state of this beautiful island and its interesting and fascinating natives at the time when Captain Wallis first discovered and Lieutenant Cook shortly afterwards visited it. What they now are, as described by Captain Beechey, it is lamentable to reflect. All their usual and innocent amusements have been denounced by the missionaries, and, in lieu of them, these poor people have been driven to seek for resources in habits of indolence and apathy: that simplicity of character, which atoned for many of their faults, has been converted into cunning and hypocrisy; and drunkenness, poverty, and disease have thinned the island of its former population to a frightful degree. There is but too much reason to ascribe this diminution to praying, psalm-singing, and dram-drinking. . . .

The Bread-fruit
First discovered by Mendana de Neyra in 1598, its potential as a food was popularised by William Dampier in 1729 and by Hawkesworth in his 1773 account of Cook's voyage. Both over-sold its virtues: the plantation slaves found it indigestible.

Deptford dockyard, painted by John Clevely in 1792.
Naval dockyards were administered by the Navy Board separately from the Admiralty prior to 1832 and one wonders how Barrow found time to write his account of the *Bounty* mutiny during the year in which the two offices were being merged. Deptford is on the south bank of the River Thames, near the Royal Naval Hospital at Greenwich. It was while the ship was fitting out at Deptford that James Morrison accused Bligh of misappropriating two cheeses from the ship's stores. Bligh claimed that the cheeses were stolen by the crew. John Clevely's brother James sailed with Bligh as carpenter on the *Resolution* and Clevely used a drawing by his brother as the basis for his famous painting of Cook's death at Kealakekua Bay.

CHAPTER TWO

The Bread-fruit

In the year 1787, merchants and planters interested in the West India possessions having represented to his Majesty that the introduction of the bread-fruit tree into the islands of those seas, to constitute an article of food, would be of benefit to the inhabitants, the king was graciously pleased to comply with their request; and a vessel was accordingly purchased, and fitted at Deptford with the necessary fixtures and preparations, for carrying into effect the benevolent object of the voyage. The arrangements for disposing the plants were undertaken by Sir Joseph Banks, who superintended the whole equipment of the ship with the greatest assiduity till she was in all respects ready for sea. He named the ship the *Bounty*, and recommended Lieutenant Bligh, who had been with Captain Cook [in the *Resolution*, during Cook's last voyage], to command her. Her burden was about two hundred and fifteen tons; and her establishment consisted of one lieutenant, who was commanding officer, one master, three warrant officers, one surgeon, two master's mates, two midshipmen, and thirty-four petty officers and seamen, making in all forty-four; to which were added two skilful and careful men, recommended by Sir Joseph Banks, to have the management of the plants intended to be carried to the West Indies, and others to be brought home for his Majesty's garden at Kew: one was David Nelson, who had served in a similar situation in Captain Cook's last voyage; the other William Brown, as an assistant to him.

The object of all the former voyages to the South Seas, undertaken by command of his Majesty George III, was the increase of knowledge by new discoveries; the intention of the present voyage was to derive some practical benefit from the discoveries that had already been made; and no object was deemed more likely to realise the expectation of benefit than the bread-fruit, which afforded to the natives of Otaheite so very considerable a portion of their food, and which it was hoped it might also do for the black population of the West India Islands.

The bread-fruit plant was no new discovery of either Wallis or Cook. So early as the year 1688, that excellent old navigator, Dampier, thus describes it:- 'The bread-fruit, as we call it, grows on a large tree, as big and high as our largest apple-trees; it hath a spreading head, full of branches and dark leaves. The fruit grows on the boughs like apples; it is as big as a penny-loaf, when wheat is at five shillings the bushel; it is of a round shape, and hath a thick tough rind; when the fruit is ripe it is yellow and soft, and the taste is sweet and pleasant. The natives of Guam use it for bread. They gather it, when full grown, while it is green and hard; then they bake it in an oven, which scorcheth the rind and makes it black, but they scrape off the outside

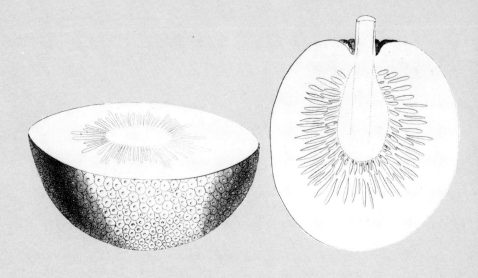

Sections of the Bread-fruit. (*above*)
The effect of the American War of Independence on the food supplies of the slave colonies of the West Indies, combined with the desire of the slave owners to feed their people at no cost to themselves, persuaded the British Government to attempt to transplant the bread-fruit from Tahiti. Bligh's name will evermore be associated with the bread-fruit and in his own day he was teasingly nicknamed 'Bread-fruit Bligh' (and sometimes, more offensively, 'the *Bounty* Bastard').

Bounty Armed Transport, Carrying four 4-pounders and 10 Swivels. (*above right*)
The *Bethia* was purchased by the Navy Board from Messrs Wellbank, Sharp and Brown for £1950 (the asking price was £2600) on 26 May, 1787, and was taken to Deptford for refitting and supply. This added a further £4456: in all £6406 at a time when, for comparison, Bligh's salary as a lieutenant was about £70 a year. While the *Bethia*, renamed *Bounty*, was 'an excellent sea boat', it was far too small and cramped for its long mission. Bligh reported to Banks that 'the burthen of this ship is nearly 215 tons, her length on deck 90ft 10in, and breadth outside to outside of bends 24ft 3in; a flush deck, and a pretty figurehead of a woman in riding habit.' Lord Selkirk considered the vessel, 'highly improper for so long a voyage.' Cook's *Endeavour* weighed 368 tons and the *Resolution* 462 tons. Cook also had a party of marines and a second ship in attendance, while Bligh was given a very small ship, was denied a marine contingent and was effectively told to get on with the job.

Deck plans of the *Bounty*. (*right*)
Refitting of the *Bounty* commenced at Deptford in June 1787 under the control of Banks and the gardener David Nelson. The great cabin was converted to house the pots holding the bread-fruit plants and on 25 June the Navy Board reported to the Admiralty that Banks had proposed, 'to have as many Gratings on the Upper deck as conveniently can be given air: likewise to have Scuttles through the side for the same reason . . . leading the upper part of the Deck, that the water which may drain through the several pots may run to the fore part and be convey'd to a reservoir for the saving of it, which being submitted for your Consideration, we pray your directions thereon.' Bligh was appointed commander on the 16th August.

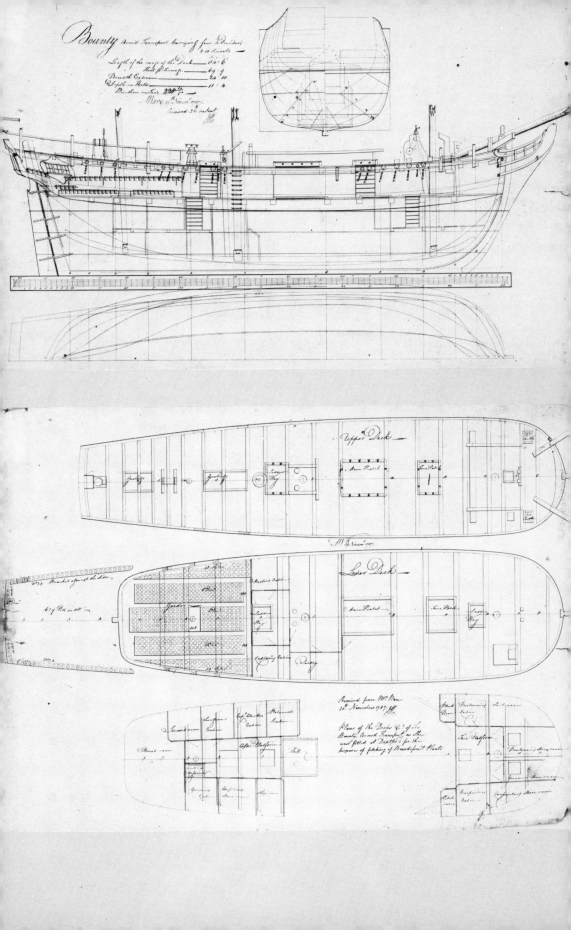

The Town and Harbor of Portsmouth, with a View of His Majesty's fleet at Spithead.
When John Bowles made this painting, in about 1812, Portsmouth was the main base for
the Royal Navy's Channel Fleet. It was from Spithead, the anchorage between the
mainland and the Isle of Wight, that the *Bounty* sailed in 1787.

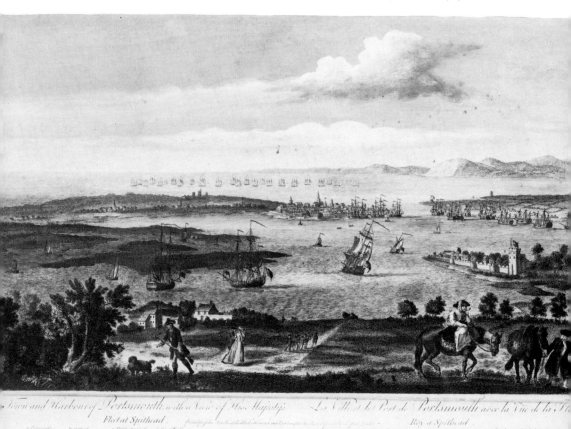

black crust, and there remains a tender thin crust; and the inside is soft,
tender, and white, like the crumb of a penny-loaf. This fruit lasts in season
eight months in the year, during which the natives eat no other sort of food
of bread kind. . . .'

Cook says also that its taste is insipid, with a slight sweetness, somewhat
resembling that of the crumb of wheaten bread mixed with a Jerusalem
artichoke. It is not surprising that the West India planters should have
felt desirous of introducing it into those islands; and accordingly the introduction of it was subsequently accomplished, notwithstanding the failure
of the present voyage; it has not, however, been found to answer the
expectation that had reasonably been entertained. The climate, as to latitude,
ought to be the same, or nearly so, as that of Otaheite, but there would appear
to be some difference in the situation or nature of the soil, that prevents it
from thriving in the West India Islands.

Bounty before and after the mutiny
Bligh charted the Bounty Isles (off New Zealand) and Aitutaki during the fateful voyage,
and after leaving Tahiti, Christian discovered Rarotonga and possibly also Ono-i-Lau
while seeking a refuge. His search covered 7,800 miles before landing was made at Pitcairn.

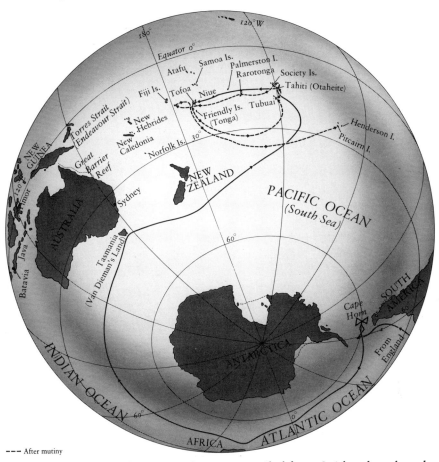

- - - After mutiny

On the 23rd December, 1787, the *Bounty* sailed from Spithead, and on the
26th it blew a severe storm of wind from the eastward, which continued to
the 29th, in the course of which the ship suffered greatly. One sea broke
away the spare-yards and spars out of the starboard main-chains. Another
heavy sea broke into the ship and stove all the boats. Several casks of beer
that had been lashed upon deck, were broke loose and washed overboard;
and it was not without great difficulty and risk that they were able to secure
the boats from being washed away entirely. Besides other mischief done to
them in this storm, a large quantity of bread was damaged and rendered
useless, for the sea had stove in the stern and filled the cabin with water.

This made it desirable to touch at Teneriffe to put the ship to rights, where
they arrived on the 5th January, 1788, and having refitted and refreshed, they
sailed again on the 10th.

'I now,' says Bligh, 'divided the people into three watches, and gave the charge of the third watch to Mr. Fletcher Christian, one of the mates. I have always considered this a desirable regulation when circumstances will admit of it, and I am persuaded that unbroken rest not only contributes much towards the health of the ship's company, but enables them more readily to exert themselves in cases of sudden emergency.'

Wishing to proceed to Otaheite without stopping, and the late storm having diminished their supply of provisions, it was deemed expedient to put all hands on an allowance of two-thirds of bread. It was also decided that water for drinking should be passed through filtering stones that had been procured at Teneriffe. 'I now,' says Bligh, 'made the ship's company acquainted with the object of the voyage, and gave assurances of the certainty of promotion to every one whose endeavours should merit it.' Nothing, indeed, seemed to be neglected on the part of the commander to make his officers and men comfortable and happy. He was himself a thorough-bred sailor, and availed himself of every possible means of preserving the health of his crew. Continued rain and a close atmosphere had covered everything in the ship with mildew. She was therefore aired below with fires, and frequently sprinkled with vinegar, and every interval of dry weather was taken advantage of to open all the hatchways, and clean the ship, and to have all the people's wet things washed and dried. With these precautions to secure health, they passed the hazy and sultry atmosphere of the low latitudes without a single complaint.

On Sunday, the 2nd of March, Lieutenant Bligh observes, 'after seeing that every person was clean, Divine service was performed, according to my usual custom. On this day I gave to Mr. Fletcher Christian, whom I had before desired to take charge of the third watch, a written order to act as lieutenant.'

Having reached as far as the latitude of 36° south, on the 9th March, 'the change of temperature,' he observes, 'began now to be sensibly felt, there being a variation in the thermometer, since yesterday, of eight degrees. That the people might not suffer by their own negligence, I gave orders for their light tropical clothing to be put by, and made them dress in a manner more suited to a cold climate. On this day, on a complaint of the master, I found it necessary to punish Matthew Quintal, one of the seamen, with two dozen lashes, for insolence and mutinous behaviour. Before this I had not had occasion to punish any person on board.'

The sight of New Year's Harbour, in Staaten Land [Staten Island, off the tip of Tierra del Fuego], almost tempted him, he says, to put in; but the lateness of the season, and the people [crew] being in good health, determined him to lay aside all thoughts of refreshment until they should reach Otaheite. Indeed the extraordinary care he had taken to preserve the health of the ship's company rendered any delay in this cold and inhospitable region unnecessary.

They soon after this had to encounter tremendous weather off Cape Horn, storms of wind, with hail and sleet, which made it necessary to keep a

A View of the Streight le Maire between Terra del Fuego and Staten Land.
George (later Lord) Anson circumnavigated the world in 1740–1744 in the *Centurion*
accompanied by five warships and two supply ships. He intended to open the Pacific to
Britain. In the course of the voyage he lost 1300 men and seven ships but captured bullion
valued at more than a million pounds. Bligh had a copy of Anson's *Voyage* with him on
the *Bounty* and wrote in his Log, 'I am fortunate perhaps in seeing the Coast of Terra del
Fuego at a time when it is freest of snow, however I cannot help remarking that at this
time it has not shewn itself with all the horrors mentioned by former Navigators. . . . But
Staten Land does at first bear a most desolate appearance.'

A View of Streight le Maire between Terra del Fuego, and Staten Land, in ⅌ Latᵈ of 54:45 Sᵒ, and Longᵈ from London 70:04 W⅌, with a Squadron ⅌ Ships under ⅌ Command of Commodore GEO. ANSON Esqᵣ. A Part of Staten Land. b Cape Sᵗ Bartholomew. C Part of Terra del Fuego. d Pᵗ Maurice. by some taken for ⅌ Bay of good Succefs, by others for Valentines Bay. We Steer'd thro'⅌ Streights Sᵒ within three Leagᵉ of Terra del Fuego, and found ⅌ ⅌ rapid current set to ⅌ Southward. till past ⅌ Streights, then it set to ⅌ Eastward along Staten-land. agreable to Monſr Freſier's account: We had soundings from 5 to 8 fathoms all Stones and ſhells between two and three Leagᵉ from Terra del Fuego. Variation of ⅌ Compaſs 22:30 Easterly

constant fire night and day; and one of the watch always attended to dry the
people's wet clothes. This stormy weather continued for nine days; the
ship began to complain, and required pumping every hour; the decks became
so leaky that the commander was obliged to allot the great cabin to those
who had wet births, to hang their hammocks in. Finding they were losing
ground every day, and that it was hopeless to persist in attempting a passage
by this route, at this season of the year, to the Society Islands, and after
struggling for thirty days in this tempestuous ocean, it was determined to
bear away for the Cape of Good Hope. The helm was accordingly put a-
weather, to the great joy of every person on board.

They arrived at the Cape on the 23rd of May, and having remained there ✓
thirty-eight days to refit the ship, replenish provisions, and refresh the
crew, they sailed again on the 1st July, and anchored in Adventure Bay, in
Van Dieman's Land [Tasmania], on the 20th August. [At this time Tasmania
was not known to be an island: it was thought to be the southernmost point
of Australia – or New Holland as it was then called.] Here they remained
taking in wood and water till the 4th September, and on the evening of the
25th October they saw Otaheite; and the next day came to anchor in
Matavai Bay, after a distance since leaving England, of twenty-seven
thousand and eighty-six miles. . . .

Otoo, the chief of the district, on hearing of the arrival of the *Bounty*, sent
a small pig and a young plantain tree, as a token of friendship. The ship was
now plentifully supplied with provisions; every man on board having as
much as he could consume.

Otoo, King of Tahiti.
Bligh first met Tu (from O Too) on Cook's Third Voyage in 1777. When the *Bounty*
visited Tahiti in 1788, Tu was thirty-five years old and six feet three inches tall. He was not
the king of Tahiti as Cook and Bligh believed, but the chief of Pare, a small district
behind One Tree Hill at Matavai, and when the *Bounty* arrived he was in hiding after his
district had been sacked by a rival. Bligh considered him 'one of the most timorous men
existing,' but timorous or not he was clearly a consummate politician in Tahitian terms. He
never made the mistake of correcting the Europeans' erroneous view of his status, and he
very quickly grasped the strategic importance of Matavai Bay as the only safe anchorage
for European ships, spending much of his life getting control (mainly by guile) of the
surrounding districts. He later declared himself *King Pomare I.*

As soon as the ship was secured, Lieutenant Bligh went on shore with the
chief, Poeeno, passing through a walk delightfully shaded with bread-fruit
trees, to his own house, where his wife and her sister were busily employed
staining a piece of cloth red. They desired him to sit down on a mat, and
with great kindness offered him refreshments. Several strangers were now
introduced, who came to offer their congratulations, and behaved with great
decorum and attention. On taking leave, he says, 'the ladies, for they deserve
to be called such from their natural and unaffected manners, and elegance of
deportment, got up, and taking some of their finest cloth and a mat, clothed
me in the Otaheitan fashion, and then said, "We will go with you to your
boat;" and each taking me by the hand, amidst a great crowd, led me to the
water side, and then took their leave.' In this day's walk, Bligh had the
satisfaction to see that the island had received some benefit from the former
visits of Captain Cook. Two shaddocks were brought to him, a fruit which
they had not till Cook introduced it; and among the articles which they
brought off to the ship, and offered for sale, were capsicums, pumpkins, and
two young goats. 'In the course of two or three days,' says he, 'an intimacy
between the natives and the ship's company was become so general, that
there was scarcely a man in the ship who had not already his *tayo* or friend.'

Nelson, the gardener, and his assistant, being sent out to look for young
plants, it was no small degree of pleasure to find them report on their return,
that, according to appearances, the object of the voyage would probably be

accomplished with ease; the plants were plentiful, and no apparent objection on the part of the natives to collect as many as might be wanted.

Presents were now given to Otoo, the Chief of Matavai, who had changed his name to Tinah. He was told that, on account of the kindness of his people to Captain Cook, King George had sent out those valuable presents to him; and 'will you not, Tinah,' said Bligh, 'send something to King George in return?' 'Yes,' he said, 'I will send him anything I have;' and then began to enumerate the different articles in his power, among which he mentioned the bread-fruit. This was the exact point to which Bligh was endeavouring to lead him, and he was immediately told that the bread-fruit trees were what King George would like very much, on which he promised that a great many should be put on board.

Hitherto no thefts had been committed, and Bligh was congratulating himself on the improvement of the Otaheitans in this respect, as the same facilities and the same temptations were open to them as before. The ship, as on former occasions, was constantly crowded with visitors. One day, however, the gudgeon of the rudder belonging to the large cutter was drawn out and stolen, without being perceived by the man who was stationed to take care of her; and as this and some other petty thefts, mostly owing to the negligence of the men, were commencing, and would have a tendency to interrupt the good terms on which they were with the chiefs, 'I thought,' says Bligh, 'it would have a good effect to punish the boat-keeper in their presence, and accordingly I ordered him a dozen lashes.'

The longer they remained on the island, the more they had occasion to be pleased with the conduct of the islanders. Into every house they wished to enter, they always experienced a kind reception. The Otaheitans, we are told, have the most perfect easiness of manner, equally free from forwardness and formality; and that 'there is a candour and sincerity about them that is quite delightful.'

On one occasion the *Bounty* had nearly gone ashore in a tremendous gale of wind, and on another did actually get aground; on both which accidents, these kind-hearted people came in crowds to congratulate the captain on her escape; and many of them are stated to have been affected in the most lively manner, shedding tears while the danger in which the ship was placed continued.

On the 9th December, the surgeon of the *Bounty* died from the effects of intemperance and indolence. This unfortunate man is represented to have been in a constant state of intoxication, and was so averse from any kind of exercise, that he never could be prevailed on to take half a dozen hours upon deck at a time in the whole course of the voyage. Lieutenant Bligh had obtained permission to bury him on shore; and on going with the chief Tinah to the spot intended for his burial place, 'I found,' says he, 'the natives had already begun to dig his grave.' Tinah asked if they were doing it right? 'There,' says he, 'the sun rises, and there it sets.' Whether the idea of making the grave east and west is their own, or whether they learnt it from the

Sketch of the North Part of Otaheite.
The *Bounty* was hit by gales while at Matavai Bay in December and on Christmas Day
Bligh ordered a move to a safer anchorage at Toaroa (from Toahroah). During the move,
the ship ran aground and Bligh expressed his displeasure with both John Fryer, the Master,
whose job it was to act as lookout and who had also previously surveyed the route, and
Fletcher Christian, the Acting Lieutenant, who was supposed to guide the ship from the
launch. While the poor weather conditions might in part excuse Fryer's failings, Christian
had only himself to blame in allowing the launch to become becalmed in the lee of the
Bounty. Bligh was attempting a very difficult maneuvre through a channel only 200 yards
wide into a harbor only 350 yards across, and his temper was tried even further when the
anchor cables were entangled during the refloating routine.

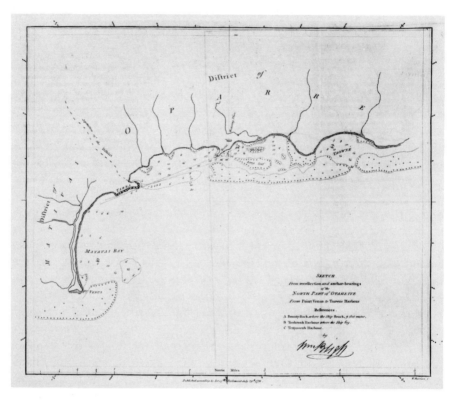

Spaniards, who buried the captain of their ship on the island in 1774, there
were no means of ascertaining; but it was certain they had no intimation of
that kind from anybody belonging to the *Bounty*. When the funeral took
place, the chiefs and many of the natives attended the ceremony, and shewed
great attention during the service.

The border of low land, which is of the breadth of about three miles,
between the sea-coast and the foot of the hills, consists of a very delightful
country, well covered with bread-fruit and cocoa-trees, and strewed with
houses in which are swarms of children playing about. 'It is delightful,'
Bligh observes, 'to see the swarms of little children that are everywhere to be
seen employed at their several amusements; some flying kites, some swinging
in ropes suspended from the boughs of trees, others walking on stilts, some

wrestling, and others playing all manner of antic tricks such as are common to boys in England. The little girls have also their amusements, consisting generally of heivahs or dances. On an evening, just before sunset the whole beach abreast the ship is described as being like a parade, crowded with men, women, and children, who go on with their sports and amusements till nearly dark, when every one peaceably returns to his home.

It did not appear that much pains were taken in their plantations, except those of the ava and the cloth-plant; many of the latter are fenced with stone, and surrounded with a ditch. In fact, Nature has done so much for them, that they have no great occasion to use exertion in obtaining a sufficient supply of either food or raiment. Yet when Bligh commenced taking up the bread-fruit plants, he derived much assistance from the natives in collecting and pruning them, which they understood perfectly well.

The behaviour of these people on all occasions was highly deserving of praise. One morning, at the relief of the watch, the small cutter was missing. The ship's company were immediately mustered, when it appeared that three men were absent. They had taken with them eight stand of arms and ammunition; but what their plan was, or which way they had gone, no one on board seemed to have the least knowledge. Information being given of the route they had taken, the master was dispatched to search for the cutter, and one of the chiefs went with him; but before they had got half way, they met the boat with five of the natives, who were bringing her back to the ship. For this service they were handsomely rewarded. The chiefs promised to use every possible means to detect and bring back the deserters, which, in a few days, some of the islanders had so far accomplished as to seize and bind them, but let them loose again on a promise that they would return to their ship. This they did not exactly fulfil, but gave themselves up soon after on a search being made for them.

A few days after this, a much more serious occurrence happened. The wind had blown fresh in the night, and at daylight it was discovered that the cable, by which the ship rode, had been cut near the water's edge, in such a manner, that only one strand remained whole. While they were securing the ship, Tinah came on board; and, though there was no reason whatever to suppose otherwise than that he was perfectly innocent of the transaction, nevertheless, says the commander, 'I spoke to him in a very peremptory manner, and insisted upon his discovering and bringing to me the offender. He promised to use his utmost endeavours to discover the guilty person. The next morning he and his wife came to me, and assured me that they had made the strictest inquiries without success. This was not at all satisfactory, and I behaved towards them with great coolness, at which they were much distressed; and the lady at length gave vent to her sorrow by tears. I could no longer keep up the appearance of mistrusting them, but I earnestly recommended to them, as they valued the King of England's friendship, that they would exert their utmost endeavours to find out the offenders, which they faithfully promised to do.'

Facsimile: Log of the *Bounty*, 7 July 1788.

Bligh's Log recorded all events, routine, serious and trivial, and as it was written up each day, rather than retrospectively, it attracts a high degree of credibility. Thomas Huggan, the *Bounty's* Surgeon, mentioned in this extract, was in the final stages of alcoholic collapse when appointed in August 1787. The Log includes many statements about Huggan's drunkenness: on 21 October 1788 the following is recorded. 'The Surgeon kept to his Bed all this day and always drunk, without eating an ounce of food. If it is ever necessary this should be publickly known, I may be blamed for not searching his Cabbin and taking all liquor from him; but my motive is that, altho Every person on board is acquainted with his ebreity, yet hoping every day will produce change in him, I forebear making a publick matter of My disapprobation of his conduct, in expectation as he has done many times this Voyage, he may turn sober again.' Huggan's carelessness directly caused the death of James Valentine, seaman, from an infection. This incident mortified Bligh. Huggan fell into an alcoholic coma on 10 December 1788, at Tahiti and died that same night.

Here Bligh observes, it had since occurred to him, that this attempt to cut the ship adrift was most probably the act of some of his own people; whose purpose of remaining at Otaheite might have been effectually answered without danger, if the ship had been driven on shore. At the time it occurred, he says, he entertained not the least thought of this kind, having no suspicion that so strong an attachment to these islands could prevail among his people as to induce them to abandon every prospect of returning to their native country.

This after-thought of Bligh will appear in the sequel to be wholly gratuitous. Yet he might naturally enough have concluded that so long and unrestrained an intercourse with a people among whom every man had his *tayo* or friend; where he found himself surrounded by female allurements in the midst of ease and indolence, and living in a state of luxury without submitting to any kind of labour – might be supposed to create a desire for a longer residence in such a country. But this supposition is not borne out by subsequent events. The damage done to the cable was, in all probability, owing to its chafing over the rocky bottom.

The *Bounty* arrived on the 26th October, 1788, and remained till the 4th April, 1789. On the 31st March, the Commander says, 'To-day, all the plants were on board, being in seven hundred and seventy-four pots, thirty-nine tubs, and twenty-four boxes. The number of bread-fruit plants were one thousand and fifteen; besides which, we had collected a number of other plants: the *avee*, which is one of the finest flavoured fruits in the world; the *ayyah*, which is a fruit not so rich, but of a fine flavour and very refreshing; the *rattah*, not much unlike a chestnut; and the *orai-ab*, which is a very superior kind of plantain.'

While these active preparations for departure were going on, there appeared among the natives an evident degree of sorrow that they were so soon to leave them, which they showed by a more than usual degree of kindness and attention. The excellent chief Tinah, with his wife, brothers, and sister, requested permission to remain on board for the night previous to the sailing of the *Bounty*. The ship was crowded the whole day with the natives, and she was loaded with presents of cocoa-nuts, plantains, bread-fruits, hogs, and goats. Contrary to what had been the usual practice, there was this evening no dancing or mirth on the beach, but all was silent.

At sunset, the boat returned from landing Tinah and his wife, and the ship made sail, bidding farewell to Otaheite, where, Bligh observes, 'for twenty-three weeks we had been treated with the utmost affection and regard, and which seemed to increase in proportion to our stay. That we were not insensible to their kindness, the events which followed more than sufficiently prove; for to the friendly and endearing behaviour of these people, may be ascribed the motives for that event which effected the ruin of an expedition, that there was every reason to hope would have been completed in the most fortunate manner.' . . .

A few days after sailing, the weather became squally, and a thick body of black clouds collected in the east. A water-spout was in a short time seen at no great distance from the ship, which appeared to great advantage from the darkness of the clouds behind it. The upper part is described as being about two feet in diameter; and the lower about eight inches. It advanced rapidly towards the ship, when it was deemed expedient to alter the course, and to take in all the sails, except the foresail; soon after which it passed within ten yards of the stern, making a rustling noise, but without their feeling the least effect from its being so near. The rate at which it travelled was judged to be about ten miles per hour, going towards the west, in the direction of the wind; and in a quarter of an hour after passing the ship, it dispersed.

The *Bounty* anchored at Anamooka on the 23rd April. . . . 'I landed,' says Bligh, 'in order to procure some bread-fruit plants to supply the place of one that was dead, and two or three others that were a little sickly. I walked to the west part of the bay, where some plants and seeds had been sown by Captain Cook; and had the satisfaction to see, in a plantation close by, about twenty fine pineapple plants, but no fruit, this not being the proper season. They told me that they had eaten many of them, that they were very fine and large, and that at Tongataboo there were great numbers.'

A brisk trade soon began to be carried on for yams; some plantains and bread-fruit were likewise brought on board, but no hogs. Some of the sailing

---

War Canoes

In its heyday the Tahitian fleet of war canoes numbered more than 300. Their magnificent design and decoration made an enormous impression on Cook who wrote, 'the whole made a grand and Noble appearance such as was never seen before in this Sea.' The interesting bow design had a practical purpose: the Tahitians would drive their canoes right onto the beach like modern landing craft and the warriors would storm ashore to attack their enemies. The largest double canoe Cook saw was 108 feet long – longer than the *Bounty*. King Tu tried many times to persuade Cook and Bligh to subdue his enemies. Wisely both refused, realising that European fire-power would devastate Tahitian culture. The *Bounty* mutineers did allow themselves to become embroiled in local disputes – with the almost inevitable result that within a few years the population and economy were in decline, and the ability to build these superb craft was destined soon to be lost.

Table Bay

The *Bounty* spent thirty-eight days refitting at Cape Town, and here Morrison accused Bligh and the officers of being 'base enough to sign false *Survey Books* and papers to the prejudice of his Majesty & Government,' and that, 'the Bills drawn at the Cape of Good Hope, will prove, that Wm. Muspratt and Thos. Hayward, both belonging to the *Bounty*, have signed as respectable merchants of that place.' Morrison also claimed that it was 'well known to every Officer and Seaman that belonged to the *Bounty* that there never were any Masts, Yards or Sails lost . . . or any purchased in their stead, or any Provisions lost or condemned by Survey, or any stores of any kind . . . after the said Ship sailed from Spithead.' (*Memorandums and Particulars*, 1792.) Bligh replied, 'Surely if anything will refute this assertion, & show this Morrison, (who was the worst of the Mutineers next to Christian and Churchill, if not their adviser) in the light he ought to be held in, it is this – Musprat & Hayward signed only as witnesses on C. Bligh's behalf that He payed the Money to Mr C. Brandt. . . . These papers are now to be seen at the Publick Boards.' (Bligh: *Remarks on Morrison's Journal*, 1794.)

canoes, which arrived in the course of the day, were large enough to contain not less than ninety passengers. From these the officers and crew purchased hogs, dogs, fowls, and shaddocks; yams, very fine and large; one of them actually weighed above forty-five pounds. The crowd of natives had become so great the next day, Sunday 26th, that it became impossible to do anything. The watering party were therefore ordered to go on board, and it was determined to sail; the ship was accordingly unmoored and got under weigh. A grapnel, however, had been stolen, and Bligh informed the chiefs that were still on board, that unless it was returned, they must remain in the ship, at which they were surprised and not a little alarmed. 'I detained them,' he says, 'till sunset, when their uneasiness and impatience increased to such a degree, that they began to beat themselves about the face and eyes, and some of them cried bitterly. As this distress was more than the grapnel was worth, I could not think of detaining them longer, and called their canoes alongside. I told them they were at liberty to go, and made each of them a present of a hatchet, a saw, with some knives, gimlets, and nails. This unexpected present, and the sudden change in their situation affected them not less with joy than they had before been with apprehension. They were unbounded in their acknowledgements; and I have little doubt but that we parted better friends than if the affair had never happened.'

From this island the ship stood to the northward all night, with light winds; and on the next day, the 27th, at noon, they were between the islands Tofoa and Kotoo.

'Thus far,' says Bligh, 'the voyage had advanced in a course of uninterrupted prosperity, and had been attended with many circumstances equally pleasing and satisfactory. A very different scene was now to be experienced. A conspiracy had been formed, which was to render all our past labour productive only of extreme misery and distress. The means had been concerted and prepared with so much secrecy and circumspection, that no one circumstance appeared to occasion the smallest suspicion of the impending calamity, the result of an act of piracy the most consummate and atrocious that was probably ever committed.'

How far Bligh was justified in ascribing the calamity to a conspiracy will be seen hereafter. The following chapter will detail the facts of the mutinous proceedings as stated by the Lieutenant, in his own words.

Matavai Bay, Tahiti

The *Bounty* spent five months at Tahiti, two of them at the anchorage in Matavai Bay which had earlier been used by Cook. The Tahitians did not live in large villages but in individual huts scattered throughout the low-lying areas close to the shore. The high mountains in the background provided a refuge for the oppressed, those out of favor with their chiefs, and for the victims of the occasional wars that erupted when local disputes or chiefly ambitions got out of control. Some of the mutineers sought refuge in these mountains when the *Pandora* arrived in 1791. It took the naval parties several days to capture them, which they did after pursuing them into the hills with assistance from some of the Tahitians who were doubtless relieved to be rid of some of the wilder members of the group.

A View of Anamooka.
Bligh visited Nomuka in the Tonga Islands in 1777 with Captain Cook, whose account
notes the proclivity of the islanders for thievery – outrageous even by Polynesian standards.
Bligh's version of what happened when the *Bounty* called at the island contains his only
direct criticism of Fletcher Christian. His Log entry for 15 April 1789 reads, 'At Day break
I sent the Parties away. Those a Watering under the Command of Mr Christian and
consisting of 11 Men, and the Wooders under the direction of Mr Elphinstone, Mate of the
Ship, consisting of four Men. To the Waterers I ordered Arms, but to be kept in the Boat
. . . and to the Wooders I gave none. To these people I not only gave my Orders but also
my advice, that they were to keep themselves unconnected with the Natives. They however
had not been an hour on shore before one Man had lost his Axe and another his Adz.
The cause of this was that the Officers contrary to my direct orders suffered the Indians to
crowd round them and amuse them, and by that means the Theft was committed. The Men
cleared themselves of the Neglect as they could not comply with any part of their duty and
keep their Tools in their Hands, and therefore merit no punishment. As to the Officers I
have no recourse, or do I ever feel myself safe in the few instances I trust them.'

CHAPTER THREE

The Mutiny

'In the morning of the 28th April, the north-westernmost of the Friendly Islands, called Tofoa, bearing north-east, I was steering to the westward with a ship in most perfect order, all my plants in a most flourishing condition, all my men and officers in good health, and in short, everything to flatter and insure my most sanguine expectations. On leaving the deck I gave directions for the course to be steered during the night. The master had the first watch; the gunner, the middle watch; and Mr. Christian, the morning watch. This was the turn of duty for the night.

'Just before sun-rising on Tuesday the 28th, while I was yet asleep, Mr. Christian, officer of the watch, Charles Churchill, ship's corporal, John Mills, gunner's mate, and Thomas Burkitt, seaman, came into my cabin, and seizing me, tied my hands with a cord behind my back, threatening me with instant death if I spoke or made the least noise. I called, however, as loud as I could in hopes of assistance; but they had already secured the officers who were not of their party, by placing sentinels at their doors. There were three men at my cabin door, besides the four within; Christian had only a cutlass in his hand, the others had muskets and bayonets. I was hauled out of bed, and forced on deck in my shirt, suffering great pain from the tightness with which they had tied my hands behind my back. [I was] held by Fletcher Christian, and Charles Churchill, with a bayonet at my breast, and two men, Alexander Smith and Thomas Burkitt behind me, with loaded muskets cocked and bayonets fixed. I demanded the reason of such violence, but received no other answer than abuse, for not holding my tongue. The master, the gunner, Mr. Elphinstone, the master's mate, and Nelson, were kept confined below; and the fore-hatchway was guarded by sentinels. The boatswain and carpenter, and also Mr. Samuel the clerk, were allowed to come upon deck, where they saw me standing abaft the mizen-mast, with my hands tied behind my back, under a guard, with Christian at their head. The boatswain was ordered to hoist the launch out, with a threat, if he did not do it instantly, to take care of himself.

'When the boat was out, Mr. Hayward and Mr. Hallet, two of the midshipmen, and Mr. Samuel, were ordered into it. I demanded what their intention was in giving this order, and endeavoured to persuade the people near me not to persist in such acts of violence; but it was to no effect – "Hold your tongue, Sir, or you are dead this instant," was constantly repeated to me.

'The master by this time had sent to request that he might come on deck, which was permitted; but he was soon ordered back again to his cabin.

Facsimile: Bligh's *Voyage of the Bounty's Launch* (below)
Aiutaki (from Whytootaikee), the island discovered by Bligh in the *Bounty* and mentioned
in this extract from his journal of the launch voyage after the mutiny, was named by the
mutineers as their rendevous with Captain Cook. They lied to the gullible Tahitians in
order to explain their return so soon with the *Bounty* without Bligh and played upon the
islanders' ignorance of Cook's death ten years earlier. The extract also includes Bligh's
description of his arrest by Fletcher Christian.

The Seizure of Lieutenant Bligh. (*opposite*)
The artist has captured some aspects of the seizure of Bligh and confused others but the
overall truth is represented: Christian's mutiny was possible because his party was armed
and the majority of the crew were not. Bligh, however, was roused from his sleep shortly
before sunrise in his nightshirt. He was bound with rope which had caught up his shirt
and exposed his buttocks. He was certainly not dressed in trousers and with his stockings
and shoes on. Of the four men who seized Bligh only one, Thomas Burkitt, Seaman, was
caught by the Royal Navy. He was hanged at Spithead in October 1792.

Having thus far most effectually completed the object of my Voyage, I sailed from the
Island Otaheite on the 4th of April 1789 with
1015 fine Breadfruit Plants, besides many other
valuable Fruits of that Country, which for three
and twenty weeks we had been collecting and
with an unremitted attention had now got them
to the highest state of perfection. —

My orders were to return home through
Endeavor Streights a Pass not much known but
for its dangers, which it was expected I would
take great pains to encounter to the advantage
of future Navigation. It was absolutely necessary for this to be my route that I might be
able to perform the Voyage expeditiously, as the
success of the undertaking depended very materially
on it. —

On the 11 April I discovered an
Island in latitude 18°.52'S and long.° 200°.19' E.
called Whytootackee, and on the 24th I anch.°
in Annamooka Road at the Friendly Islands
where after completing my Water & Wood I

sailed on the 27th following with the most sanguine expectations of my Plants doing exceedingly
well.

In the Evening of the 20th owing to light
Winds we were not clear of the Islands & at
Night I directed my Course towards Tofoa — The
Master had the first Watch. The Gunner the mid-
dle, and Mr. Christian one of the Mates the Morn-
ing Watch. — This was the Tour of duty for the
Night.

Just before sun rising Mr. Christian, the
Master at Arms, Gunners Mate, & Thos. Burket
Seaman, came into my Cabbin while I was a
sleep and seizing me tied my hands with a
Cord behind my back and threatned me with
instant Death if I spoke or made the least
noise. I however called so loud as to alarm every
one, but the Officers found themselves secured
by Centinels at their Doors. — There were now
three Men at my Cabbin Door, besides the four
inside. Christian had only a Cutlass in his
hand, the others had Musquets and bayonets.
They soon got the better of me, & I was hauled
out of Bed and forced on Deck in my shirt

'When I exerted myself in speaking loud, to try if I could rally any with a sense of duty in them, I was saluted with – "d—n his eyes, the ——, blow his brains out"; while Christian was threatening me with instant death, if I did not hold my tongue.

'I continued my endeavours to turn the tide of affairs, when Christian changed the cutlass which he had in his hand for a bayonet that was brought to him, and holding me with a strong grip by the cord that tied my hands, he threatened, with many oaths, to kill me immediately, if I would not be quiet; the villains round me had their pieces cocked and bayonets fixed. Particular persons were called on to go into the boat and were hurried over the side; whence I concluded that with these people I was to be set adrift. I therefore made another effort to bring about a change, but with no other effect than to be threatened with having my brains blown out.

'The boatswain and seamen who were to go in the boat, were allowed to collect twine, canvas, lines, sails, cordage, an eight-and-twenty gallon cask of water; and Mr. Samuel got one hundred and fifty pounds of bread, with a small quantity of rum and wine, also a quadrant and compass; but he was forbidden, on pain of death, to touch either map, ephemeris, book of astronomical observations, sextant, timekeeper, or any of my surveys or drawings.

'The mutineers having forced those of the seamen whom they meant to get rid of into the boat, Christian directed a dram to be served to each of his own crew. I then unhappily saw that nothing could be done to effect the recovery of the ship: there was no one to assist me, and every endeavour on my part was answered with threats of death.

'The officers were next called upon deck, and forced over the side into the boat, while I was kept apart from every one, abaft the mizen-mast; Christian, armed with a bayonet, holding me by the bandage that secured my hands. The guard round me had their pieces cocked, but on my daring the ungrateful wretches to fire, they uncocked them.

'Isaac Martin, one of the guard over me, I saw had an inclination to assist me, and as he fed me with shaddock (my lips being quite parched) we explained our wishes to each other by our looks; but this being observed, Martin was removed from me. He then attempted to leave the ship, for which purpose he got into the boat; but with many threats they obliged him to return.

'The armourer, Joseph Coleman, and two of the carpenters, M'Intosh and Norman, were also kept, contrary to their inclination; and they begged of me, after I was astern in the boat, to remember that they declared they had no hand in the transaction. Michael Byrne, I am told, likewise wanted to leave the ship.

'It is of no moment for me to recount my endeavours to bring back the offenders to a sense of their duty; all I could do was by speaking to them in general; but it was to no purpose, for I was kept securely bound, and no one except the guard suffered to come near me.

'To Mr. Samuel (clerk) I am indebted for securing my journals and commission, with some material ship papers. Without these I had nothing to certify what I had done, and my honour and character might have been suspected, without my possessing a proper document to have defended them. All this he did with great resolution, though guarded and strictly watched. He attempted to save the timekeeper, and a box with my surveys, drawings, and remarks, for fifteen years past, which were numerous; when he was hurried away with "D—n your eyes, you are well off to get what you have."

'It appeared to me that Christian was some time in doubt whether he should keep the carpenter, or his mates; at length he determined on the latter, and the carpenter was ordered into the boat. He was permitted, but not without some opposition, to take his tool-chest.

'Much altercation took place among the mutinous crew during the whole business: some swore "I'll be d—d if he does not find his way home, if he gets anything with him"; and when the carpenter's chest was carrying away, "D—n my eyes, he will have a vessel built in a month"; while others laughed at the helpless situation of the boat, being very deep, and so little room for those who were in her. As for Christian, he seemed as if meditating destruction on himself and every one else.

'I asked for arms, but they laughed at me, and said I was well acquainted with the people among whom I was going, and therefore did not want them; four cutlasses, however, were thrown into the boat, after we were veered astern.

'The officers and men being in the boat, they only waited for me, of which the master-at-arms informed Christian; who then said – "Come, Captain Bligh, your officers and men are now in the boat, and you must go with them; if you attempt to make the least resistance, you will instantly be put to death"; and without further ceremony, with a tribe of armed ruffians about me, I was forced over the side, when they untied my hands. Being in the boat, we were veered astern by a rope, a few pieces of pork were thrown to us, and some clothes, also the cutlasses I have already mentioned; and it was then that the armourer and carpenters called out to me to remember that they had no hand in the transaction. After having undergone a great deal of ridicule, and been kept for some time to make sport for these unfeeling wretches, we were at length cast adrift in the open ocean.

Bligh and his companions in the launch.

Bligh is standing in the boat looking dishevelled in contrast to the other men who had been given time to dress. The launch had been veered astern. The mutineers refused Bligh any muskets but someone threw in four cutlasses. Some of the food thrown to the boat fell into the sea and one man is seen here trying to pick something out of the water. Eighteen men can be seen on the *Bounty*, some with muskets, one of which is being pointed menacingly at the boat. Shouts of, 'shoot the Bugger', were heard and Mr Cole, the boatswain, recommended that they cast off because, 'they certainly will do some mischief if we stay much longer'. Bligh agreed: 'After having undergone a great deal of ridicule, and being kept for some time to make sport for these unfeeling wretches, we were at length cast adrift in the open ocean.' Apart from having too little food, Bligh also had to contend with only seven inches of freeboard and the absolute minimum of navigation aids. He had an old book of latitudes and longitudes which belonged to midshipman Hallet (probably Hamilton Moore's *Practical Navigator*) and he devised a log-line to get an account of the daily run. Christian had given him a sextant and the Master had a compass and a quadrant. Using his knowledge of the approximate location of Fiji, Bligh steered a course which enabled him to use the parallels of latitude to best advantage. Once he reached Australia he followed the coast to Cape York and then steered for Timor, reaching it exactly as planned. Given his resources it was a remarkable exercise in navigation.

'I had with me in the boat the following persons:

Names.	Stations.
JOHN FRYER	Master.
THOMAS LEDWARD	Acting Surgeon.
DAVID NELSON	Botanist.
WILLIAM PECKOVER	Gunner.
WILLIAM COLE	Boatswain.
WILLIAM PURCELL	Carpenter.
WILLIAM ELPHINSTONE	Master's Mate.
THOMAS HAYWARD	} Midshipmen.
JOHN HALLET	
JOHN NORTON	} Quarter-Masters.
PETER LINKLETTER	
LAWRENCE LEBOGUE	Sailmaker.
JOHN SMITH	} Cooks.
THOMAS HALL	
GEORGE SIMPSON	Quarter-Master's Mate.
ROBERT TINKLER	A boy.
ROBERT LAMB	Butcher.
MR. SAMUEL	Clerk.

In all eighteen.

'There remained in the *Bounty*:

Names.	Stations.
FLETCHER CHRISTIAN	Master's Mate.
PETER HEYWOOD	
EDWARD YOUNG	} Midshipmen.
GEORGE STEWART	
CHARLES CHURCHILL	Master-at-Arms.
JOHN MILLS	Gunner's Mate.
JAMES MORRISON	Boatswain's Mate.
THOMAS BURKITT	
MATTHEW QUINTAL	
JOHN SUMNER	
JOHN MILLWARD	
WILLIAM M'KOY	
HENRY HILLBRANT	
MICHAEL BYRNE	} Able Seamen.
WILLIAM MUSPRATT	
ALEXANDER SMITH	
JOHN WILLIAMS	
THOMAS ELLISON	
ISAAC MARTIN	
RICHARD SKINNER	
MATTHEW THOMPSON	
WILLIAM BROWN	Gardener.
JOSEPH COLEMAN	Armourer.
CHARLES NORMAN	Carpenter's Mate.
THOMAS M'INTOSH	Carpenter's Crew.

In all twenty-five – and the most able of the ship's company.

Observations.. Sextants.. Time Keeper or any of my Surveys or drawings. —

The Mutineers were now hurrying every one into the Boat, and the most of them being in, Christian directed a Dram to be served to each of his Crew. — I was now exceedingly fatigued, and unhappily saw I could do nothing to effect the Recovery of the Ship. every endeavour was threatened with death, and the following People were now in the Boat. —

John Fryer	Master
Tho.ᵈ Denmᵈ Ledward	Surgeon
David Nelson	Botanist
Willᵐ Peckover	Gunner
Willᵐ Cole	Boatswain
Willᵐ Purcell	Carpenter
Willᵐ Elphinstone	Masters Mate
Thoˢ Hayward	Midⁿ
John Hallett	Midⁿ
John Norton	Quʳ Master
Peter Linkletter	Quʳ Master
Sawᵃ Lebogue	Sail maker
John Smith	Ab
Thoˢ Hall	Ab
Geo: Simpson	Quʳ Masters Mate
Robᵗ Tinkler	Ab
Robᵗ Lamb	Ab
John Samuel	Clerk —

There remained on board as Pirates and under Arms

Fletcher Christian	Masters Mate
Peter Heywood	Midⁿ
George Stewart	Midⁿ
Edⁿ dⁿʳ Young	Midⁿ

Facsimile: Log of the *Bounty*.
Nineteen men, including Bligh, went into the *Bounty*'s launch. Twenty-five others stayed on board, including four (Byrne, Coleman, Norman and McIntosh) who were reported by Bligh to have 'had no hand in the transaction.' Morrison and Heywood claimed to have been against the mutiny but Bligh thought otherwise and said so. The hard core of the mutineers numbered eleven only of the *Bounty*'s forty-four men.

Facsimile: Signatures of some of the *Bounty*'s officers.
This is the only known signature of Fletcher Christian to appear on any document
connected with the *Bounty*. The document is incomplete but appears to be an official
affidavit to do with some business transacted on 1 December 1788. It may have been
connected with an incident in which a boat's rudder was stolen, 'by the remissness of my
Officers and People at the Tent,' described in Bligh's Log entry for that date. Christian
was in command of the shore camp and it is significant that he signed the document as one
of the master's mates and not as acting lieutenant.

'Christian, the chief of the mutineers, is of a respectable family in the
North of England. This was the third voyage he had made with me; and as I
found it necessary to keep my ship's company at three watches, I had given
him an order to take charge of the third, his abilities being thoroughly equal
to the task; and by this means the master and gunner were not at watch and
watch.

'Heywood is also of a respectable family in the North of England [he was
born in the Isle of Man], and a young man of abilities as well as Christian.
These two had been objects of my particular regard and attention, and I had
taken great pains to instruct them, having entertained hopes that, as professional men, they would have become a credit to their country.

'Young was well recommended, and had the look of an able, stout seaman; he, however, fell short of what his appearance promised.

'Stewart was a young man of creditable parents in the Orkneys; at which
place, on the return of the *Resolution* from the South Seas, in 1780, we
received so many civilities that, on that account only, I should gladly have
taken him with me: but, independent of this recommendation, he was a
seaman, and had always borne a good character.

'Notwithstanding the roughness with which I was treated, the remembrance of past kindnesses produced some signs of remorse in Christian.
When they were forcing me out of the ship, I asked him if this treatment was

a proper return for the many instances he had received of my friendship? he appeared disturbed at my question, and answered with much emotion, "That, – Captain Bligh, – that is the thing; – I am in hell, – I am in hell!"

'As soon as I had time to reflect, I felt an inward satisfaction, which prevented any depression of my spirits: conscious of my integrity, and anxious solicitude for the good of the service in which I had been engaged, I found my mind wonderfully supported, and I began to conceive hopes, notwithstanding so heavy a calamity, that I should one day be able to account to my king and country for the misfortune. . . .

'It will very naturally be asked, what could be the reason for such a revolt? In answer to which I can only conjecture that the mutineers had flattered themselves with the hopes of a more happy life among the Otaheitans than they could possibly enjoy in England; and this, joined to some female connexions, most probably occasioned the whole transaction. The ship, indeed, while within our sight, steered to the W.N.W., but I considered this only as a feint; for when we were sent away, – "Huzza for Otaheite!" – was frequently heard among the mutineers.

'The women of Otaheite are handsome, mild, and cheerful in their manners and conversation, possessed of great sensibility, and have sufficient delicacy to make them admired and beloved. The chiefs were so much attached to our people, that they rather encouraged their stay among them than otherwise, and even made them promises of large possessions. Under these and many other attendant circumstances, equally desirable, it is now perhaps not so much to be wondered at, though scarcely possible to have been foreseen, that a set of sailors, most of them void of connexions, should be led away; especially when, in addition to such powerful inducements, they imagined it in their power to fix themselves in the midst of plenty, on one of the finest islands in the world, where they need not labour, and where the allurements of dissipation are beyond anything that can be conceived. The utmost, however, that any commander could have supposed to have happened is, that some of the people would have been tempted to desert. But if it should be asserted that a commander is to guard against an act of mutiny and piracy in his own ship, more than by the common rules of service, it is as much as to say that he must sleep locked up, and when awake, be girded with pistols.

'Desertions have happened, more or less, from most of the ships that have been at the Society Islands; but it has always been in the commander's power to make the chiefs return their people; the knowledge, therefore, that it was unsafe to desert, perhaps first led mine to consider with what ease so small a ship might be surprised, and that so favourable an opportunity would never offer to them again.

'The secrecy of this mutiny is beyond all conception. Thirteen of the party, who were with me, had always lived forward among the seamen; yet neither they, nor the messmates of Christian, Stewart, Heywood, and Young, had ever observed any circumstance that made them in the least suspect

VOYAGES AND TRAVELS

OF

FLETCHER CHRISTIAN,

AND A NARRATIVE OF

THE MUTINY,

𝕺𝕹 𝕭𝖔𝖆𝖗𝖉

HIS MAJESTY'S SHIP

BOUNTY, AT OTAHEITE.

With a fuccinct account of the Proceedings of the
Mutineers, with a Defcription of the Manners, Cuſtoms
Religious Ceremonies, Diverfions Faſhions, Arts, Commerce; Method of Fighting; the Breadfruit, and every
intereſting particular relating to

𝕿𝖍𝖊 𝕾𝖔𝖈𝖎𝖊𝖙𝖞 𝕴𝖘𝖑𝖆𝖓𝖉𝖘.

ALSO

His Shipwreck on the coaſt of America, and travels
in that extenfive Country; with a hiſtory of the Gold
Mines and general account of the poffeffions of

𝕿𝖍𝖊 𝕾𝖕𝖆𝖓𝖎𝖆𝖗𝖉𝖘.

IN CHILI, PERU, MEXICO &c

PRINTED for H. LEMOINE.

1798.

Price Two Shillings.

Facsimile: *Voyages and Travels of Fletcher Christian.*
This book appeared two years after another volume claiming to be *Letters from Mr
Fletcher Christian*. Both were almost certainly spurious. Neither account fits the known
activities of the mutineers though both do show considerable knowledge of the west coast
of South America. In both books 'Christian' praises Captain Bligh and apologises for the
mutiny. Bligh's reaction was to write to Banks, 'I can only say that I heartily dispise the
praise of any of the family of Christian and I hope & trust yet that the mutineer will meet
with his deserts.' William Wordsworth, the poet and friend of the Christian family, stated
enigmatically, 'I have the best authority for saying that this publication is spurious.'

what was going on. To such a close-planned act of villainy, my mind being entirely free from any suspicion, it is not wonderful that I fell a sacrifice. Perhaps, if there had been marines on board, a sentinel at my cabin-door might have prevented it; for I slept with the door always open, that the officer of the watch might have access to me on all occasions, the possibility of such a conspiracy being ever the farthest from my thoughts. Had their mutiny been occasioned by any grievances, either real or imaginary, I must have discovered symptoms of their discontent, which would have put me on my guard; but the case was far otherwise. Christian, in particular, I was on the most friendly terms with: that very day he was engaged to have dined with me; and the preceding night he excused himself from supping with me, on pretence of being unwell; for which I felt concerned, having no suspicions of his integrity and honour.'

Such is the story published by Lieutenant Bligh immediately on his return to England, after one of the most distressing and perilous passages over nearly four thousand miles of the wide ocean, with eighteen persons, in an open boat. The story obtained implicit credit; and though Lieutenant Bligh's character never stood high in the navy for suavity of manners or mildness of temper, he was always considered as an excellent seaman, and his veracity stood unimpeached. But in this age of refined liberality, when the most atrocious criminals find their apologists, it is not surprising it should now be discovered, when all are dead that could either prove or disprove it, that it was the tyranny of the commander alone, and not the wickedness of the ringleader of the mutineers of the *Bounty*, that caused that event. 'We all know,' it is said, [in the *United Service Journal* of April, 1831] 'that mutiny can arise but from one of these two sources, excessive folly or excessive tyranny; therefore as it is admitted that Bligh was no idiot, the inference is obvious. Not only was the *narrative* which he published proved to be false in many material bearings, by evidence before a court-martial, but every act of his public life after this event, from his successive command of the *Director*, the *Glatton*, and the *Warrior*, to his disgraceful expulsion from New South Wales, – was stamped with an insolence, an inhumanity, and coarseness, which fully developed his character.'

There is no intention, in narrating this eventful history, to accuse or defend either the character or the conduct of the late Admiral Bligh; it is well known his temper was irritable in the extreme; but the circumstance of his having been the friend of Captain Cook, with whom he sailed as his master, – of his ever afterwards being patronised by Sir Joseph Banks, – of the Admiralty promoting him to the rank of commander, appointing him immediately to the *Providence*, to proceed on the same expedition to Ota-heite, – and of his returning in a very short time to England with complete success, and recommending all his officers for promotion on account of their exemplary conduct; – of his holding several subsequent employments in the service, – of his having commanded ships of the line in the battles of Copen-hagen and Camperdown, – and risen to the rank of flag-officer, – these may perhaps be considered to speak something in his favour, and be allowed to stand as some proof that, with all his failings, he had his merits. That he was a man of coarse habits, and entertained very mistaken notions with regard to discipline, is quite true: yet he had many redeeming qualities. The accusation, by the writer in question, of Bligh having falsified his 'narrative,' is a very heavy charge, and, it is to be feared, is not wholly without foundation; though it would perhaps be more correct to say, that in the printed narrative of his voyage, and the narrative on which the mutineers were tried, there are many important omissions from his original manuscript journal, some of which it will be necessary to notice presently.

The same writer further says, 'We know that the officers fared in every way worse than the men, and that even young Heywood was kept at the mast head no less than eight hours at one spell, in the worst weather which they encountered off Cape Horn.'

Perhaps Heywood may himself be brought forward as authority, if not to disprove, at least to render highly improbable, his experiencing any such treatment on the part of his captain. This young officer, in his defence, says, 'Captain Bligh, in his narrative, acknowledges that he had left some friends on board the *Bounty*, and no part of my conduct could have induced him to believe that I ought not to be reckoned of the number. Indeed, from his attention to, *and very kind treatment of me personally*, I should have been a monster of depravity to have betrayed him.'

In looking over a manuscript journal, kept by Morrison, the boatswain's mate, who was tried and convicted as one of the mutineers, but received the king's pardon, the conduct of Bligh appears in a very unfavourable point of view. This Morrison was a person, from talent and education, far above the situation he held in the *Bounty*; he had previously served in the navy as midshipman, and, after his pardon, was appointed gunner of the *Blenheim*, in which her perished with Sir Thomas Troubridge. In comparing this journal with other documents, the dates and transactions appear to be correctly stated, though the latter may occasionally be somewhat too highly coloured. How he contrived to preserve this journal, in the wreck of the *Pandora*, does not appear; but there can be no doubt of its authenticity, having been kept among the late Captain Heywood's papers; various passages in it have been corrected either by this officer or some other person, but without altering their sense.

It would appear from this important document that the seeds of discord, in the unfortunate ship *Bounty*, were sown at a very early period of the voyage. It happened, as was the case in all small vessels, that the duties of commander and purser were united in the person of Lieutenant Bligh; and it would seem that this proved the cause of very serious discontent among the officers and crew; of the mischief arising out of this union, the following statement of Mr. Morrison may serve as a specimen. At Teneriffe, Lieutenant Bligh ordered the cheese to be hoisted up and exposed to the air; which was no sooner done, than he pretended to miss a certain quantity, and declared that it had been stolen. The cooper, Henry Hillbrant, informed him that the cask in question had been opened by the orders of Mr. Samuel, his clerk, who acted also as steward, and the cheese sent on shore to his own house, previous to the *Bounty* leaving the river on her way to Portsmouth. Lieutenant Bligh, without making any further inquiry, immediately ordered the allowance of that article to be stopped, both from *officers* and *men*, until the deficiency should be made good, and told the cooper he would give him a d—d good flogging if he said another word on the subject. It can hardly be supposed that a man of Bligh's shrewdness, if disposed to play the rogue, would have placed himself so completely in the hands of the cooper, in a transaction which, if revealed, must have cost him his commission.

Again, on approaching the equator, some decayed pumpkins, purchased at Teneriffe, were ordered to be issued to the crew, at the rate of *one* pound of pumpkin for *two* pounds of biscuit. The reluctance of the men to accept this proposed substitute, *on such terms*, being reported to Lieutenant Bligh, he flew upon deck in a violent rage, saying, 'I'll see who will dare to refuse the pumpkin, or any thing else I may order to be served out;' to which he added, 'You d—d infernal scoundrels, I'll make you eat grass, or any thing you can catch, before I have done with you.' This speech had the desired effect, every one receiving the pumpkins, even the *officers*.

Next comes a complaint respecting the mode of issuing beef and pork: but when a representation was made to Lieutenant Bligh in the quiet and orderly manner prescribed by the twenty-first article of war [*see* page 199], he called the crew aft, told them that every thing relative to the provisions was transacted by his orders; that it was therefore needless for them to complain, as they would get no redress, he being the fittest judge of what was right or wrong, and that he would flog the first man who should dare attempt to make any complaint in future.

According to this Journalist, 'the seeds of eternal discord were sown between Lieutenant Bligh and some of his officers,' while in Adventure Bay, Van Dieman's Land; and on arriving at Matavai Bay, in Otaheite, he is accused of taking the officers' hogs and bread-fruit, and serving them to the ship's company; and when the master remonstrated with him on the subject, he replied that 'he would convince him that every thing became *his* as soon as it was brought on board; that he would take nine-tenths of every man's property, and let him see who dared to say anything to the contrary.' The sailors' pigs were seized without ceremony, and it became a favour for a man to obtain an extra pound of his own meat.

The writer then says, 'the object of our visit to the Society Islands being at length accomplished, we weighed on the 4th April, 1789. Every one seemed in high spirits, and began to talk of home, as though they had just left Jamaica instead of Otaheite, so far onward did their flattering fancies waft them. On the 23rd, we anchored off Annamooka, the inhabitants of which island were very rude, and attempted to take the casks and axes from the parties sent to fill water and cut wood. A musket pointed at them produced no other effect than a return of the compliment, by poising their clubs or spears with menacing looks; and, as it was Lieutenant Bligh's orders, that no person should affront them on any occasion, they were emboldened by meeting with no check to their insolence. They at length became so troublesome, that Mr. Christian, who commanded the watering party, found it difficult to carry on his duty; but on acquainting Lieutenant Bligh with their behaviour, he received a volley of abuse, was d—d as a cowardly rascal, and asked if he were afraid of naked savages whilst he had weapons in his hand? To this he replied in a respectful manner, "The arms are of no effect, Sir, while your orders prohibit their use." '

This happened but three days before the mutiny, and the same circumstance is noticed, but somewhat differently, in Bligh's MS. Journal, where he says, 'the men cleared themselves, and they therefore merit no punishment. As to the officers I have no resource, nor do I ever feel myself safe in the few instances I trust to them.' A perusal of all the documents certainly leads to the conclusion that all his officers were of a very inferior description; they had no proper feeling of their own situation; and this, together with the contempt in which they were held by Bligh, and which he could not disguise, may account for that perfect indifference, with regard both to the captain and the ship, which was manifested on the day of the mutiny.

That sad catastrophe, if the writer of the Journal be correct, was hastened, if not brought about by, the following circumstance, of which Bligh takes no notice. 'In the afternoon of the 27th, Lieutenant Bligh came upon deck, and missing some of the cocoa-nuts, which had been piled up between the guns, said they had been stolen, and could not have been taken away without the knowledge of the officers, all of whom were sent for and questioned on the subject. On their declaring that they had not seen any of the people touch them, he exclaimed, "Then you must have taken them yourselves"; and proceeded to inquire of them separately, how many they had purchased. On coming to Mr. Christian, that gentleman answered, "I do not know, Sir, but I hope you do not think me so mean as to be guilty of stealing yours." Mr. Bligh replied, "Yes, you d—d hound, I do – you must have stolen them from me, or you would be able to give a better account of them;" then turning to the other officers, he said, "God d—n you, you scoundrels, you are all thieves alike, and combine with the men to rob me: I suppose you will steal my yams next; but I'll sweat you for it, you rascals – I'll make half of you jump overboard, before you get through Endeavour Straits." This threat was followed by an order to the clerk "to stop the villains' grog, and give them but half a pound of yams to-morrow; if they steal them, I'll reduce them to a quarter." '

It is difficult to believe that an officer in his Majesty's service could condescend to make use of such language to the meanest of the crew, much less to gentlemen: it is to be feared, however, that there is sufficient ground for the truth of these statements: with regard to the last, it is borne out by the evidence of Mr. Fryer, the master, on the court-martial. This officer, being

John Fryer's telescope.

John Fryer, Master.

Fryer was appointed Master of the *Bounty* and brought with him his thirteen-year-old brother-in-law, Robert Tinkler. Bligh and Fryer quarrelled frequently on the *Bounty* and in the open boat after the mutiny, mainly over Fryer's incompetence and insubordination. Bligh refused Fryer a reference when he was offered an appointment by Captain Riou. Fryer remained in the rank of master but Tinkler became a lieutenant and commander. They were present at the Battle of Copenhagen in 1801 in which Bligh commanded HMS *Glatton* under Nelson.

Page from John Fryer's journal.

John Fryer was a constant source of trouble for Bligh. He failed to meet Bligh's high standards; he tried, during the outward voyage, to blackmail Bligh by refusing to sign the expense books until Bligh wrote a reference for him, and he was so concerned about Bligh's possible actions when he returned to Britain that he wrote up his own journal, stressing his own version of the events, claiming that Bligh had refused to let him see the official Log after the mutiny. According to *his* journal, Fryer could have navigated the launch to Timor, and indeed he gives himself credit for virtually everything that was accomplished on that hazardous voyage.

asked, 'what did you suppose to be Mr. Christian's meaning, when he said he had been in hell for a fortnight?' answered, 'From the frequent quarrels they had had, and the abuse which he had received from Mr. Bligh'. – 'Had there been any very recent quarrel?' – 'The day before Mr. Bligh challenged all the young gentlemen and people with stealing his cocoa-nuts.' It was on the evening of this day that Lieutenant Bligh, according to his printed narrative, says Christian was to have supped with him; but excused himself on account of being unwell; and that he was invited to dine with him on the day of the mutiny.

Every one of these circumstances, and many others, which might be stated from Mr. Morrison's Journal, are omitted in Bligh's published narrative; but many of them are alluded to in his original Journal, and others that prove distinctly the constant reproofs to which his officers were subject, and the bad terms on which they stood with their commander. A few extracts from this Journal will sufficiently establish this point.

In so early a part of the voyage as their arrival in Adventure Bay, he found fault with his officers, and put the carpenter into confinement. Again, at Matavai Bay, on the 5th December, Bligh says, 'I ordered the carpenter to cut a large stone that was brought off by one of the natives, requesting me to get it made fit for them to grind their hatchets on, but to my astonishment he refused, in direct terms, to comply, saying, "I will not cut the stone, for it will spoil my chisel; and though there may be law to take away my clothes, there is none to take away my tools." This man having before shown his mutinous and insolent behaviour, I was under the necessity of confining him to his cabin.'

On the 5th January three men deserted in the cutter, on which occasion Bligh says, 'Had the mate of the watch been awake, no trouble of this kind would have happened. I have therefore disrated and turned him before the mast; such neglectful and worthless petty officers, I believe, never were in a ship as are in this. No orders for a few hours together are obeyed by them, and their conduct in general is so bad, that no confidence or trust can be reposed in them; in short, they have driven me to every thing but corporal punishment, and that must follow if they do not improve.'

By Morrison's Journal it would appear that 'corporal punishment' was not long delayed; for, on the very day, he says, the midshipman was put in irons, and confined from the 5th January to the 23rd March – eleven weeks!

On the 17th January, orders being given to clear out the sail-room and to air the sails, many of them were found very much mildewed and rotten in many places, on which he observes, 'If I had any officers to supersede the master and boatswain, or was capable of doing without them, considering them as common seamen, they should no longer occupy their respective stations; scarcely any neglect of duty can equal the criminality of this.'

On the 24th January, the three deserters were brought back and flogged, then put in irons for further punishment. 'As this affair,' he says, 'was solely caused by the neglect of the officers who had the watch, I was induced to give them all a lecture on this occasion, and endeavour to show them that, however exempt they were at present from the like punishment, yet they were equally subject, by the articles of war, to a condign one.' He then tells them, that it is only necessity that makes him have recourse to reprimand, because there are no means of trying them by court-martial. . . .

These extracts show the terms on which Bligh was with his officers; and these few instances, with others from Morrison's Journal, make it pretty clear, that though Christian, as fiery and passionate a youth as his commander could well be, and with feelings too acute to bear the foul and opprobrious language constantly addressed to him, was the sole instigator of the mutiny; – the captain had no support to expect, and certainly received none, from the rest of his officers. That Christian was the sole author appears still more strongly from the following passage in Morrison's Journal. 'When Mr. Bligh found he must go into the boat, he begged of Mr. Christian to desist, saying "I'll pawn my honour, I'll give my bond, Mr. Christian, never to think of this, if you'll desist," and urged his wife and family; to which Mr. Christian replied, "No, Captain Bligh, if you had any honour, things had not come to this; and if you had any regard for your wife and family, you should have thought on them before, and not behaved so much like a villain." Lieutenant Bligh again attempted to speak, but was ordered to be silent. The boatswain also tried to pacify Mr. Christian, to whom he replied, "It is too late, I have been in hell for this fortnight past, and am determined to bear it no longer; and you know, Mr. Cole, that I have been used like a dog all the voyage." '

It is pretty evident, therefore, that the mutiny was not, as Bligh in his narrative states it to have been, the result of a conspiracy. It will be seen by the minutes of the court-martial, that the whole affair was planned and executed between the hours of four and eight o'clock, on the morning of the 28th April, when Christian had the watch upon deck; that Christian, unable longer to bear the abusive and insulting language, had meditated his own escape from the ship the day before, choosing to trust himself to fate, rather than submit to the constant upbraiding to which he had been subject; but the unfortunate business of the cocoa-nuts drove him to the commission of the rash and felonious act, which ended, as such criminal acts usually do, in his own destruction, and that of a great number of others, many of whom were wholly innocent.

Lieutenant Bligh, like most passionate men, whose unruly tempers get the better of their reason, having vented his rage about the cocoa-nuts, became immediately calm, and by inviting Christian to sup with him the same evening, evidently wished to renew their friendly intercourse. On the same night, towards ten o'clock, when the master had the watch, Bligh came on deck, as was his custom, before retiring to sleep. It was one of those calm and beautiful nights, so frequent in tropical regions, whose soothing influence can be appreciated only by those who have felt it, when, after a scorching day, the air breathes a most refreshing coolness. . . . While, on this lovely night, Bligh and his master were congratulating themselves on the pleasing prospect of fine weather and a full moon, to light them through Endeavour's dangerous straits, the unhappy and deluded Christian was, in all probability, brooding over his wrongs, and meditating on the criminal act he was to perpetrate the following morning; for he has himself stated, that he had just fallen asleep about half after three in the morning, and was much out of order.

The evidence on the court-martial is sufficiently explicit as to the mode in which this act of piracy was committed. By the Journal of James Morrison, the following is the account of the transaction, as given by Christian himself to the two midshipmen, Heywood and Stewart (both of whom had been kept below), the moment they were allowed to come upon deck, after the boat, in which were Bligh and his companions, had been turned adrift.

He said, that, 'finding himself much hurt by the treatment he had received from Lieutenant Bligh, he had determined to quit the ship the preceding evening, and had informed the boatswain, carpenter, and two midshipmen (Stewart and Hayward), of his intention to do so; that by them he was supplied with part of a roasted pig, some nails, beads, and other articles of trade, which he put into a bag that was given him by the last-named gentleman; that he put this bag into the clue of Robert Tinkler's hammock, where it was discovered by that young gentleman when going to bed at night, but the business was smothered, and passed off without any further notice. He said he had fastened some staves to a stout plank, with which he intended to make his escape; but finding he could not effect it during the first and middle watches, as the ship had no way through the water, and the people were all moving about, he laid down to rest about half-past three in the morning; that when Mr. Stewart called him to relieve the deck at four o'clock, he had but just fallen asleep, and was much out of order; upon observing which, Mr. Stewart strenuously advised him to abandon his intention; that as soon as he had taken charge of the deck, he saw Mr. Hayward, the mate of his watch, lie down on the arm-chest to take a nap; and finding that Mr. Hallet, the other midshipman, did not make his appearance, he suddenly formed the resolution of seizing the ship. Disclosing his intention to Matthew Quintal and Isaac Martin, both of whom had been flogged by Lieutenant Bligh, they called up Charles Churchill, who had also tasted the cat, and Matthew Thompson, both of whom readily joined in the plot. That Alexander Smith (*alias* John Adams), John Williams, and William M'Koy, evinced equal willingness, and went with Churchill to the armourer, of whom they obtained the keys of the arm-chest, under pretence of wanting a musket to fire at a shark, then alongside; that finding Mr. Hallet asleep on an arm-chest, in the main-hatchway, they roused and sent him on deck. Charles Norman, unconscious of their proceedings, had in the meantime awaked Mr. *Hayward*, and directed his attention to the shark, whose movements he was watching at the moment that Mr. Christian and his confederates came up the fore-hatchway, after having placed arms in the hands of several men who were not aware of their design. One man, Matthew Thompson, was left in charge of the chest, and he served out arms to Thomas Burkitt and Robert Lamb. Mr. Christian said he then proceeded to secure Lieutenant Bligh, the master, gunner, and botanist.'

'When Mr. Christian,' observes Morrison in his Journal, 'related the above circumstances, I recollected having seen him fasten some staves to a plank lying on the larboard gangway, as also having heard the boatswain say to the carpenter, "it will not do to-night," I likewise remembered that Mr. Christian had visited the fore-cockpit several times that evening, although he had very seldom, if ever, frequented the warrant-officers' cabins before.'

If this be a correct statement, and the greater part of it is borne out by evidence on the court-martial, it removes every doubt of Christian being the sole instigator of the mutiny, and that no conspiracy nor preconcerted measures had any existence, but that it was suddenly conceived by a hot-headed young man, in a state of great excitement of mind, amounting to a temporary aberration of intellect, caused by the frequent abusive and insulting language of his commanding officer. Waking out of a short half hour's disturbed sleep, to take the command of the deck – finding the two mates of the watch, Hayward and Hallet, asleep (for which they ought to have been dismissed the service instead of being, as they were, promoted) – the opportunity tempting, and the ship completely in his power, with a momentary impulse he darted down the fore-hatchway, got possession of the keys of the arm-chest, and made the hazardous experiment of arming such of the men as he thought he could trust, and effected his purpose.

There is a passage in Captain Beechey's account of Pitcairn Island [written many years later], which, if correct, would cast a stain on the memory of the unfortunate Stewart – who, if there was one innocent man in the ship, was that man. Captain Beechey says (speaking of Christian), 'His plan, strange as it must appear for a young officer to adopt, who was fairly advanced in an honourable profession, was to set himself adrift upon a raft, and make his way to the island (Tofoa) then in sight. The raft was soon constructed and he was on the point of launching it, when a young officer, *who afterwards perished in the Pandora*, to whom Christian communicated his intention, recommended him, rather than risk his life on so hazardous an expedition, *to endeavour to take possession of the ship*, which he thought would not be very difficult, as many of the ship's company were not well disposed towards the commander, and would all be very glad to return to Otaheite, and reside among their friends in that island. This daring proposition is even more extraordinary than the premeditated scheme of his companion, and, if true, certainly relieves Christian from part of the odium which has hitherto attached to him as the sole instigator of the mutiny.' Relieve him? – not a jot – but on the best authority it may boldly be stated, that it is *not* true – the authority of Stewart's friend and messmate, the late Captain Heywood.

Captain Beechey very properly sent his chapter on Pitcairn's Island for any observations Captain Heywood might have to make on what was said therein regarding the mutiny; observing in his note which accompanied it, that this account, received from Adams, differed materially from a footnote in Marshall's *Naval Biography*; to which Captain Heywood returned the following reply.

'*5th April*, 1830.

'DEAR SIR, – I have perused the account you received from Adams of the mutiny in the *Bounty*, which does indeed differ very materially from a footnote in Marshall's *Naval Biography*, by the editor, to whom I verbally detailed the facts, which are strictly true.

'That Christian informed the boatswain and the carpenter, Messrs. Hayward and Stewart, of his determination to leave the ship upon a raft, on the night preceding the mutiny, is certain; but that any one of them (Stewart in particular) should have "recommended, rather than risk his life on so hazardous an expedition, that he should try the expedient of taking the ship from the captain, etc.," is entirely at variance with the whole character and conduct of the latter, both before and after the mutiny; as well as with the assurance of Christian himself, the very night he quitted Taheité, that the idea of attempting to take the ship had never entered his distracted mind, until the moment he relieved the deck, and found his mate and midshipman [Hayward and Hallet] asleep.

'At that last interview with Christian he also communicated to me, for the satisfaction of his relations, other circumstances connected with that unfortunate disaster, which, after their deaths, may or may not be laid before the public. And although they can implicate none but himself, either living or dead, they may extenuate but will contain not a word of his in defence of the crime he committed against the laws of his country. – I am, etc.,

'P. HEYWOOD.'

The temptations, therefore, which it was supposed Otaheite held out to the deluded men of the *Bounty*, had no more share in the transaction than the supposed conspiracy; it does not appear, indeed, that the cry of 'Huzza for Otaheite!' was ever uttered; if this island had been the object of either Christian or the crew, they would not have left it three hundred miles behind them, before they perpetrated the act of piracy; but after the deed had been committed, it would be natural enough that they should turn their minds to the lovely island and its fascinating inhabitants, which they had but just quitted, and that in the moment of excitement some of them should have so called out; but Bligh is the only person who has said they did so.

If, however, the recollection of the 'sunny isle' and its 'smiling women' had really tempted the men to mutiny, Bligh would himself not be free from blame, for having allowed them to indulge for six whole months among this voluptuous and fascinating people. . . . Bligh would appear to have been sensible of this on his next expedition in the *Providence*, for on that occasion he collected more bread-fruit plants than on the former, and spent only half the time in doing so. . . .

As far, however, as the mutiny of his people was concerned, we must wholly discard the idea thrown out by Bligh, that the seductions of Otaheite had any share in producing it. It could not have escaped a person of

Christian's sagacity, that certain interrogatories would unquestionably be put by the natives of Otaheite, on finding the ship return so soon without her commander, without the bread-fruit plants, and with only about half her crew; questions he knew to which no satisfactory answer could be made; and though, at subsequent periods, he twice visited that island, it was some time afterwards, and not from choice but necessity; his object was to find a place of concealment, where he might pass the remainder of his days, unheard of and unknown, and where it is to be hoped he had time for sincere repentance, the only atonement he could make for the commission of a crime, which involved so many human beings in misery, and brought others to an untimely end – but of this hereafter.

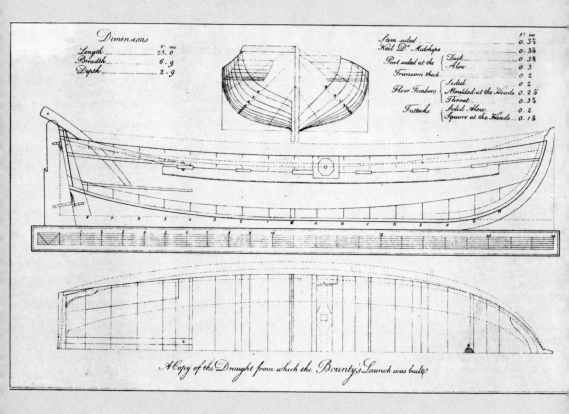

Dimensions

	Fᵗ	ins
Length	23	0
Breadth	6	9
Depth	2	9

		Fᵗ	ins
Stem sided		0	3¾
Keel Dº Midships		0	3¾
Post sided at the	Tuck	0	3¾
	Alow	0	3
Transom thick		0	2
Floor Timbers	Sided	0	2
	Moulded at the Heads	0	2½
	Throat	0	3¾
Futtocks	Sided Alow	0	2
	Square at the Heads	0	1¾

A Copy of the Draught from which the Bounty's Launch was built

Copy of the Draught from which the *Bounty*'s launch was built.
John Burr, contractor, supplied a twenty-foot launch for the *Bounty*, but Bligh exchanged
it at Deptford for a larger one of twenty-three feet length. This proved fortuitous for the
men who undertook the open-boat voyage. The lines of the launch are well proportioned
and its stout construction and excellent sea-worthiness were well proven in the perilous and
stormy voyage to Timor. The launch was equipped with six oars and a mast, though
Bligh, in his Log entry for 9 May, enigmatically refers to 'each mast.' He clearly intended
to bring the launch home but was forced to sell it. In his *Narrative of the Mutiny* (1790) he
wrote, 'The services she had rendered us made me feel great reluctance at parting with her,
which I would not have done if I could have found a convenient opportunity of getting
her conveyed to Europe.'

CHAPTER FOUR

The Open-boat Navigation

Christian had intended to send away his captain and associates in the cutter – a small wretched boat, that could hold but eight or ten men at the most, with a very small additional weight; and, what was still worse, she was so worm-eaten and decayed, especially in the bottom planks, that the probability was, she would have gone down before she had proceeded a mile from the ship. But the remonstrances of the master, boatswain, and carpenter prevailed on him to let those unfortunate men have the launch, into which nineteen persons were thrust, whose weight, together with that of the few articles they were permitted to take, brought down the boat so near to the water, as to endanger her sinking with but a moderate swell of the sea – and to all human appearance, in no state to survive the length of voyage they were destined to perform.

The first consideration of Lieutenant Bligh and his eighteen unfortunate companions, on being cast adrift in their open boat, was to examine the state of their resources. The provisions which they found to have been thrown into the boat, by some few kind-hearted messmates, amounted to one hundred and fifty pounds of bread, sixteen pieces of pork, each weighing two pounds, six quarts of rum, six bottles of wine, with twenty-eight gallons of water, and four empty barricoes [small casks]. Being so near to the island of Tofoa, it was resolved to seek there a supply of bread-fruit and water, to preserve if possible the above-mentioned stock entire; but after rowing along the coast, they discovered only some cocoa-nut trees, on the top of high precipices, from which, with much danger owing to the surf, and great difficulty in climbing the cliffs, they succeeded in obtaining about twenty nuts. The second day they made excursions into the island, but without success. They met however with a few natives, who came down with them to the cove where the boat was lying; and others presently followed. They made inquiries after the ship, and Bligh unfortunately advised they should say that the ship had overset and sunk, and that they only were saved. The story might be innocent, but it was certainly indiscreet to put the people in possession of their defenceless situation; however, they brought in small quantities of bread-fruit, plantains, and cocoa-nuts, but little or no water could be procured. These supplies, scanty as they were, served to keep up the spirits of the men: 'They no longer,' says Bligh, 'regarded me with those anxious looks, which had constantly been directed towards me, since we lost sight of the ship; every countenance appeared to have a degree of cheerfulness, and they all seemed determined to do their best.'

The numbers of the natives having so much increased as to line the whole beach, they began knocking stones together, which was known to be the preparatory signal for an attack. With some difficulty on account of the surf, our seamen succeeded in getting the things that were on shore into the boat, together with all the men, except John Norton, quarter-master, who was casting off the stern-fast. The natives immediately rushed upon this poor man, and actually stoned him to death. A volley of stones was also discharged at the boat, and every one in it was more or less hurt. This induced the people to push out to sea with all the speed they were able to give to the launch, but to their surprise and alarm, several canoes, filled with stones, followed close after them and renewed the attack; against which, the only return the unfortunate men in the boat could make, was with the stones of the assailants that lodged in her, a species of warfare in which they were very inferior to the Indians. The only expedient left was to tempt the enemy to desist from the pursuit, by throwing overboard some clothes, which fortunately induced the canoes to stop and pick them up; and night coming on, they returned to the shore, leaving the party in the boat to reflect on their unhappy situation.

The men now intreated their commander to take them towards home; and on being told that no hope of relief could be entertained till they reached Timor, a distance of full twelve hundred leagues, they all readily agreed to be content with an allowance, which, on calculation of their resources, the commander informed them would not exceed one ounce of bread, and a quarter of a pint of water, per day. Recommending them, therefore, in the most solemn manner, not to depart from their promise in this respect, 'we bore away,' says Bligh, 'across a sea where the navigation is but little known, in a small boat twenty-three feet long from stem to stern, deeply laden with eighteen men. I was happy, however, to see that every one seemed better satisfied with our situation than myself. It was about eight o'clock at night on the 2nd May, when we bore away under a reefed lug-foresail; and having divided the people into watches, and got the boat into a little order, we returned thanks to God for our miraculous preservation.'

At day-break on the 3rd, the forlorn and almost hopeless navigators saw with alarm the sun to rise fiery and red, – a sure indication of a severe gale of wind; and accordingly, at eight o'clock it blew a violent storm, and the sea ran so very high, that the sail was becalmed when between the seas, and too much to have set when on the top of the sea; yet it is stated that they could not venture to take it in, as they were in very imminent danger and distress, the sea curling over the stern of the boat, and obliging them to bale with all their might.

The bread, being in bags, was in the greatest danger of being spoiled by the wet, the consequence of which, if not prevented, must have been fatal, as the whole party would inevitably be starved to death, if they should fortunately escape the fury of the waves. It was determined, therefore, that all superfluous clothes, with some rope and spare sails, should be thrown overboard, by which the boat was considerably lightened. The carpenter's tool-chest was cleared, and the tools stowed in the bottom of the boat, and the bread secured in the chest. All the people being thoroughly wet and cold, a teaspoonful of rum was served out to each person, with a quarter of a bread-fruit, which is stated to have been scarcely eatable, for dinner; Bligh having determined to preserve sacredly, and at the peril of his life, the engagement they entered into, and to make their small stock of provisions last eight weeks, let the daily proportion be ever so small.

The sea continuing to run even higher than in the morning, the fatigue of baling became very great; the boat was necessarily kept before the sea. The men were constantly wet, the night very cold, and at daylight their limbs were so benumbed, that they could scarcely find the use of them. At this time a teaspoonful of rum served out to each person was found of great benefit to all. Five small cocoa-nuts were distributed for dinner, and every one was satisfied; and in the evening, a few broken pieces of bread-fruit were served for supper, after which prayers were performed.

On the night of the 4th and morning of the 5th, the gale had abated; the first step to be taken was to examine the state of the bread, a great part of which was found to be damaged and rotten – but even this was carefully preserved for use. The boat was now running among some islands, but after their reception at Tofoa, they did not venture to land. On the 6th, they still continued to see islands at a distance; and this day, for the first time, they hooked a fish, to their great joy; 'but', says the commander, 'we were miserably disappointed by its being lost in trying to get it into the boat.' In the evening, each person had an ounce of the damaged bread, and a quarter of a pint of water for supper.

Lieutenant Bligh observes, 'it will readily be supposed our lodgings were very miserable, and confined for want of room'; but he endeavoured to remedy the latter defect, by putting themselves at watch and watch; so that one half always sat up, while the other lay down on the boat's bottom, or upon a chest, but with nothing to cover them except the heavens. Their limbs, he says, were dreadfully cramped, for they could not stretch them out; and the nights were so cold, and they were so constantly wet, that, after a few hours' sleep, they were scarcely able to move. At dawn of day on the 7th, being very wet and cold, he says, 'I served a spoonful of rum and a morsel of bread for breakfast.'

In the course of this day they passed close to some rocky isles, from which two large sailing-canoes came swiftly after them, but in the afternoon gave over the chase. They were of the same construction as those of the Friendly Islands, and the land seen for the last two days was supposed to be the Fiji Islands. But being constantly wet, Bligh says, 'it is with the utmost difficulty I can open a book to write, and I feel truly sensible I can do no more than point out where these lands are to be found, and give some idea of their extent.' Heavy rain came on in the afternoon, when every person in the boat did his utmost to catch some water, and thus succeeded in increasing their stock to thirty-four gallons, besides quenching their thirst for the first time since they had been at sea: but having no dry things to shift or cover themselves, they experienced cold and shiverings scarcely to be conceived.

On the 8th, the allowance issued was an ounce and a half of pork, a teaspoonful of rum, half a pint of cocoa-nut milk, and an ounce of bread. The rum, though so small in quantity, is stated to have been of the greatest service. In the afternoon, they were employed in cleaning out the boat, which occupied them until sunset before they got every thing dry and in order. 'Hitherto,' Bligh says, 'I had issued the allowance by guess, but I now made a pair of scales with two cocoa-nut shells; and having accidentally some pistol-balls in the boat, twenty-five of which weighed one pound or sixteen ounces, I adopted one of these balls as the proportion of weight that each person should receive of bread at the times I served it. I also amused all hands with describing the situations of New Guinea and New Holland, and gave them every information in my power, that in case any accident should happen to me, those who survived might have some idea of what they were about, and be able to find their way to Timor. At night I served a quarter of a pint of water and half an ounce of bread for supper.'

On the morning of the 9th, a quarter of a pint of cocoa-nut milk and some of the decayed bread were served for breakfast; and for dinner, the kernels of four cocoanuts, with the remainder of the rotten bread, which, he says, was eatable only by such distressed people as themselves. A storm of thunder and lightning gave them about twenty gallons of water. 'Being miserably wet and cold, I served to the people a teaspoonful of rum each, to enable them to bear with their distressing situation. The weather continued extremely bad, and the wind increased; we spent a very miserable night, without sleep, except such as could be got in the midst of rain.'

The following day, the 10th, brought no relief. The sea broke over the boat so much, that two men were kept constantly baling; and it was necessary to keep the boat before the waves for fear of its filling. The allowance now served regularly to each person was one twenty-fifth part of a pound of bread and a quarter of a pint of water, at eight in the morning, at noon, and at sunset. To-day was added about half an ounce of pork for dinner.

The morning of the 11th did not improve. 'At day-break I served to every person a teaspoonful of rum, our limbs being so much cramped that we could scarcely move them. Our situation was now extremely dangerous, the sea frequently running over our stern, which kept us baling with all our strength. At noon the sun appeared, which gave us as much pleasure as is felt when it shows itself on a winter's day in England.

'In the evening of the 12th it still rained hard, and we again experienced a dreadful night. At length the day came, and showed a miserable set of beings, full of wants, without any thing to relieve them. Some complained of great pain in their bowels, and every one of having almost lost the use of his limbs. The little sleep we got was in no way refreshing, as we were constantly covered with the sea and rain. The weather continuing, and no sun affording the least prospect of getting our clothes dried, I recommended to every one to strip and wring them through the sea-water, by which means they received a warmth that, while wet with rain-water, they could not have.' The shipping of seas and constant baling continued; and though the men were shivering with wet and cold, the commander was under the necessity of informing them, that he could no longer afford them the comfort they had derived from the teaspoonful of rum.

On the 13th and 14th the stormy weather and heavy sea continued unabated, and on these days they saw distant land, and passed several islands. The sight of these islands, it may well be supposed, served only to increase the misery of their situation. They were as men very little better than starving

Dangerous Situation of Captain and his Crew.
In his *Notebook*, dated 21 May 1789, Bligh wrote a prayer which he read to the crew in the open boat. 'We most devoutly thank thee for our preservation & are truly conscious that only through thy Divine Mercy we have been saved – We supplicate thy glorious Majesty to accept our unfeigned Prayers and thanksgivings for thy Glorious Protection – Thou has showed us wonders in the Deep, that we might see how powerfull gracious a God thou art; how able and ready to help those that trust in thee. – Thou has given us strength & fed us, hast shown how both Winds and Seas obey thy command, that we may learn even from them to hereafter obey thy holy word and to do as Thou hast ordered. We bless and glorify thy name for this thy Mercy in saving us from perishing, and we humbly beseech thee to make us truly sensible of thy Almighty goodness that we may be always ready to express a thankfullness not only by our Words, but also by our lives in living more obediently to thy Holy Commandments. . . . Grant unto us health & strength to continue our Voyage, & so bless our miserable morsel of Bread, that it may be sufficient for our undertaking. O Almighty God relieve us from our extreme distress, such as Men never felt, – conduct us through thy Mercy to a Safe Haven, and in the End restore us to our disconsolate Families and Friends. We promise O Lord with full & contrite hearts never to forget thy great Mercies vouchsafed unto us – We promise to renew our unfeigned thanks at thy Divine Altar & mend our lives according to thy Holy Word. . . .'

with plenty in their view; yet, to attempt procuring any relief was considered to be attended with so much danger, that the prolongation of life, even in the midst of misery, was thought preferable, while there remained hopes of being able to surmount their hardships.

The whole day and night of the 15th were still rainy; the latter was dark, not a star to be seen by which the steerage could be directed, and the sea was continually breaking over the boat. On the next day, the 16th, was issued for dinner an ounce of salt pork, in addition to their miserable allowance of one twenty-fifth part of a pound of bread. The night was again truly horrible, with storms of thunder, lightning, and rain; not a star visible, so that the steerage was quite uncertain.

On the morning of the 17th, at dawn of day, 'I found,' says the commander, 'every person complaining, and some of them solicited extra allowance, which I positively refused. The little rum we had was of the greatest service: when our nights were particularly distressing, I generally served a teaspoonful or two to each person, and it was always joyful tidings when they heard of my intentions. It was my intention, if possible, to make the coast of New Holland [Australia] to the southward of Endeavour Straits, being sensible that it was necessary to preserve such a situation as would make a southerly wind a fair one; that we might range along the reefs till an opening should be found into smooth water, and we the sooner be able to pick up some refreshments.'

On the 18th the rain abated, when, at their commander's recommendation, they all stripped and wrung their clothes through the sea-water, from which, as usual, they derived much warmth and refreshment; but every one complained of violent pains in their bones. At night the heavy rain recommenced, with severe lightning, which obliged them to keep baling without intermission. The same weather continued through the 19th and 20th; the rain constant – at times a deluge – the men always baling; the commander, too, found it necessary to issue for dinner only half an ounce of pork.

At dawn of day, Lieutenant Bligh states, that some of his people seemed half dead; that their appearances were horrible; 'and I could look,' says he, 'no way, but I caught the eye of some one in distress. Extreme hunger was now too evident, but no one suffered from thirst, nor had we much inclination to drink, that desire perhaps being satisfied through the skin. The little sleep we got was in the midst of water, and we constantly awoke with severe cramps and pains in our bones. At noon the sun broke out and revived every one.

Facsimile: Log of the *Bounty*'s Launch.
Such was Bligh's supreme seamanship that he found time and energy to survey and fix many of the islands and channels through which the near-starving boat party passed, and testimony to his navigational skills has been given by many cartographers who have compared Bligh's positions with those of Captain Cook, and even with those given on modern charts.

H	K	F	Courses	Winds	Rem^s Wednesday 20th May 1789 In the Bountys Launch
1	3	4	West	E.N.E	Moderate and Rainy W^r
2	3	4			
3	3				
4	2	4		..	Deluge of Rain — Constantly bailing
5	3				
6	3			..	Servd ¼ lb of Bread for Supper — Water we want none for our thirst
7	2	6			seems to be quenched through our Skin. —
8	4				
9	3	2			
10	3	2			
11	3	2			
12	3	2		..	No intermission of Rain and at times a Deluge. —
1	3	2			
2	4				
3	3	6			
4	5				
5	4			..	At Dawn of day some of my people half dead. the Weather continuing
6	4				the Same. I now servd two tea spoonfulls of Rum to each person.
7	4				
8	4				
9	3	4			
10	2	4			
11	2	4		..	Tropic Gulls Men of War Birds and Boobies
12	3			..	Towards Noon the Rain abated and had the Sun out. Hung up our
	102				Wet things to dry — Servd ¼ lb of Bread and 2 Gills of Water for
	149½				Dinner
	15	73	Merid Alt^d ⊙ ..	;	
			⊙ Center 34..54		

		Latitude		Longitude	
Course	Dis^t	Obs^d	DR	DR	
N80W	101	14..49 S	14..40 S	159..34 E	

'During the whole of the afternoon of the 21st we were so covered with rain and salt water, that we could scarcely see. Sleep, though we longed for it, afforded no comfort; for my own part, I almost lived without it. On the 22nd, our situation was extremely calamitous. We were obliged to take the course of the sea, running right before it, and watching with the utmost care, as the least error in the helm would in a moment have been our destruction. It continued through the day to blow hard, and the foam of the sea kept running over our stern and quarters.

'The misery we suffered this night exceeded the preceding. The sea flew over us with great force, and kept us baling with horror and anxiety. At dawn of day I found every one in a most distressed condition, and I began to fear that another such night would put an end to the lives of several, who seemed no longer able to support their sufferings. I served an allowance of *two* teaspoonfuls of rum; after drinking which, and having wrung our clothes and taken our breakfast of bread and water, we became a little refreshed.

'On the evening of the 24th, the wind moderated and the weather looked much better. The night also was fair; but being always wet with the sea, we suffered much from the cold. I had the pleasure to see a fine morning produce some cheerful countenances; and for the first time, during the last fifteen days, we experienced comfort from the warmth of the sun. We stripped and hung up our clothes to dry, which were by this time become so threadbare, that they could not keep out either wet or cold. In the afternoon we had many birds about us, which are never seen far from land, such as boobies and noddies.'

As the sea now began to run fair, and the boat shipped but little water, Lieutenant Bligh took the opportunity to examine into the state of their bread; and it was found that, according to the present mode of living, there was a sufficient quantity remaining for twenty-nine days' allowance, by which time there was every reason to expect they would be able to reach

---

Mother Carey's Chicken, or Pairooi of Otaheite. (*above*)
Wherever he went on his voyages, William Bligh worked ceaselessly to record everything that came within his experience, charting and positioning islands and passages, recording the appearance, customs and social systems of the peoples he encountered, noting areas offering trading potential, and describing native plant and animal life. Many of his paintings show a sensitive touch and a naturalist's eye for detail, offering a glimpse of another facet of this complex and often unjustly maligned character.

Noddy of Otahytey . . . about one-half life size. (*below*)
The noddy caught flying close to the open boat on 25 May 1789 was like manna from heaven to the starving occupants. Only the previous day Bligh had been forced to cut their pitiful rations still further, noting in his diary that it was 'like robbing them of life.' The entire bird, beak, claws and all, was devoured. As the boat drew nearer to the coast of Australia, more birds were caught, among them boobies (*centre*), and the threat of starvation gradually receded. The birds illustrated here were painted by George Tobin in 1792.

Mother Carey's Chicken or Fairsoni of Otaheite

Booha, so called by Tamien. One third its natural size. Lat.ᵈ 9.00 South. Long.ᵈ 151.00 East. G.ᵗᵉ 1792. Page 253.

Noddie of Otaheitey. About one half the size of life. G.ᵗᵉ 1792. Page 100.

Timor. But as this was still uncertain, and it was possible that, after all, they might be obliged to go to Java, it was determined to proportion the allowance, so as to make the stock hold out six weeks. 'I was apprehensive,' he says, 'that this would be ill received, and that it would require my utmost resolution to enforce it; for, small as the quantity was which I intended to take away for our future good, yet it might appear to my people like robbing them of life; and some who were less patient than their companions, I expected would very ill brook it. However, on my representing the necessity of guarding against delays that might be occasioned by contrary winds, or other causes, and promising to enlarge upon the allowance as we got on, they cheerfully agreed to my proposal.' It was accordingly settled that every person should receive one twenty-fifth part of a pound of bread for breakfast, and the same quantity for dinner as usual, but that the proportion for supper should be discontinued; this arrangement left them forty-three days' consumption.

On the 25th about noon, some noddies came so near to the boat that one of them was caught by hand. This bird was about the size of a small pigeon. 'I divided it,' says Bligh, 'with its entrails, into eighteen portions, and by a well-known method at sea, of "*Who shall have this?*" it was distributed, with the allowance of bread and water for dinner, and eaten up, bones and all, with salt water for sauce. [To ensure absolute fairness, the food is divided into portions and one man turns his back on them. Another then points to each portion, at random, asking, 'Who shall have this?', to which the first responds by calling someone's name. Bligh later spoke of the great amusement caused by the beak and claws falling to his share.] In the evening, several boobies flying very near to us, we had the good fortune to catch one of them. This bird is as large as a duck. They are the most presumptive proof of being near land, of any sea-fowl we are acquainted with. I directed the bird to be killed for supper, and the blood to be given to three of the people who were the most distressed for want of food. The body, with the entrails, beak, and feet, I divided into eighteen shares, and with the allowance of bread, which I made a merit of granting, we made a good supper compared with our usual fare.

'On the next day, the 26th, we caught another booby, so that Providence appeared to be relieving our wants in an extraordinary manner. The people were overjoyed at this addition to their dinner, which was distributed in the same manner as on the preceding evening; giving the blood to those who were the most in want of food. To make the bread a little savoury, most of the men frequently dipped it in salt water, but I generally broke mine into small pieces, and ate it in my allowance of water, out of a cocoa-nut shell, with a spoon, economically avoiding to take too large a piece at a time, so that I was as long at dinner as if it had been a much more plentiful meal.'

The weather was now serene, which, nevertheless, was not without its inconveniences, for, it appears, they began to feel distress of a different kind from that which they had hitherto been accustomed to suffer. The heat of the sun was now so powerful, that several of the people were seized with a languor and faintness, which made life indifferent. But the little circumstance of catching two boobies in the evening, trifling as it may appear, had the effect of raising their spirits. The stomachs of these birds contained several flying-fish, and small cuttle-fish, all of which were carefully saved to be divided for dinner the next day; 'so that to-day,' says the Lieutenant, 'with the usual allowance of bread at breakfast and at dinner, I was happy to see that every person thought he had feasted.' From the appearance of the clouds in the evening, Mr. Bligh had no doubt they were then near the land.

Accordingly, at one in the morning of the 28th, the person at the helm heard the sound of breakers. It was the 'barrier reef' which runs along the eastern coast of New Holland, through which it now became the anxious object to discover a passage; Mr. Bligh says this was now become absolutely necessary, without a moment's loss of time. The idea of getting into smooth water and finding refreshments kept up the people's spirits. The sea broke furiously over the reef in every part; within, the water was so smooth and calm, that every man already anticipated the heartfelt satisfaction he was about to receive, as soon as he should have passed the barrier. At length a break in the reef was discovered, a quarter of a mile in width, and through this the boat rapidly passed with a strong stream running to the westward, and came immediately into smooth water, and all the past hardships seemed at once to be forgotten.

They now returned thanks to God for His generous protection, and with much content took their miserable allowance of the twenty-fifth part of a pound of bread, and a quarter of a pint of water, for dinner.

The coast now began to show itself very distinctly, and in the evening they landed on the sandy point of an island, when it was soon discovered there were oysters on the rocks, it being low water. The party sent out to reconnoitre returned highly rejoiced at having found plenty of oysters and fresh water. By help of a small magnifying-glass a fire was made, and among the things that had been thrown into the boat was a tinder-box and a piece of brimstone, so that in future they had the ready means of making a fire. One of the men too had been so provident as to bring away with him from the ship a copper pot; and thus with a mixture of oysters, bread, and pork, a stew was made, of which each person received a full pint.

The general complaints among the people were a dizziness in the head, great weakness in the joints, and violent tenesmus [straining of the bowel], but none of them are stated to have been alarming; and notwithstanding their sufferings from cold and hunger, all of them retained marks of strength. Mr. Bligh had cautioned them not to touch any kind of berry or fruit that they might find; yet it appears they were no sooner out of sight, than they began to make free with three different kinds that grew all over the island, eating without any reserve. The symptoms of having eaten too much began at last to frighten some of them; they fancied they were all poisoned, and regarded each other with the strongest marks of apprehension, uncertain

Bounty's launch: the open boat voyage.
Bligh's handling of the *Bounty*'s launch was a superb feat of seamanship. It required the strictest attention and fine judgement. If too much sail had been carried, the boat would have been swamped: if too little, she would have been too slow and the crew would have starved to death. If the sail had been too low she would have been becalmed in the troughs: too high and she would have been overturned. If she had been allowed to come broadside on she would again have been swamped by the huge seas. Bligh had to run her before the wind, even when it meant losing distance, if he was to avoid a capsize. And all this, day after day, in a boat dangerously overladen and with the crew half starved. The Log showed a voyage of 3618 miles. Stepping off the distance on a modern chart suggests it was nearer 3870.

Bligh's chart of the coast of northeastern Australia. (*opposite*)
Matthew Flinders, who sailed with the *Providence* and later became Australia's most famous maritime explorer, praised Bligh's survey of northeastern Australia in these words: 'It has been to me a cause of much surprise, that under such distress of hunger and fatigue, and of anxiety still greater than these, and while running before a strong breeze in an open boat, Captain Bligh should have been able to gather material for a chart; but that this chart should possess a considerable share of accuracy is a subject for admiration.' The Fiji government named a channel in the archipelago 'Bounty Boat Passage' in honour of Bligh's discovery of many of the Fijian islands.

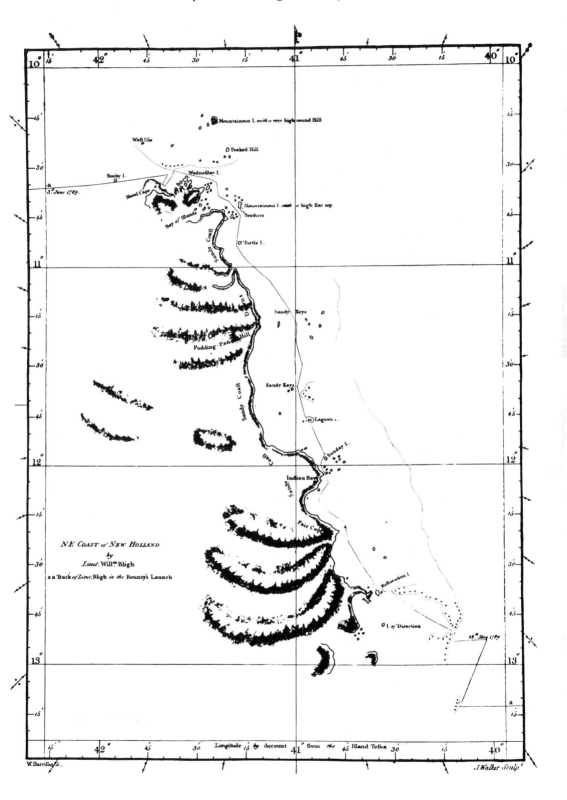

what might be the issue of their imprudence; fortunately the fruit proved to be wholesome and good.

'This day (29th May) being,' says Lieutenant Bligh, 'the anniversary of the restoration of King Charles II, and the name not being inapplicable to our present situation (for we were *restored* to fresh life and strength), I named this "Restoration Island"; for I thought it probable that Captain Cook might not have taken notice of it.'

With oysters and palm-tops stewed together the people now made excellent meals, without consuming any of their bread. In the morning of the 30th, Mr. Bligh saw with great delight a visible alteration in the men for the better, and he sent them away to gather oysters, in order to carry a stock of them to sea, for he determined to put off again that evening. They also procured fresh water, and filled all their vessels to the amount of nearly sixty gallons. On examining the bread, it was found there still remained about thirty-eight days' allowance.

Being now ready for sea, every person was ordered to attend prayers; but just as they were embarking, about twenty naked savages made their appearance, running and hallooing, and beckoning the strangers to come to them; but, as each was armed with a spear or lance, it was thought prudent to hold no communication with them. They now proceeded to the northward, having the continent on their left, and several islands and reefs on their right.

On the 31st they landed on one of these islands, to which was given the name of 'Sunday.' 'I sent out two parties (says Bligh), one to the northward and the other to the southward, to seek for supplies, and others I ordered to stay by the boat. On this occasion, fatigue and weakness so far got the better of their sense of duty, that some of the people expressed their discontent at having worked harder than their companions, and declared that they would rather be without their dinner than go in search of it. One person, in particular, went so far as to tell me, with a mutinous look, that he was as good a man as myself. It was not possible for one to judge where this might have an end, if not stopped in time; to prevent therefore such disputes in future, I determined either to preserve my command or die in the attempt; and seizing a cutlass, I ordered him to lay hold of another and defend himself; on which he called out that I was going to kill him, and immediately made concessions. I did not allow this to interfere further with the harmony of the boat's crew, and every thing soon became quiet.'

On this island they obtained oysters, and clams, and dog-fish; also a small bean, which Nelson, the botanist, pronounced to be a species of dolichos. On the 1st of June, they stopped in the midst of some sandy islands, such as are known by the name of *keys*, where they procured a few clams. Here Nelson was taken very ill with a violent heat in his bowels, a loss of sight, great thirst, and an inability to walk. A little wine, which had carefully been saved, with some pieces of bread soaked in it, was given to him in small quantities, and he soon began to recover. The boatswain and carpenter were also ill, and complained of headache and sickness of the stomach. Others became shockingly distressed with tenesmus; in fact, there were few without complaints.

A party was sent out by night to catch birds; they returned with only twelve noddies, but it is stated, that, had it not been for the folly and obstinacy of one of the party, who separated from the others and disturbed the birds, a great many more might have been taken. The offender was Robert Lamb, who acknowledged, when he got to Java, that he had that night eaten *nine* raw birds, after he separated from his two companions. The birds, with a few clams, were the whole of the supplies afforded at these small islands.

On the 3rd of June, after passing several keys and islands, and doubling Cape York, the north-easternmost point of New Holland, at eight in the evening the little boat and her brave crew once more launched into the open ocean. 'Miserable,' says Bligh, 'as our situation was in every respect, I was secretly surprised to see that it did not appear to affect any one so strongly as myself; on the contrary, it seemed as if they had embarked on a voyage to Timor in a vessel sufficiently calculated for safety and convenience. So much confidence gave me great pleasure, and I may venture to assert that to this cause our preservation is chiefly to be attributed.

'We had been just six days on the coast of New Holland, in the course of which we found oysters, a few clams, some birds and water. But a benefit, probably not less than this, was that of being relieved from the fatigue of sitting constantly in the boat, and enjoying good rest at night. These advantages certainly preserved our lives; and small as the supply was, I am very sensible how much it alleviated our distresses. Before this time nature must have sunk under the extremes of hunger and fatigue. Even in our present situation, we were most deplorable objects, but the hopes of a speedy relief kept up our spirits.' . . .

On the 5th a booby was caught by the hand, the blood of which was divided among three of the men who were weakest, and the bird kept for next day's dinner; and on the evening of the 6th the allowance for supper was recommenced, according to a promise made when it had been discontinued. On the 7th, after a miserably wet and cold night, nothing more could be afforded than the usual allowance for breakfast; but at dinner each person had the luxury of an ounce of dried clams, which consumed all that remained. The sea was running high and breaking over the boat the whole of this day. Mr. Ledward, the surgeon, and Lawrence Lebogue, an old hardy seaman, appeared to be giving way very fast. No other assistance could be given to them than a teaspoonful or two of wine, that had been carefully saved for such a melancholy occasion, which was not at all unexpected.

On the 8th the weather was more moderate, and a small dolphin was caught, which gave about two ounces to each man: in the night it again blew strong, the boat shipped much water, and they all suffered greatly from wet and cold. The surgeon and Lebogue still continued very ill, and the only relief that could be afforded them was a small quantity of wine, and encouraging them with the hope that a very few days more, at the rate they were then sailing, would bring them to Timor.

'In the morning of the 10th, after a very comfortless night, there was a visible alteration for the worse,' says Mr. Bligh, 'in many of the people, which gave me great apprehensions. An extreme weakness, swelled legs, hollow and ghastly countenances, a more than common inclination to sleep, with an apparent debility of understanding, seemed to me the melancholy presages of an approaching dissolution. The surgeon and Lebogue, in particular, were most miserable objects. I occasionally gave them a few teaspoonfuls of wine, out of the little that remained, which greatly assisted them. The hope of being able to accomplish the voyage was our principal support. The boatswain very innocently told me that he really thought I looked worse than any in the boat. The simplicity with which he uttered such an opinion amused me, and I returned him a better compliment.'

On the 11th Lieutenant Bligh announced to his wretched companions that he had no doubt they had now passed the meridian of the eastern part of Timor, a piece of intelligence that diffused universal joy and satisfaction. Accordingly at three in the morning of the following day Timor was discovered at the distance only of two leagues from the shore.

'It is not possible for me,' says this experienced navigator, 'to describe the pleasure which the blessing of the sight of this land diffused among us. It appeared scarcely credible to ourselves that, in an open boat, and so poorly provided, we should have been able to reach the coast of Timor in forty-one days after leaving Tofoa, having in that time run, by our log, a distance of three thousand six hundred and eighteen nautical miles; and that, notwithstanding our extreme distress, no one should have perished in the voyage.'

On Sunday the 14th they came safely to anchor in Coupang Bay, where they were received with every mark of kindness, hospitality, and humanity. The houses of the principal people were thrown open for their reception. The poor sufferers when landed were scarcely able to walk; their condition is described as most deplorable. 'An indifferent spectator (if such could be found) would have been at a loss which most to admire, the eyes of famine sparkling at immediate relief, or the horror of their preservers at the sight of so many spectres. Our bodies were nothing but skin and bones, our limbs were full of sores, and we were clothed in rags; in this condition, with the tears of joy and gratitude flowing down our cheeks, the people of Timor beheld us with a mixture of horror, surprise, and pity.

'When,' continues the commander, 'I reflect how providentially our lives were saved at Tofoa, by the Indians delaying their attack; and that, with scarcely anything to support life, we crossed a sea of more than twelve hundred leagues, without shelter from the inclemency of the weather; when I reflect that in an open boat, with so much stormy weather, we escaped foundering, that not any of us were taken off by disease, that we had the great good fortune to pass the unfriendly natives of other countries without accident, and at last to meet with the most friendly and best of people to

Bligh and his Companions Landing at Coupang.
'Soon after daybreak a Soldier hailed me to land, which I instantly did among a Crowd of Malays,' wrote Bligh in the Log of the *Bounty*'s Launch for 14 June 1789. Bligh's party was received with great hospitality by the Dutch and their generous assistance was never forgotten by him. In 1796 Bligh interceded with the Admiralty on behalf of the widow of a Dutch surgeon who tended the boat crew, to get returned to her some official receipts which the British had impounded during the Anglo-Dutch war. Mrs Abegg needed the receipts to claim her late husband's estate in the Netherlands, and Bligh wrote in a letter to the Admiralty on 10 May 1796, 'I hope their Lordships will pardon the liberty I have taken to trouble them with this circumstance. I feel it in some way my duty, to show the high confidence the petitioners have that such services as their relatives rendered to us will not be forgotten.'

relieve our distresses – I say, when I reflect on all these wonderful escapes, the remembrance of such great mercies enables me to bear with resignation and cheerfulness the failure of an expedition, the success of which I had so much at heart.'

Having recruited their strength by a residence of two months among the friendly inhabitants of Coupang, they proceeded to the westward on the 20th August in a small schooner, which was purchased and armed for the purpose, and arrived on the 1st October in Batavia Road [Djakarta], where Mr. Bligh embarked in a Dutch packet, and was landed on the Isle of Wight on the 14th March, 1790. The rest of the people had passages provided for them in ships of the Dutch East India Company, then about to sail for Europe. All of them, however, did not survive to reach England. Nelson, the botanist, died at Coupang; Mr. Elphinstone, master's-mate, Peter Linkletter and Thomas Hall, seamen, died at Batavia; Robert Lamb, seaman (the booby-eater), died on the passage; and Mr. Ledward, the surgeon, was left behind, and not afterwards heard of. These six, with John Norton, who was stoned to death, left twelve of the nineteen, forced by the mutineers into the launch, to survive the difficulties and dangers of this unparalleled voyage, and to revisit their native country.

Sir

         I am now unfortunately to acquaint you
that His Majesty's Armed Vessel Bounty under my Command
was taken from me by the greatest part of the inferior Officers &
Men, on the 28th April 1789 in the following manner. — At day
light Fletcher Christian who was Mate of the Ship and Officer of
the Watch, with the Ships Corporal came into my Cabbin while
I was asleep, and seizing me tied my hands with a Cord, assisted
by others who were also in the Cabbin all armed. — I was now
threatned with instant death if I spoke a word. I however
called for Assistance and awakened every one, but the Officers
who were in their Cabbins were secured by armed Centinels
at their doors, so that no one could come to me. — The Arms
were all secured, & I was forced on Deck in my shirt with
my hands tied behind my back in so severe a manner that
I suffered the severest torture. I was now put under a Guard
about the Mizen Mast, during which the Mutineers expressed
much joy that they would soon again see Otaheite. —

         I now demanded the cause of such a Violent Act,
but no other answer could I get, but hold your tongue Sir
or you are dead this instant, and holding me by the Cord

It is impossible not fully to accord with Bligh when he says, 'Thus happily ended, through the assistance of Divine Providence, without accident, a voyage of the most extraordinary nature that ever happened in the world, let it be taken either in its extent, duration, or the want of every necessary of life.' We may go further and say, it is impossible to read this extraordinary and unparalleled voyage, without bestowing the meed of unqualified praise on the able and judicious conduct of its commander, who is in every respect, as far as this extraordinary enterprise is concerned, fully entitled to rank with Parry, Franklin and Richardson. To his discreet management of the men, and their scanty resources, and to his ability as a thorough seaman, eighteen souls were saved from imminent and otherwise inevitable destruction. It was not alone the dangers of the sea, in an open boat, crowded with people, that he had to combat, though they required the most consummate nautical skill, to contend successfully against them; but the unfortunate situation, to which the party were exposed, rendered him subject to the almost daily murmuring and caprice of people less conscious than himself of their real danger. From the experience they had acquired at Tofoa of the savage disposition of the people against the defenceless boat's crew, a lesson was learned how little was to be trusted, even to the mildest of uncivilized people, when a conscious superiority was in their hands. Lieutenant Bligh, fully aware of his own weakness, deemed it expedient, therefore, to resist all desires and temptations to land at any of those islands, among which they passed in the course of the voyage.

But the circumstance of being tantalized with the appearance of land, clothed with perennial verdure, whose approach was forbidden to men chilled with wet and cold, and nearly perishing with hunger, was by no means the most difficult against which the commander had to struggle. 'It was not the least of my distresses,' he observes, 'to be constantly assailed with the melancholy demands of my people for an increase of allowance, which it grieved me to refuse.' He well knew that to reason with men reduced to the last stage of famine, yet denied the use of provisions within their reach, would be to no purpose. The first thing he set about, therefore, was to ascertain the exact state of their provisions, which were found to amount to the ordinary consumption of five days, but which were to be spun out so as to last fifty days. This was at once distinctly stated to the men, and a solemn promise made by all, that the settled allowance should never be deviated from, as they were made clearly to understand that on the strict observance

Facsimile: Bligh's letter from Batavia to the Admiralty, dated 12 October 1789, reporting the mutiny.
Bligh sent an identical letter from Coupang on 18 August 1789, which was used in evidence at the court-martial of the captured mutineers in September 1792. He also sent reports to the British Governors of India and New South Wales in case the mutineers took the *Bounty* to any port within their jurisdiction. Such was the lottery of the sea post in the eighteenth century that duplicate letters and reports were sent at every opportunity.

of this agreement rested the only hope of their safety; and by reminding them of this compact, whenever they became clamorous for more, Lieutenant Bligh succeeded in resisting all their solicitations. . . .

But the great art of all was to divert the men's attention from the almost hopeless situation in which they were placed, and to prevent despondency from taking possession of their minds; and in order to assist in effecting this, some employment was devised for them; among other things, a logline, an object of interest to all, was measured and marked; and the men were practised in counting seconds correctly, that the distance run on each day might be ascertained with a nearer approach to accuracy than by mere guessing. These little operations afforded them a temporary amusement; and the log being daily and hourly hove gave them also some employment, and diverted their thoughts for the moment from their melancholy situation. Then, every noon, when the sun was out, or at other times before and after noon, and also at night when the stars appeared, Lieutenant Bligh never neglected to take observations for the latitude, and to work the day's work for ascertaining the ship's place. The anxiety of the people to hear how they had proceeded, what progress had been made, and whereabouts they were on the wide ocean, also contributed for the time to drive away gloomy thoughts. These observations were rigidly attended to, and sometimes made under the most difficult circumstances, the sea breaking over the observer, and the boat pitching and rolling so much, that he was obliged to be 'propped up,' while taking them. In this way, with now and then a little interrupted sleep, about a thousand long and anxious hours were consumed in pain and peril, and a space of sea passed over equal to four thousand five hundred miles, being at the rate of four and one-fifth miles an hour, or one hundred miles a day.

Lieutenant Bligh has expressed his conviction, that the six days spent among the coral islands, off the coast of New Holland, were the salvation of the whole party; for such, he says, was the exhausted condition of all on their arrival at the 'barrier reef,' that a few days more at sea must have terminated the existence of many of them. This stoppage, however, had been nearly productive of another mutiny. Bligh mentions in his printed narrative, the mutinous conduct of a person to whom he gave a cutlass to defend himself. This affair, as stated in his original manuscript journal, wears a far more serious aspect.

'The carpenter (Purcell) began to be insolent to a high degree, and at last told me, with a mutinous aspect, he was as good a man as I was. I did not just now see where this was to end; I therefore determined to strike a final blow at it, and either to preserve my command or die in the attempt; and taking hold of a cutlass, I ordered the rascal to take hold of another and defend himself, when he called out that I was going to kill him, and began to make concessions. I was now only assisted by Mr. Nelson; and the master (Fryer) very deliberately called out to the boatswain, to put me under an arrest, and was stirring up a greater disturbance, when I declared if he interfered, when I was in the execution of my duty to preserve order and regularity, and that in consequence any tumult arose, I would certainly put him to death the first person. This had a proper effect on this man, and he now assured me that, on the contrary, I might rely on him to support my orders and directions for the future.' He adds, 'I was told that the master and carpenter, at the last place, were endeavouring to produce altercations, and were the principal cause of their murmuring there.' This carpenter he brought to a court-martial on their arrival in England, on various charges, of which he was found guilty in part, and reprimanded. Purcell is said to be at this time in a madhouse.

On another occasion, when a stew of oysters was distributed among the people, Lieutenant Bligh observes (in the MS. Journal), 'The *master* began to be dissatisfied, because it was not made into a larger quantity by the addition of water, and showed a turbulent disposition, until I laid my commands on him to be silent.' Again, on his refusing bread to the men, because they were collecting oysters, he says, 'this occasioned some murmuring with the master and carpenter, the former of whom endeavoured to prove the propriety of such an expenditure, and was troublesomely ignorant, tending to create disorder.'

If what Bligh states with regard to the conduct of the master and the carpenter be true, it was such, on several occasions, as to provoke a man much less irritable than himself. He thus speaks of the latter, when in the ship and in the midst of the mutiny. 'The boatswain and carpenter were fully at liberty; the former was employed, on pain of death, to hoist the boats out, but the latter I saw acting the part of an idler, with an impudent and ill-looking countenance, which led me to believe he was one of the mutineers, until he was among the rest ordered to leave the ship, for it appeared to me to be a doubt with Christian, at first, whether he should keep the carpenter or his mate (Norman), but knowing the former to be a troublesome fellow, he determined on the latter.'

The following paragraph also appears in his original journal, on the day of the mutiny, but is not alluded to in his printed narrative. 'The master's cabin was opposite to mine; he saw them (the mutineers) in my cabin, for our eyes met each other through his door-window. He had a pair of ship's pistols loaded, and ammunition in his cabin – a firm resolution might have made a good use of them. After he had sent twice or thrice to Christian to be allowed to come on deck, he was at last permitted, and his question then was, "Will you let me remain in the ship?" – "No," "Have *you* any objection, Captain Bligh?" I whispered to him to knock him [Christian] down – Martin is good [a potential ally] (this is the man who gave the shaddock), for this was just before Martin was removed from me. Christian, however, pulled me back, and sent away the master, with orders to go again to his cabin, and I saw no more of him, until he was put into the boat. He afterwards told me that he could find nobody to act with him; that by staying in the ship he hoped to have retaken her, and that, as to the pistols, he was so flurried and surprised, that he did not recollect he had them.' This master tells a very different story respecting the pistols, in his evidence before the court-martial.

Whatever, therefore, on the whole, may have been the conduct of Bligh towards his officers, that of some of the latter appears to have been on several occasions provoking enough, and well calculated to stir up the irascible temper of a man, active and zealous in the extreme, as Bligh always was, in the execution of his duty. Some excuse may therefore be found for Bligh's hasty expressions uttered in moments of irritation. But no excuse can be found for his deeply and unfeelingly, without provocation, and in cold blood, inflicting a wound on the heart of a widowed mother, already torn with anguish and tortured with suspense for a beloved son, whose life was in imminent jeopardy. This charge is not loosely asserted; it is founded on documentary evidence under his own hand. Since the death of the late Captain Heywood, some papers have been brought to light, that throw a still more unfavourable stigma on the character of the two commanders, Bligh and Edwards, than any censure that his hitherto appeared in print, though the conduct of neither of them has been spared, whenever an occasion has presented itself for bringing their names before the public.

Bligh, it may be recollected, mentions young Heywood only as one of those left in the ship; he does not charge him with taking any active part in the mutiny; there is every reason, indeed, to believe that Bligh did not, and indeed could not, see him on the deck on that occasion: in point of fact, he never was within thirty feet of Captain Bligh, and the booms were between them. About the end of March, 1790, two months subsequent to the death of a most beloved and lamented husband, Mrs. Heywood received the afflicting information, but by report only, of a mutiny having taken place on board the Bounty. In that ship Mrs. Heywood's son had been serving as midshipman, who, when he left his home, in August, 1787, was under fifteen years of age, a boy deservedly admired and beloved by all who knew him. In a state of mind little short of distraction, on hearing this fatal intelligence, his mother addressed a letter to Captain Bligh, dictated by a mother's tenderness, and strongly expressive of the misery she must necessarily feel on such an occasion. The following is Bligh's reply:–

'*London, April 2nd.* 1790.

'MADAM, – I received your letter this day, and feel for you very much, being perfectly sensible of the extreme distress you must suffer from the conduct of your son Peter. *His baseness is beyond all description*, but I hope you will endeavour to prevent the loss of him, heavy as the misfortune is, from afflicting you too severely. I imagine he is, with the rest of the mutineers, returned to Otaheite. – I am, Madam,

(Signed) 'Wm. BLIGH.'

Colonel Holwell, the uncle of young Heywood, had previously addressed Bligh on the same melancholy subject, to whom he returned the following answer:–

'26th March, 1790.

'SIR, – I have just this instant received your letter. With much concern I inform you that your nephew, Peter Heywood, is among the mutineers. *His ingratitude to me is of the blackest dye,* for I was a father to him in every respect, and he never once had an angry word from me through the whole course of the voyage, as his conduct always gave me much pleasure and satisfaction. I very much regret *that so much baseness formed the character of a young man* I had a real regard for, and it will give me much pleasure to hear that his friends *can bear the loss of him without much concern.* – I am, Sir, etc.

(Signed) 'Wm. BLIGH.'

The only way of accounting for this ferocity of sentiment towards a youth, who had in point of fact no concern in the mutiny, is by a reference to certain points of evidence given by Hayward, Hallet, and Purcell on the court-martial, each point wholly unsupported. Those in the boat would no doubt, during their long passage, often discuss the conduct of their messmates left in the *Bounty*, and the unsupported evidence given by these three was well calculated to create in Bligh's mind a prejudice against young Heywood; yet, if so, it affords but a poor excuse for harrowing up the feelings of near and dear relatives.

As a contrast to these ungracious letters, it is a great relief to peruse the correspondence that took place, on this melancholy occasion, between this unfortunate young officer and his amiable but dreadfully afflicted family. The letters of his sister, Nessy Heywood (extracts from a few of which will be inserted in the course of this narrative), exhibit so lively and ardent an affection for her beloved brother, are couched in so high a tone of feeling for his honour, and confidence in his innocence, and are so nobly answered by the suffering youth, that no apology seems to be required for their introduction. After a state of long suspense, this amiable and accomplished young lady thus addresses her brother:–

'Isle of Man, 2nd June, 1792.

'In a situation of mind only rendered supportable by the long and painful state of misery and suspense we have suffered on his account, how shall I address my dear, my fondly beloved brother! Oh! my ever dearest boy, when I look back to that dreadful moment which brought us the fatal intelligence that you had remained in the *Bounty* after Mr. Bligh had quitted her, and were looked upon by him as a *mutineer!* – when I contrast that day of horror with my present hopes of again beholding you, I know not which is the most predominant sensation, – pity, compassion, and terror for your sufferings, or joy and satisfaction at the prospect of their being near a termination.

'I will not ask you, my beloved brother, whether you are innocent of the dreadful crime of mutiny; if the transactions of that day were as Mr. Bligh has represented them, such is my conviction of your worth and honour, that I will, without hesitation, stake my life on your innocence. If, on the contrary, you were concerned in such a conspiracy against your commander, I shall be as firmly persuaded *his* conduct was the occasion of it. Nothing but conviction from your own mouth can possibly persuade me, that you would commit an action in the smallest degree inconsistent with honour and duty; and the circumstance of your having swam off to the *Pandora* on her arrival at Otaheite is sufficient to convince all who know you, that you certainly staid behind either by force or from views of preservation.

'Gracious God, grant that we may be at length blessed by your return! but, alas! the *Pandora*'s people have been long expected, and are not even yet arrived. I send this to the care of Mr. Hayward, of Hackney, father to the young gentleman you so often mention in your letters while you were on board the *Bounty*, and who went out as third lieutenant of the *Pandora* – a circumstance which gave us infinite satisfaction, as you would, on entering the *Pandora*, meet your old friend. On discovering old Mr. Hayward's residence, I wrote to him, as I hoped he could give me some information respecting the time of your arrival, and in return he sent me a most friendly letter, and has promised this shall be given to you when you reach England. Let me conjure you, my dearest Peter, to write to us the very first moment – do not lose a post – 'tis of no consequence how short your letter may be, if it only informs us you are well.

'We are at present making all possible interest with every friend and connexion we have, to ensure you a sufficient support and protection at your approaching trial; for a trial you must unavoidably undergo, in order to convince the world of that innocence, which those who know you will not for a moment doubt; but, alas! while circumstances are against you, the generality of mankind will judge severely. Bligh's representations to the Admiralty are, I am told, very unfavourable, and hitherto the tide of public opinion has been greatly in his favour.

'Farewell, my most beloved brother! My mamma, brothers, and sisters, join with me in every sentiment of love and tenderness.

(Signed) 'NESSY HEYWOOD.'

The gleam of joy which this unhappy family derived from the circumstance, which had been related to them, of young Heywood's swimming off to the *Pandora*, was dissipated by a letter from himself to his mother, soon after his arrival in England, in which he says:– 'The question, my dear mother, in one of your letters, concerning my swimming off to the *Pandora*, is one falsity among the too many, in which I have often thought of undeceiving you, and as frequently forgot. The story was this:– On the morning she arrived, accompanied by two of my friends (natives), I was going up the mountains, and having got about a hundred yards from my own house, another of my friends came running after me, and informed me there was a ship coming. I immediately ascended a rising ground, and saw, with indescribable joy, a ship laying-to off Hapiano; it was just after daylight, and thinking Coleman might not be awake, I sent one of my servants to inform him of it, upon which he immediately went off in a single canoe. He no sooner got alongside than rippling capsized the canoe, and he being obliged to let go the tow-rope to get her righted, went astern, and was picked up the next tack and taken on board the *Pandora*, he being the first person. I, along with my messmate Stewart, was then standing upon the beach with a double canoe, manned with twelve paddles ready for launching; and just as she made her last tack into her berth, we put off and got alongside just as they streamed the buoy; and being dressed in the country manner, tanned as brown as themselves, and I *tattooed* like them in the most curious manner, I do not in the least wonder at their taking us for natives.' . . .

Among the many anxious friends and family connexions of the Heywoods, was Commodore Pasley, to whom Nessy Heywood addressed herself on the melancholy occasion; and the following is the reply she received from this officer.

'*Sheerness, June 8th*, 1792.

'Would to God, my dearest Nessy, that I could rejoice with you on the early prospect of your brother's arrival in England. One division of the *Pandora*'s people has arrived, and now on board the *Vengeance* (my ship). Captain Edwards with the remainder, and all the prisoners late of the *Bounty*, in number ten (four having been drowned on the loss of that ship), are daily expected. They have been most rigorously and closely confined since taken, and will continue so, no doubt, till Bligh's arrival. You have no chance of seeing him, for no bail can be offered. Your intelligence of his swimming off on the *Pandora*'s arrival is not founded; a man of the name of Coleman swam off ere she anchored – your brother and Mr. Stewart the next day; this last youth, when the *Pandora* was lost, refused to allow his irons to be taken off to save his life.

'I cannot conceal it from you, my dearest Nessy, neither is it proper I should – your brother appears, by all accounts, to be the greatest culprit of all, Christian alone excepted. Every exertion, you may rest assured, I shall use to save his life, but on trial I have no hope of his not being condemned. Three of the ten who are expected are mentioned, in Bligh's narrative, as men detained against their inclination. Would to God your brother had been one of that number! Adieu! my dearest Nessy – present my affectionate remembrances to your mother and sisters, and believe me always, with the warmest affection, – Your uncle,

'THOS. PASLEY.'

How unlike is this from the letter of Bligh! While it frankly apprises this amiable lady of the real truth of the case, without disguise, as it was then understood to be from Mr. Bligh's representations, it assures her of his best exertions to save her brother's life. Every reader of sensibility will sympathise in the feeling displayed in her reply.

'*Isle of Man, 22nd June*, 1792.

'Harassed by the most torturing suspense, and miserably wretched as I have been, my dearest uncle, since the receipt of your last, conceive, if it is possible, the heartfelt joy and satisfaction we experienced yesterday morning, when, on the arrival of the packet, the dear delightful letter from our beloved Peter (a copy of which I send you enclosed) was brought to us. Surely, my excellent friend, you will agree with me in thinking there could not be a stronger proof of his innocence and worth, and that it must prejudice every person who reads it most powerfully in his favour. Such a letter would, I am persuaded, reflect honour on the pen of a person much older than my poor brother. . . . Let it speak for him; the perusal of his artless and pathetic story will, I am persuaded, be a stronger recommendation in his favour than any thing I can urge. . . . Your most affectionate niece,

NESSY HEYWOOD.'

[Extracts from Peter Heywood's letter are given in the following chapter, to which they appropriately belong.]

Pandora 26 Augᵗ 1791

It being the unanimous opinion of
the 3 Lieu^t & master that nothing further
could be done for the preservation of
H.M. Ship it was concluded at next day dawn
we endeavour to save the lives of the Crew

To the truth whereof we this day
put our hands

Geo. Hamilton Surgeon

G. Bentham Purser

George Hamilton
SURGEON,
Royal Navy

Facsimile: Hamilton's Statement about the loss of the *Pandora*.
The loss of one of His Majesty's ships, for any reason, automatically resulted in the court-martial of the captain and officers. Captain Edwards prudently made sure that the lieutenants and the master concurred with the decision to abandon ship and also that their 'unanimous opinion' was witnessed by the surgeon and the purser. These, and other documents such as the ship's Log and the officers' and master's journals, would be presented in evidence at the court hearing. The court honorably acquitted him for the loss of his ship and he went on to become a Rear-Admiral in 1799. He died in 1815 at the age of seventy-three.

George Hamilton, Surgeon, HMS *Pandora*
Barrow is very critical of Hamilton, calling him 'coarse, vulgar and illiterate,' but Hamilton's assessment of the impact of the Europeans on the Tahitians was very much in line with the views of both Cook and Bligh. He wrote, '. . . for to our shame be it spoken, disease and gunpowder is all the benefit they have received from us in return for their hospitality and kindness.' Hamilton considered the prisoners' cage, 'the most desirable place in the ship,' and noted that the prisoners, contrary to 'the established laws of the service,' were put on full rations instead of two-thirds rations. Morrison described Hamilton as, 'a very humane gentleman.'

CHAPTER FIVE

The 'Pandora'

The tide of public applause set as strongly in favour of Bligh, on account of his sufferings and successful issue of his daring enterprise, as its indignation was launched against Christian and his associates, for the audacious and criminal deed they had committed. Bligh was promoted by the Admiralty to the rank of Commander, and speedily sent out a second time to transport the bread-fruit to the West Indies, which he without the least obstruction successfully accomplished; and his Majesty's government were no sooner made acquainted with the atrocious act of piracy and mutiny, than it determined to adopt every possible means to apprehend and bring to condign punishment the perpetrators of so foul a deed. For this purpose, the *Pandora* frigate, of twenty-four guns and one hundred and sixty men, was despatched under the command of Captain Edward Edwards, with orders to proceed, in the first instance, to Otaheite, and not finding the mutineers there, to visit the different groups of the Society and Friendly Islands, and others in the neighbouring parts of the Pacific, using his best endeavours to seize and bring home in confinement the whole or such part of the delinquents as he might be able to discover.

This voyage was in the sequel almost as disastrous as that of the *Bounty*, but from a different cause. The waste of human life was much greater, occasioned by the wreck of the ship, and the distress experienced by the crew not much less, owing to the famine and thirst they had to suffer in a navigation of eleven hundred miles in open boats; but the Captain succeeded in fulfilling a part of his instructions, by taking fourteen of the mutineers, of whom ten were brought safe to England, the other four being drowned when the ship was wrecked.

The only published account of this voyage is contained in a small volume by Mr. George Hamilton, the surgeon, who appears to have been a coarse, vulgar, and illiterate man, more disposed to relate licentious scenes and adventures than to give any information about the main object of the voyage. In a more modern publication, many abusive epithets have been bestowed on Captain Edwards, and observations made on the conduct of this officer highly injurious to his reputation, in regard to his inhuman treatment of, and disgraceful acts of cruelty towards, his prisoners, which it is to be feared have but too much foundation in fact.

The account of his proceedings, rendered by himself to the Admiralty, is vague and unsatisfactory; and had it not been for the journal of Morrison, and a circumstantial letter of young Heywood to his mother, no record would have remained of the unfeeling conduct of this officer towards his unfortunate

Point Venus, Island of Otahytey.
The *Pandora* remained at Tahiti from 23 March to 8 May 1791 and George Tobin's painting, dated 1792, shows Bligh's *Providence* and *Assistant* at the same anchorage the following year. On the outward voyage to Tahiti the *Pandora* passed a little to the north of Pitcairn Island, where the mutineers took refuge unbeknown to the world until 1808. At Tahiti the men of the *Pandora* received the usual unrestrained welcome. But venereal disease was by this time rife and Hamilton, the ship's surgeon, noted ruefully, 'We now discover that the ladies of Otaheite have left us many warm tokens of their affection.' Clearly, Point Venus had taken on a new meaning.

prisoners, who were treated with a rigour which could not be justified on any ground of necessity or prudence.

The *Pandora* anchored in Matavai Bay on the 23rd March 1791. Captain Edwards, in his narrative, states that Joseph Coleman, the armourer of the *Bounty*, attempted to come on board before the *Pandora* had anchored; that on reaching the ship, he began to make inquiries of him after the *Bounty* and her people, and that he seemed to be ready to give him any information that was required; that the next who came on board, just after the ship had anchored, were Mr. Peter Heywood and Mr. Stewart, before any boat had been sent on shore; that they were brought down to his cabin, when, after come conversation, Heywood asked if Mr. Hayward (midshipman of the *Bounty*, but now lieutenant of the *Pandora*) was on board, as he had heard that he was; that Lieutenant Hayward, whom he sent for, treated Heywood with a sort of contemptuous look, and began to enter into conversation with him respecting the *Bounty*; but Edwards ordered him to desist, and called in the sentinel to take the prisoners into safe custody, and to put them in irons; that four other mutineers soon made their appearance; and that, from them and some of the natives, he learned that the rest of the *Bounty*'s people had built a schooner, with which they had sailed the day before from Matavai Bay to the north-west part of the island.

He goes on to say that, on this intelligence, he despatched the two lieutenants, Corner and Hayward, with the pinnace and launch, to endeavour to intercept her. They soon got sight of her and chased her out to sea, but the schooner gained so much upon them, and night coming on, they were compelled to give up the pursuit and return to the ship. It was soon made known however, that she had returned to Paparré, on which they were again despatched in search of her. Lieutenant Corner had taken three of the mutineers, and Hayward, on arriving at Paparré, found the schooner there, but the mutineers had abandoned her and fled to the mountains. He carried off the schooner, and returned next day, when he learned they were not far off; and the following morning, on hearing they were coming down, he drew up his party in order to receive them, and when within hearing, called to them to lay down their arms and to go on one side, which they did, when they were confined and brought as prisoners to the ship.

The following were the persons received on board the *Pandora*:

PETER HEYWOOD	Midshipman.
GEORGE STEWART	Ditto.
JAMES MORRISON	Boatswain's mate.
CHARLES NORMAN	Carpenter's mate.
THOMAS M'INTOSH	Carpenter's crew.
JOSEPH COLEMAN	Armourer.
RICHARD SKINNER	
THOMAS ELLISON	
HENRY HILLBRANT	
THOMAS BURKITT	
JOHN MILLWARD	Seamen.
JOHN SUMNER	
WILLIAM MUSPRATT	
MICHAEL BYRNE	

In all fourteen. The other two, which made up the sixteen that had been left on the island, had been murdered, as will appear presently.

Captain Edwards himself explains how he disposed of his prisoners. 'I put the pirates,' he says, 'into a round-house which I built on the after part of the quarter-deck, for their more effectual security in this airy and healthy situation, and to separate them from, and to prevent their having communication with, or to crowd and incommode, the ship's company.' Dr. Hamilton calls it the most desirable place in the ship, and adds, that 'orders were given that the prisoners should be victualled, in every respect, the same as the ship's company, both in meat, liquor, and all the extra indulgences with which they were so liberally supplied, notwithstanding the established laws of the service, which restrict prisoners to two-thirds allowance. Mr. Morrison, one of the prisoners, gives a very different account of their treatment. He says that Captain Edwards put both legs of the two midshipmen in irons, and that he branded them 'piratical villains'; that they, with the rest, being strongly handcuffed, were put into a kind of round-house only eleven feet long, built as a prison, and aptly named '*Pandora*'s Box,' which was entered by a scuttle in the roof, about eighteen inches square. This was done in order that they might be kept separate from the crew, and also the more effectually to prevent them from having any communication with the natives; that such of those friendly creatures as ventured to look pitifully towards them were instantly turned out of the ship, and never again allowed to come on board. But two sentinels were kept constantly upon the roof of the prison, with orders to shoot the first of its inmates who should attempt to address another in the Otaheitan dialect.

That Captain Edwards took every precaution to keep his prisoners in safe custody, and place them in confinement, as by his instructions he was directed to do, may be well imagined, but Mr. Morrison will probably be thought to go somewhat beyond credibility in stating that orders were given 'to *shoot* any of the prisoners,' when confined in irons. Captain Edwards must have known that such an act would have cost him his commission or something more. The fact is, that information was given to Edwards, at least he so asserts, by the brother of the King of Otaheite, that a conspiracy was formed among the natives to cut the ship's cables the first strong wind that should blow on the shore. This was considered to be probable, as many of the prisoners were said to be married to the most respectable chiefs' daughters in the district opposite to the anchorage, and the midshipman Stewart, in particular, had married the daughter of a man of great landed property near Matavai Bay. This intelligence, no doubt, weighed with the Captain in restricting the visits of the natives. But so far is it from being true that all communication between the mutineers and the natives was cut off, that we are distinctly told by Mr. Hamilton, that 'the prisoners' wives visited the ship daily, and brought their children, who were permitted to be carried to their unhappy fathers. Their wives brought them ample supplies of every delicacy that the country afforded, while we lay there, and behaved with the greatest fidelity and affection to them.'

Of the fidelity and attachment of these simple-minded creatures an instance is afforded in the affecting story which is told, in the first *Missionary Voyage of the Duff*, of the unfortunate wife of the reputed mutineer Mr. Stewart. It would seem also to exonerate Edwards from some part of the charges which have been brought against him.

'The history of Peggy Stewart marks a tenderness of heart that never will be heard without emotion: she was the daughter of a chief, and taken for his wife by Mr. Stewart, one of the unhappy mutineers. A beautiful little girl had been the fruit of their union, and was at the breast when the *Pandora* arrived, seized the criminals, and secured them in irons on board the ship. Frantic with grief, the unhappy Peggy (for so he had named her) flew with her infant in a canoe to the arms of her husband. The interview was so affecting and afflicting, that Stewart himself, unable to bear the heartrending scene, begged she might not be admitted again on board. She was separated from him by violence, and conveyed on shore in a state of despair and grief too big for utterance. Withheld from him, and forbidden to come any more on board, she sunk into the deepest dejection; she lost all relish for food and life, rejoiced no more, pined under a rapid decay of two months, and fell a victim to her feelings, dying literally of a broken heart. Her child is yet alive, and the tender object of our care.' . . .

All the mutineers that were left on the island being received on board the *Pandora*, that ship proceeded in search of those who had gone away in the *Bounty*. It may be mentioned, however, that two of the most active in the mutiny, Churchill and Thompson, had perished on the island before the *Pandora*'s arrival, by violent deaths. These two men had accompanied a chief, who was the *tayo*, or sworn friend, of Churchill, and having died without children, this mutineer succeeded to his property and dignity, according to the custom of the country. Thompson, for some real or fancied insult, took an opportunity of shooting his companion. The natives assembled, stoned Thompson to death, and later brought his skull on board the *Pandora*. This horrible wretch had some time before slain a man and a child through mere wantonness, but escaped punishment by a mistake that had nearly proved fatal to young Heywood. It seems that the description of a person in Otaheite is usually given by some distinguishing figure of the *tattoo*, and Heywood, having the same marks as Thompson, was taken for him; and as the club was raised to dash out his brains, the interposition of an old chief, with whom he was travelling round the island, was just in time to avert the blow.

Captain Edwards had no clue to guide him as to the route taken by the *Bounty*, but he learnt from different people and from journals kept on board that ship, which were found in the chests of the mutineers at Otaheite, the proceedings of Christian and his associates after Lieutenant Bligh and his companions had been turned adrift in the launch. From these it appears that the pirates proceeded in the first instance to the island of Toobouai, in lat. 20° 13' S., long. 149° 35' W., where they anchored on the 25th May, 1789. They had thrown overboard the greater part of the bread-fruit plants, and divided among themselves the property of the officers and men who had been so inhumanly turned adrift. At this island they intended to form a settlement, but the opposition of the natives, the want of many necessary materials, and quarrels among themselves, determined them to go to Otaheite to procure what might be required to effect their purpose, provided they should agree to prosecute their original intention. They accordingly sailed from Toobouai about the latter end of the month, and arrived at Otaheite on the 6th June. The Otoo, or reigning sovereign, and other principal natives, were anxious to know what had become of Lieutenant Bligh and the rest of the crew, and also what had been done with the bread-fruit plants? They were told they had most unexpectedly fallen in with Captain Cook at an island he had just discovered, called Whytootakee [Aitutaki], where he intended to form a settlement, and where the plants had been landed; and that Lieutenant Bligh and the others were stopping there to assist Captain Cook in the business he had in hand, and that he had appointed Mr. Christian commander of the *Bounty*; and that he was now come by his orders for an additional supply of hogs, goats, fowls, bread-fruit, and various other articles which Otaheite could supply.

This artful story was quite sufficient to impose on the credulity of these humane and simple-minded islanders; and so overcome with joy were they to hear that their old friend Captain Cook was alive, and about to settle so near them, that every possible means were forthwith made use of to procure the things that were wanted; so that in the course of a very few days the *Bounty* received on board three hundred and twelve hogs, thirty-eight goats, eight dozen of fowls, a bull and a cow, and a large quantity of bread-fruit, plantains, bananas, and other fruits. They also took with them eight men, nine women, and seven boys. With these supplies they left Otaheite on the 19th June, and arrived a second time at Toobouai on the 26th. They warped the ship up the harbour, landed the live stock, and set about building a fort of fifty yards square.

While this work was carrying on, quarrels and disagreements were daily happening among them, and continual disputes and skirmishes were taking place with the natives, generally brought on by the violent conduct of the invaders, and by depredations committed on their property. Retaliations were attempted by the natives without success, numbers of whom being pursued with fire-arms were put to death. Still the situation of the mutineers became so disagreeable and unsafe, the work went on so slowly and reluctantly, that the building of the fort was agreed to be discontinued. Christian in fact, had very soon perceived that his authority was on the wane, and that no peaceful establishment was likely to be accomplished at Toobouai; he therefore held a consultation as to what would be the most advisable step to take. After much angry discussion, it was at length determined that Toobouai should be abandoned; that the ship should once more be taken to Otaheite; and that those who might choose to go on shore there might do so, and those who preferred to remain in the ship might proceed in her to whatever place they should agree upon among themselves.

In consequence of this determination they sailed from Toobouai on the 15th, and arrived at Matavai Bay on the 20th September, 1789. Here sixteen of the mutineers were put on shore, at their own request, fourteen of whom were received on board the *Pandora*, and two of them, as before mentioned, were murdered on the island. The remaining nine agreed to continue in the *Bounty*. The small arms, powder, canvas, and the small stores belonging to the ship, were equally divided among the whole crew. The *Bounty* sailed finally from Otaheite on the night of the 21st September, and was last seen the following morning to the north-west of Point Venus. They took with them seven Otaheitan men and twelve women. It was not even conjectured whither they meant to go; but Christian had frequently been heard to say, that his object was to discover some unknown or uninhabited island, in which there was no harbour for shipping; that he would run the *Bounty* on shore, and make use of her materials to form a settlement; but this was the only account, vague as it was, that could be procured to direct Captain Edwards in his intended search.

It appears that when the schooner, of which we have spoken, had been finished, six of the fourteen mutineers that were left on Otaheite embarked in her, with the intention of proceeding to the East Indies, and actually put to sea; but meeting with bad weather, and suspecting the nautical abilities of Morrison, whom they had elected as commanding officer, to conduct her in safety, they resolved on returning to Otaheite.

Morrison, it seems, first undertook the construction of this schooner, being himself a tolerable mechanic, in which he was assisted by the two

---

Whytootackay – about three miles distant.
'I had little reason to expect making any New Discovery, as my Track altho not traversed by any one before, yet was bordering so near on others that I scarce thought it probable to meet with any land. At day light however we discovered an Island of Moderate height with a round conical Hill towards the northern extreme. The NW part made in a perpendicular head but the SE sloped off to a point. As I advanced towards it, a Number of Small Keys were seen from the Mast head lying to the SE, and at Noon could Count nine of them. They were all covered with Trees, and the large Island had a most fruitful Appearance. The Shore was bordered with Flat land with innumerable Cocoa Nutt and other Trees, and the higher Grounds were beautifully interspersed with Lawns. I saw no Smoke or any sign of Inhabitants but it is scarcely to be imagined that so charming a little Spot is without them.' (Log of the *Bounty*, 11 April 1789.) Captain Edwards in the *Pandora* searched Aiutaki for the mutineers and Bligh also believed they would head there.

carpenters, the cooper, and some others. Conscious of his innocence, his object is stated to have been that of reaching Batavia in time to secure a passage home in the next fleet bound to Holland; but that their return was occasioned, not by any distrust of Morrison's talents, but by a refusal, on the part of the natives, to give them a sufficient quantity of matting and other necessaries for so long a voyage, being, in fact, desirous of retaining them on the island. Stewart and young Heywood took no part in this transaction, having made up their minds to remain at Otaheite, and there to await the arrival of a king's ship, it being morally certain that ere long one would be sent out thither to search for them, whatever might have been the fate of Bligh and his companions; and that this was really their intention is evident by the alacrity they displayed in getting on board the *Pandora*, the moment of her arrival.

On the 8th of May, the *Pandora* left Otaheite, accompanied by the little schooner which the mutineers had built. In point of size she was not a great deal larger than Lieutenant Bligh's launch, her dimensions being thirty feet length of keel; thirty-five feet length on deck; nine feet and a half extreme breadth; five feet depth of the hold. She parted from the *Pandora* near the Palmerston Islands, when searching for the *Bounty*, and was not heard of till the arrival of the *Pandora*'s crew at Samarang, in Java, where they found her lying at anchor, the crew having suffered so dreadfully from famine and the want of water, that one of the young gentlemen belonging to her became delirious. She was a remarkably swift sailer, and, being afterwards employed in the sea-otter trade, is stated to have made one of the quickest passages ever known from China to the Sandwich Islands. [This claim has been disproved by recent research.]

The *Pandora* called at numerous islands without success, but on Lieutenant Corner having landed on one of the Palmerston's group, he found a yard and some spars with the broad arrow upon them, and marked *Bounty*. This induced the captain to cause a very minute search to be made in all these islands, in the course of which the *Pandora*, being driven out to sea by blowing weather, and very thick and hazy, lost sight of the little tender and a jolly boat, the latter of which was never more heard of. This gives occasion to a little splenetic effusion from a writer in the *United Service Journal*, which was hardly called for. 'When this boat,' says the writer, 'with a midshipman and several men (four), had been inhumanly ordered from alongside, it was known that there was nothing in her but one piece of salt-beef, compassionately thrown in by a seaman; and horrid as must have been their fate, the flippant surgeon, after detailing the disgraceful fact, adds – "that this is the way the world was peopled" – or words to that effect, for we quote only from memory.' The following is quoted from the book :–

'It may be difficult to surmise,' says the surgeon, 'what has been the fate of those unfortunate men. They had a piece of salt-beef thrown into the boat to them on leaving the ship; and it rained a good deal that night and the following day, which might satiate their thirst. It is by these accidents the

View of Samarang.
When Edwards called at Samarang he was reunited with the crew of the tender *Resolution*
which had become separated from the *Pandora* on 22 June while at the island of Upoli. The
Resolution had been built by the mutineers at Tahiti with a view to an escape from that
island and it was pressed into service by Edwards in the search for the *Bounty*. Mr Oliver,
Master's Mate, and Midshipman Renouard sailed the tender to Samarang, but the Dutch
suspected them of being *Bounty* mutineers. Their adventures, which included being
attacked by the islanders of Tofoa (who had killed Norton in Bligh's party), add yet
another dramatic chapter to the already overcrowded saga of the *Bounty* mutiny.

Divine Ruler of the universe has peopled the southern hemisphere.' This is
no more than asserting an acknowledged fact that can hardly admit of a
dispute, and there appears nothing in the paragraph which at all affects the
character of Captain Edwards, against whom it is levelled.

After a fruitless search of three months, the *Pandora* arrived, on the 29th
August, on the coast of New Holland, and close to that extraordinary reef
of coral rocks called the 'Barrier Reef,' which runs along the greater part of
the eastern coast, but at a considerable distance from it. The boat had been
sent out to look for an opening, which was soon discovered, but in the course
of the night the ship had drifted past it. 'On getting soundings,' says Captain Edwards, in his narrative laid before the court-martial, 'the topsails
were filled; but before the tacks were hauled on board and other sail made
and trimmed, the ship struck upon a reef; we had a quarter less two fathoms

Wreck of the *Pandora.*

Bligh doubted the ability of Captain Edwards to get the *Pandora* through the Endeavour
Straights. His professional opinion was unhappily confirmed in the wreck of the *Pandora*
with the loss of thirty-one of the crew and four of the prisoners. Edwards had already lost
five of his crew in the yawl at Palmerston Island in May and nine others were separated
from the *Pandora* in the ship's tender in June. Edwards was a trifle careless. He failed to
stock up the boats with food and water in the eleven hours he had between the *Pandora*
striking the reef and her sinking the following morning.

on the larboard side, and three fathoms on the starboard side; the sails were
braced about different ways to endeavour to get her off, but to no purpose;
they were then clewed up and afterwards furled, the top-gallant yards got
down and the top-gallant masts struck. Boats were hoisted out with a view
to carry out an anchor, but before that could be effected the ship struck so
violently on the reef, that the carpenter reported she made eighteen inches of
water in five minutes; and in five minutes after this, that there were four feet
of water in the hold. Finding the leak increasing so fast, it was thought
necessary to turn the hands to the pumps, and to bail at different hatchways;
but she still continued to gain upon us so fast, that in little more than an hour
and a half after she struck, there were eight feet and a half of water in the
hold. About ten we perceived that the ship had beaten over the reef, and was
in ten fathoms of water; we therefore let go the small bower anchor, cleared
away a cable, and let go the best bower anchor in fifteen and a half fathoms
water under foot, to steady the ship. Some of her guns were thrown overboard, and the water gained upon us only in a small degree, and we flattered
ourselves that by the assistance of a thrummed topsail, which we were
preparing to haul under the ship's bottom, we might be able to lessen the
leak, and to free her of water: but these flattering hopes did not continue
long; for, as she settled in the water, the leak increased again, and in so

great a degree, that there was reason to apprehend she would sink before daylight. During the night two of the pumps were unfortunately for some time rendered useless; one of them, however, was repaired, and we continued baling and pumping the remainder of the night; and every effort that was thought of was made to keep afloat and preserve the ship. Daylight fortunately appeared, and gave us the opportunity of seeing our situation and the surrounding danger, and it was evident the ship had been carried to the northward by a tide or current.

'The officers, whom I had consulted on the subject of our situation, gave it as their opinion that nothing more could be done for the preservation of the ship; it then became necessary to endeavour to provide and to find means for the preservation of the people. Our four boats, which consisted of one launch, one eight-oared pinnace, and two six-oared yawls, with careful hands in them, were kept astern of the ship; a small quantity of bread, water, and other necessary articles, were put into them; two canoes, which we had on board, were lashed together and put into the water; rafts were made, and all floating things upon deck were unlashed.

'About half-past six in the morning of the 29th the hold was full, and the water was between decks, and it also washed in at the upper deck ports, and there were strong indications that the ship was on the very point of sinking, and we began to leap overboard and take to the boats, and before everybody could get out of her she actually sunk. The boats continued astern of the ship in the direction of the drift of the tide from her, and took up the people that had hold of rafts and other floating things that had been cast loose, for the purpose of supporting them on the water. The double canoe, that was able to support a considerable number of men, broke adrift with only one man, and was bulged upon a reef, and afforded us no assistance when she was so much wanted on this trying and melancholy occasion. Two of the boats were laden with men and sent to a small sandy island (or key) about four miles from the wreck; and I remained near the ship for some time with the other two boats, and picked up all the people that could be seen, and then followed the two first boats to the key; and having landed the men and cleared the boats, they were immediately despatched again to look about the wreck and the adjoining reef for any that might be missing, but they returned without having found a single person. On mustering the people that were saved, it appeared that eighty-nine of the ship's company, and ten of the mutineers that had been prisoners on board, answered to their names; but thirty-one of the ship's company, and four mutineers, were lost with the ship.'

It is remarkable enough that so little notice is taken of the mutineers in this narrative of the captain; and as the following statement is supposed to come from the late Lieutenant Corner, who was second lieutenant of the *Pandora*, it is entitled to be considered as authentic. If so, Captain Edwards must have deserved the character, ascribed to him, of being altogether destitute of the common feelings of humanity.

'Three of the *Bounty*'s people, Coleman, Norman, and M'Intosh, were now let out of irons, and sent to work at the pumps. The others offered their assistance, and begged to be allowed a chance of saving their lives; instead of which, two additional sentinels were placed over them, with orders to shoot any who should attempt to get rid of their fetters. Seeing no prospect of escape, they betook themselves to prayer, and prepared to meet their fate, every one expecting that the ship would soon go to pieces, her rudder and part of the stern-post being already beat away.'

When the ship was actually sinking, and every effort making for the preservation of the crew, it is asserted that 'no notice was taken of the prisoners, as is falsely stated by the author of the *Pandora's Voyage*, although Captain Edwards was entreated by Mr. Heywood to have mercy upon them, when he passed over their prison, to make his own escape, the ship then lying on her broadside, with the larboard bow completely under water. Fortunately the master-at-arms, either by accident or design, when slipping from the roof of "*Pandora*'s Box" into the sea, let the keys of the irons fall through the scuttle or entrance, which he had just before opened, and thus enabled them to commence their own liberation, in which they were generously assisted, at the imminent risk of his own life, by William Moulter, a boatswain's mate, who clung to the coamings, and pulled the long bars through the shackles, saying he would set them free, or go to the bottom with them.

'Scarcely was this effected when the ship went down, leaving nothing visible but the top-mast cross-trees. The master-at-arms and all the sentinels sunk to rise no more. The cries of them and the other drowning men were awful in the extreme; and more than half an hour had elapsed before the survivors could be taken up by the boats. Among the former were Mr. Stewart, John Sumner, Richard Skinner, and Henry Hillbrant, the whole of whom perished with their hands still in manacles.

'On this melancholy occasion Mr. Heywood was the last person but three who escaped from the prison, into which the water had already found its way through the bulk-head scuttles. Jumping overboard, the seized a plank, and was swimming towards a small sandy quay (key) about three miles distant, when a boat picked him up, and conveyed him thither in a state of nudity. It is worthy of remark, that James Morrison endeavoured to follow his young companion's example, and, although handcuffed, managed to keep afloat until a boat came to his assistance.'

This account would appear almost incredible. It is true men are sometimes found to act the part of inhuman monsters, but then they are generally actuated by some motive or extraordinary excitement; here, however, there was neither; but on the contrary, the condition of the poor prisoners appealed most forcibly to the mercy and humanity of their jailor. The surgeon of the ship states, in his account of her loss, that as soon as the spars, booms, hen-coops, and other buoyant articles were cut loose, 'the prisoners were ordered to be let out of irons.' One would imagine, indeed, that the officers

Pandora before and after the wreck.

On its way to Tahiti, the *Pandora* passed within a day's sailing of Pitcairn Island where Christian and his comrades were hiding. After leaving Tahiti, Captain Edwards searched in the wrong direction and finally gave up the search. He also fell into the trap of carelessness and his ship was wrecked. For Lieutenant Hayward the journey to Timor meant a second dangerous open boat voyage.

– – –Pandora's boats

on this dreadful emergency would not be witness to such inhumanity, without remonstrating effectually against keeping these unfortunate men confined a moment beyond the period when it became evident that the ship must sink. It will be seen, however, presently, from Mr. Heywood's own statement, that they were so kept, and that the brutal and unfeeling conduct which has been imputed to Captain Edwards is but too true. . . .

On the sandy key which fortunately presented itself, the shipwrecked seamen hauled up the boats, to repair those that were damaged, and to stretch canvas round the gunwales, the better to keep out the sea from breaking into them. The heat of the sun and the reflection from the sand are described as excruciating, and the thirst of the men was rendered intolerable, from their stomachs being filled with salt water in the length of time they had to swim before being picked up. Mr. Hamilton says they were greatly disturbed in the night, by the irregular behaviour of one of the seamen, named Connell, which made them suspect he had got drunk with some wine that had been saved; but it turned out that the excruciating torture he suffered from thirst had induced him to drink salt water; 'by which means he went mad, and died in the sequel of the voyage.' It seems, a small keg of water, and some biscuits, had been thrown into one of the boats, which they found, by calculation, would be sufficient to last sixteen days, on an allowance of two wine-glasses of water per day to each man, and a very small quantity of bread, the weight of which was accurately ascertained by a musket-ball, and a pair of wooden scales made for each boat.

The crew and the prisoners were now distributed among the four boats. At Bligh's 'Mountainous Island,' they entered a bay where swarms of natives came down and made signs for their landing; but this they declined to do; on which an arrow was discharged and struck one of the boats; and as the savages were seen to be collecting their bows and arrows, a volley of muskets, a few of which happened to be in the boats, was discharged, which put them to flight. While sailing among the islands and near the shore, they now and then stopped to pick up a few oysters, and procure a little fresh water. On the 2nd September, they passed the north-west point of New Holland, and launched into the great Indian Ocean, having a voyage of about a thousand miles still to perform.

It will be recollected that Captain Bligh's people received warmth and comfort by wringing out their clothes in salt-water. The same practice was adopted by the crews of the *Pandora*'s boats; but the doctor observes, that 'this wetting their bodies with salt water is not advisable, if protracted beyond three or four days, as, after that time, the great absorption from the skin that takes place, taints the fluids with the bitter part of salt water, so that the saliva becomes intolerable in the mouth.' Their mouths, indeed, he says, became so parched, that few attempted to eat the slender allowance of bread. He also remarks, that as the sufferings of the people continued, their temper became cross and savage. In the captain's boat, it is stated, one of the mutineers took to praying; but that 'the captain, suspecting the purity of his doctrines, and unwilling that he should have a monopoly of the business, gave prayers himself.'

On the 13th, they saw the island of Timor, and the next morning landed and got some water, and a few small fish from the natives; and on the night of the 15th, anchored opposite the fort of Coupang. Nothing could exceed the kindness and hospitality of the governor and other Dutch officers of this settlement, in affording every possible assistance and relief in their distressed condition. Having remained here three weeks, they embarked on the 6th October, on board the *Rembang* Dutch Indiaman, and on the 30th, anchored at Samarang, where they were agreeably surprised to find their little Tender, which they had so long given up for lost. On the 7th November they arrived at Batavia, where Captain Edwards agreed with the Dutch East India

Timor

Edwards brought his four boat-loads of survivors to Coupang and received the same warm welcome from the Dutch that Bligh's party had experienced. They also found there a party of eight men, one woman and two small children who had also arrived in an open boat claiming to be the survivors of the brig *Neptune*. In fact they were escaped convicts from New South Wales who had completed a 3000-mile voyage up the Australian coast and across the straights to Coupang. Edwards took those who survived back to Britain as prisoners.

Company, to divide the whole of the ship's company and prisoners among four of their ships proceeding to Europe. The latter the captain took with him in the *Vreedenburgh*; but finding his Majesty's ship *Gorgon* at the Cape, he transhipped himself and prisoners, and proceeded in her to Spithead, where he arrived on the 19th June, 1792.

Captain Edwards, in his meagre narrative, takes no more notice of his prisoners with regard to the mode in which they were disposed of at Coupang and Batavia, than he does when the *Pandora* went down. In fact, he suppresses all information respecting them, from the day in which they were consigned to '*Pandora*'s Box.' From this total indifference towards these unfortunate men, and their almost unparalleled sufferings, Captain Edwards must be set down as a man, whose only feeling was to stick to the letter of his instructions, and rigidly to adhere to what he considered the strict line of his duty; that he was a man of a cold phlegmatic disposition, whom no distress could move, and whose feelings were not easily disturbed by the sufferings of his fellow-creatures.

There seems to have been a general feeling at and before the court-martial, that Captain Edwards had exercised a harsh, unnecessary, and undue degree of severity on his prisoners. It is the custom, sanctioned by long usage, to place in irons all such as may have been guilty of mutiny in a ship of war – to prevent communication with the rest of the ship's company, who might be contaminated by their intercourse with such mischievous and designing men; men whose crime is of that dye, that, if found guilty, they have little hope to escape the punishment of death, to which a mutineer must, by the naval articles of war, be sentenced; no alternative being left to a court-martial but to pronounce a sentence of acquittal or of death.

In the present case, however, most of the prisoners had surrendered themselves; many of them had taken no active part in the mutiny; and others had been forcibly compelled to remain in the ship. It was not likely, there-fore, that any danger could arise from indulging them occasionally, and in turns, with a few hours of fresh air on deck. As little danger was there of their escaping; where indeed could they escape to – especially when the ship was going down, at a great distance from any shore, and the nearest one known to be inhabited by savages? All or most of them were desirous of getting home, and throwing themselves on God and their country. The captain, however, had no 'compunctious visitings of nature' to shake his purpose, which seems to have been, to keep them strictly in irons during the whole passage, and to deliver them over in that state on his arrival in England. . . .

The following letter of Mr. Peter Heywood to his mother removes all doubt as to the character and conduct of this particular officer.

'*Batavia, November 20th*, 1791.

'MY EVER-HONOURED AND DEAREST MOTHER – At length the time has arrived when you are once more to hear from your ill-fated son, whose conduct at the capture of that ship, in which it was my fortune to embark, has, I fear, from what has since happened to me, been grossly misrepresented to you by Lieutenant Bligh, who, by not knowing the real cause of my remaining on board, naturally suspected me, unhappily for me, to be a coadjutor in the mutiny; but I never, to my knowledge, whilst under his command, behaved myself in a manner unbecoming the station I occupied, nor so much as even entertained a thought derogatory to his honour, so as to give him the least grounds for entertaining an opinion of me so ungenerous and undeserved. Oh! my dearest mother, I hope you have not so easily credited such an account of me; do but let me vindicate my conduct, and declare to you the true cause of my remaining in the ship, and you will then see how little I deserve censure, and how I have been injured by so gross an aspersion. . . .

'The morning the ship was taken, it being my watch below, happening to awake just after daylight, and looking out of my hammock, I saw a man sitting upon the arm-chest in the main hatchway, with a drawn cutlass in his hand, the reason of which I could not divine; so I got out of bed and inquired of him what was the cause of it. He told me that Mr. Christian, assisted by some of the ship's company had seized the captain and put him in confinement; had taken the command of the ship and meant to carry Bligh home a prisoner, in order to try him by court-martial, for his long tyrannical and oppressive conduct to his people. I was quite thunderstruck; and hurrying into my berth again, told one of my messmates, whom I awakened out of his sleep, what had happened. Then dressing myself, I went up the fore-hatchway, and saw what he had told me was but too true; and again, I asked some of the people, who were under arms, what was going to be done with the captain, who was then on the larboard side of the quarter-deck, with his hands tied behind his back, and Mr. Christian alongside him with a pistol and drawn bayonet. I now heard a very different story, and that the captain was to be sent ashore to Tofoa in the launch, and that those who would not join Mr. Christian might either accompany the captain, or would be taken in irons to Otaheite and left there. The relation of two stories so different, left me unable to judge which could be the true one; but seeing them hoisting the boats out, it seemed to prove the latter.

'In this trying situation, young and inexperienced as I was, and without an adviser (every person being as it were infatuated, and not knowing what to do), I remained for awhile a silent spectator of what was going on; and after revolving the matter in my mind, I determined to choose what I thought the lesser of two evils and stay by the ship; for I had no doubt that those who went on shore, in the launch, would be put to death by the savage natives, whereas the Otaheitans being a humane and generous race, one might have a hope of being kindly received, and remain there until the arrival of some ship, which seemed, to silly me, the most consistent with reason and rectitude.

'While this resolution possessed my mind, at the same time lending my assistance to hoist out the boats, the hurry and confusion affairs were in, and thinking my intention just, I never thought of going to Mr. Bligh for advice; besides, what confirmed me in it was, my seeing two experienced officers, when ordered into the boat by Mr. Christian, desire his permission to remain in the ship (one of whom, my own messmate, Mr. Hayward), and I being assisting to clear the launch of yams, he asked me what I intended to do? I told him, to remain in the ship. Now this answer, I imagine, he has told Mr. Bligh I made to him; from which, together with my not speaking to him that morning, his suspicions of me have arisen, construing my conduct into what is foreign to my nature.

'Thus, my dearest mother, it was all owing to my youth and unadvised inexperience, but has been interpreted into villainy and disregard of my country's laws. And now, after what I have asserted, I may still once more retrieve my injured reputation, be again reinstated in the affection and favour of the most tender of mothers, and be still considered as her ever dutiful son.

'I was not undeceived in my erroneous decision till too late, which was after the captain was in the launch; for while I was talking to the master-at-arms, one of the ring-leaders in the affair, my other messmate whom I had left in his hammock in the berth (Mr. Stewart), came up to me, and asked me, if I was not going in the launch? I replied, No – upon which he told me not to think of such a thing as remaining behind, but take his advice and go down below with him to get a few necessary things, and make haste to go with him into the launch; adding that, by remaining in the ship, I should incur an equal share of guilt with the mutineers themselves. I reluctantly followed his advice – I say *reluctantly*, because I knew no better, and was foolish; and the boat swimming very deep in the water – the land being far distant – the thoughts of being sacrificed by the natives – and the self-consciousness of my first intention being just – all these considerations almost staggered my resolution; however, I preferred my companion's judgement to my own, and we both jumped down the main-hatchway to prepare ourselves for the boat – but, no sooner were we in the berth, than the master-at-arms ordered the sentry to keep us both in the berth till he should receive orders to release us. We desired the master-at-arms to acquaint Mr. Bligh of our intention, which we had reason to think he never did, nor were we permitted to come on deck until the launch was a long way astern. I now, when too late, saw my error.

'At the latter end of May, we got to an island to the southward of Taheité, called Tooboui, where they intended to make a settlement, but finding no stock there of any kind, they agreed to go to Tahaité, and, after procuring hogs and fowls, to return to Tooboui and remain. So, on the 6th June, we arrived at Taheité, where I was in hopes I might find an opportunity of running away, and remaining on shore, but I could not effect it, as there was always too good a look-out kept to prevent any such steps being taken. And besides, they had all sworn that should any one make his escape, they would force the natives to restore him, and would then shoot him as an example to the rest; well knowing, that any one by remaining there might be the means (should a ship arrive) of discovering their intended place of abode. Finding it therefore impracticable, I saw no other alternative but to rest as content as possible and return to Tooboui, and there wait till the masts of the *Bounty* should be taken out, and then take the boat which might carry me to Taheité, and disable those remaining from pursuit. But Providence so ordered it, that we had no occasion to try our fortune at such a hazard, for, upon returning there and remaining till the latter end of August, in which time a fort was almost built, but nothing could be effected; and as the natives could not be brought to friendly terms, and with whom we had many skirmishes, and narrow escapes from being cut off by them, and, what was still worse, internal broils and discontent, – these things determined part of the people to leave the island and go to Taheité, which was carried by a majority of votes.

'This being carried into execution on the 22nd September, and having anchored in Matavai Bay, the next morning my messmate (Mr. Stewart) and I went on shore, to the house of an old landed proprietor, our former friend; and being now set free from a lawless crew, determined to remain as much apart from them as possible, and wait patiently for the arrival of a ship. Fourteen more of the *Bounty*'s people came likewise on shore, and Mr. Christian and eight men went away with the ship, but God knows whither. Whilst we remained here, we were treated by our kind and friendly natives with a generosity and humanity almost unparalleled, and such as we could hardly have expected from the most civilized people.

'To be brief – having remained here till the latter end of March, 1791, on the 26th of that month, his Majesty's ship *Pandora* arrived, and had scarcely anchored, when my messmate and I went on board and made ourselves known; and having learnt from one of the natives who had been off in a canoe, that our former messmate Mr. Hayward, now promoted to the rank of lieutenant, was on board, we asked for him, supposing he might prove the assertions of our innocence. But he (like all worldlings when raised a little in life) received us very coolly, and pretended ignorance of our affairs; yet formerly, he and I were bound in brotherly love and friendship. Appearances being so much against us, we were ordered to be put in irons, and looked upon – oh, infernal words! – as *piratical villains*.

'My sufferings I have not power to describe; but though they are great, yet I thank God for enabling me to bear them without repining. I endeavour to qualify my affliction with these three considerations, first, my innocence not deserving them; secondly, that they cannot last long; and thirdly, that the change may be for the better. The first improves my hopes; the second, my patience; and the third, my courage. . . .

'As they will no doubt proceed to the greatest lengths against me, I being the only surviving officer, and they most inclined to believe a prior story, all that can be said to confute it will probably be looked upon as mere falsity and invention. Should that be my unhappy case, and they resolved upon my destruction as an example to futurity, may God enable me to bear my fate with the fortitude of a man, conscious that misfortune, not any misconduct, is the cause, and that the Almighty can attest my innocence.

'Twelve more of the people who were at Otaheite having delivered themselves up, there was a sort of prison built on the after-part of the quarter-deck, into which we were all put in close confinement with both legs and both hands in irons, and were treated with great rigour, not being allowed ever to get out of this den; and, being obliged to eat, drink, sleep, and obey the calls of nature here, you may form some idea of the disagreeable situation I must have been in.

'On the 9th May we left Otaheite, and proceeded to the Friendly Islands, and about the beginning of August, got in among the reefs of New Holland, to endeavour to discover a passage through them; but it was not effected, for the *Pandora*, ever unlucky, and as if devoted by heaven to destruction, was driven by a current upon the patch of a reef, and on which, there being a heavy surf, she was soon almost bulged to pieces; but having thrown all the guns on one side overboard, and the tide flowing at the same time, she beat over the reef into a basin and brought up in fourteen or fifteen fathoms; but she was so much damaged while on the reef, that imagining she would go to pieces every moment, we had contrived to wrench ourselves out of our irons, and applied to the captain to have mercy on us, and suffer us to take our chance for the preservation of our lives; but it was all in vain – he was even so inhuman as to order us all to be put in irons again, though the ship was expected to go down every moment.

'In this miserable situation, with an expected death before our eyes, without the least hope of relief, and in the most trying state of suspense, we spent the night, the ship being by the hand of Providence kept up till the morning. The boats by this time had all been prepared; and as the captain and officers were coming upon the poop or roof of our prison, to abandon the ship, the water being then up to the coamings of the hatchways, we again implored his mercy; upon which he sent the corporal and an armourer down to let some of us out of irons, but three only were suffered to go up, and the scuttle being then clapped on, and the master-at-arms upon it, the armourer had only time to let two persons out of irons, the rest, except three, letting themselves out; two of these three went down with them on their hands, and the third was picked up. She now began to heel over to port so very much, that the master-at-arms, sliding overboard, and leaving the scuttle vacant, we all tried to get up, and I was the last out but three. The water was then pouring in at the bulk-head scuttles, yet I succeeded in getting out, and was scarcely in the sea when I could see nothing above it but the cross-trees, and nothing around me but a scene of the greatest distress. I took a plank (being stark-naked) and swam towards an island about three miles off, but was picked up on my passage by one of the boats. When we got ashore to the small sandy key, we found there were thirty-four men drowned, four of whom were prisoners, and among these was my unfortunate messmate (Mr. Stewart); ten of us, and eighty-nine of the *Pandora*'s crew, were saved.

'When a survey was made of what provisions had been saved, they were found to consist of two or three bags of bread, two or three breakers of water, and a little wine; so we subsisted three days upon two wine-glasses of water, and two ounces of bread per day. On the 1st September, we left the island, and on the 16th, arrived at Coupang in the island of Timor, having been on short allowance eighteen days. We were put in confinement in the castle, where we

Destruction of HMS *Pandora* and On a Sandy Islet.
Peter Heywood wrote to his sister Nessy, 'I send you two little sketches of the manner in which his Majesty's ship *Pandora* went down on the 29th August, and of the appearance which we who survived made on the small sandy key within the reef, about ninety yards long and sixty broad, in all ninety-nine souls; here we remained three days subsisting on a single glass of wine or water, and two ounces of bread a day, with no shelter from the meridian and then vertical sun.' The thoughts of Lieutenant Thomas Hayward, who had been Heywood's fellow midshipman in the *Bounty*, and had spent forty-six days in the open boat with Bligh, as he set off for a seventeen-day, 1200-mile open-boat voyage for the second time, are not recorded. He might well have thought the prisoners well provided for compared with his experience of near starvation in the *Bounty*'s launch.

remained till October, and on the 5th of that month were sent on board a Dutch ship bound for Batavia.

'Though I have been eight months in close confinement in a hot climate, I have kept my health in a most surprising manner, and am still perfectly well in mind as well as body; but without a friend, and only a shirt and pair of trousers to put on. Yet with all this I have a contented mind, entirely resigned to the will of Providence.'

In a subsequent letter to his sister he says, 'I send you two little sketches of the manner in which his Majesty's ship *Pandora* went down on the 29th August, and of the appearance which we who survived made on the small sandy key within the reef, about ninety yards long and sixty broad, in all ninety-nine souls; here we remained three days, subsisting on a single wine-glass of wine or water, and two ounces of bread a day, with no shelter from the meridian and then vertical sun. Captain Edwards had tents erected for himself and his people, and we prisoners petitioned him for an old sail which was lying useless, part of the wreck, but he refused it; and the only shelter we had was to bury ourselves up to the neck in the burning sand, which scorched the skin entirely off our bodies, for we were quite naked, and we appeared as if dipped in large tubs of boiling water. We were nineteen days in the same miserable situation before we landed at Coupang. I was in the ship, in irons, hands and feet, much longer than till the position you now see her in, the poop alone being above water (and that knee deep), when a kind Providence assisted me to get out of irons and escape from her.'

The treatment of these unhappy men was almost as bad at Batavia as in the *Pandora*, being closely confined in irons in the castle, and fed on very bad provisions; and the hardships they endured on their passage to England, in Dutch ships, were very severe, having, as he says, slept on nothing but hard boards on wet canvas, without any bed, for seventeen months, always subsisting on short allowance of execrable provisions, and without any clothes for some time, except such as the charity of two young men in the ship supplied him with. He had during his confinement at Batavia learned to make straw hats, and finished several with both his hands in fetters, which he sold for half-a-crown a-piece; and with the produce of these he procured a suit of coarse clothes, in which, with a cheerful and light heart, notwithstanding all his sufferings, he arrived at Portsmouth.

On the second day after the arrival of the *Gorgon* at Spithead the prisoners were transferred to the *Hector*, commanded by Captain (the late Admiral Sir George) Montague, where they were treated with the greatest humanity, and every indulgence allowed that could with propriety be extended to men in their unhappy situation, until the period when they were to be arraigned before the competent authority, and put on their trials for mutiny and piracy, which did not take place until the month of September.

In this period of anxious and awful suspense, a most interesting correspondence was carried on between this unfortunate youth and his numerous friends, which exhibits the character of himself and the whole family in the most amiable and affectionate colours, and in particular that of his sister Nessy.

The poor mother, on hearing of his arrival, thus addresses her unfortunate son :—

'Isle of Man, June 29th, 1792.

'Oh! my ever dearly-beloved and long-lost son, with what anxiety have I waited for this period! But now the happy time is come when, though I cannot have the unspeakable pleasure of seeing and embracing you, yet I hope we may be allowed to correspond. I have not the least doubt but that the all-gracious God, who of his good providence has protected you so long, and brought you safe through so many dangers and difficulties, will still protect you, and at your trial make your innocence appear as clear as the light. All your letters have come safe to me, and to my very dear good Nessy. Ah! Peter, with what real joy did we all receive them, and how happy are we that you are now safe in England! I will endeavour, my dearest lad, to make your present situation as comfortable as possible, for so affectionate and good a son deserves my utmost attention. Nessy has written to our faithful and kind friend, Mr. Heywood, of Plymouth, for his advice, whether it would be proper for her to come up to you; if he consents to her so doing, not a moment shall be lost, and how happy shall I be when she is with you! Such a sister as she is! Oh! Peter, she is a move valuable girl,' etc.

On the same day this 'most valuable girl' thus writes :—

'MY DEAREST AND MOST BELOVED BROTHER – Thanks to that Almighty Providence which has so miraculously preserved you, your fond, anxious, and till now, miserable Nessy, is at last permitted to address the object of her tenderest affection in England! Let me with confidence hope that the God of all mercies has not so long protected you in vain, but will at length crown your fortitude and pious resignation to His will with that peace and happiness you so richly merit. How blest did your delightful and yet dreadful letter from Batavia make us all! Surely, my beloved boy, you could not for a moment imagine we ever supposed you guilty of the crime of mutiny. No, no; believe me, no earthly power could have persuaded us that it was possible for you to do anything inconsistent with strict honour and duty; and I firmly trust that Providence will at length restore you to those dear and affectionate friends, who can know no happiness until they are blest with your loved society. Take care of your precious health, my angelic boy. I shall soon be with you; I have written to Mr. Heywood (your and our excellent friend and protector) for his permission to go to you immediately, which my uncle Heywood, without first obtaining it, would not allow, fearing lest any precipitate step might injure you at present; and I only wait the arrival of his next letter to fly into your arms.'

Mr. Heywood's sisters all address their unfortunate brother in the same affectionate, but less impassioned strain. . . .

The poor prisoner thus replies, from his Majesty's ship *Hector*, to his 'beloved sisters all' :–

'This day I had the supreme happiness of your long-expected letters, and I am not able to express the pleasure and joy they afforded me. . . . God be thanked, you still entertain such an opinion of me as I will flatter myself I have deserved. Oh! my Nessy, it grieves me to think I must be under the necessity, however heart-breaking to myself, of desiring you will relinquish your most affectionate design of coming to see me; it is too long and tedious a journey, and even on your arrival, you would not be allowed the wished-for happiness, both to you and myself, of seeing, much less conversing with, your unfortunate brother; the rules of the service are so strict, that prisoners are not permitted to have any communication with female relations; thus even the sight of, and conversation with, so truly affectionate a sister is for the present denied me! . . .

'And now, my dear Nessy, cease to anticipate the happiness of personal communication with your poor, but resigned brother, until wished-for freedom removes the indignant shackles I now bear, from the feet of your fond and most affectionate brother, P. H.'

Portrait of William Bligh as a young Midshipman
This is the most recently discovered portrait of Bligh and shows him in midshipman's uniform. It was painted in either 1770–71 or 1775–76, the only two dates during which he was in service at home before he sailed with Cook as Master on the Third Voyage. Bligh's solid middle-class background ensured him entry into the Royal Navy as a 'Young Gentleman' – his father was a Customs Officer, three of his uncles were parsons and another was a successful entrepreneur. His family was related to the line of Lord Darnley, through whose family the portrait was probably commissioned, and Bligh used the Darnley crest as his letter seal. Bligh served as a Midshipman in HMS *Hunter* 1770–71 (Irish Sea), HMS *Crescent* 1771–74 (West Indies) and HMS *Ranger* 1774–76 (Irish Sea). He had also been entered on the books of HMS *Monmouth* 1762–63 (Channel) as a 'captain's servant' while aged only seven, a practice common enough at the time.

rnyne delin Publish'd accord

The City of BATAVIA in the Island of Java and Capital of all
the Dutch Factories & Settlements in the East Indies.

London Printed for Robt

artiment.

La Ville de BATAVIA *en l'Isle de Java et Capitale de tous les*

Comptoirs et Etablissements Hollandois dans les Indes Orientales.

Fetter Lane Fleet Street.

In a subsequent letter to his sister, he says, 'Let us at present be resigned to our fate, contented with this sort of communication, and be thankful to God for having even allowed us that happiness – for be assured the present confinement is *liberty*, compared with what it has been for the fifteen months last past.'

On the 15th July, Commodore Pasley addresses the following business-like letter to Miss Heywood.

'I received your letter, my dearest Nessy, with the enclosure [her brother's narrative], but did not choose to answer it until I had made a thorough investigation; that is, seen personally all the principal evidences, which has ever since occupied my whole thoughts and time. I have also had some letters from himself; and notwithstanding he must still continue in confinement, every attention and indulgence possible is granted him by Captain Montague of the *Hector*, who is my particular friend. I have no doubt of the truth of your brother's narrative; the master, boatswain, gunner, and carpenter, late of the *Bounty*, I have seen, and have the pleasure to assure you that they are all favourable, and corroborate what he says. That *fellow*, Captain Edwards, whose inhuman rigour of confinement I shall never forget, I have likewise seen; he cannot deny that Peter avowed himself late of the *Bounty* when he came voluntarily aboard; this is a favourable circumstance. I have been at the Admiralty, and read over all the depositions taken and sent home by Bligh and his officers from Batavia, likewise the court-martial on himself; in none of which appears anything against Peter. As soon as Lieutenant Hayward arrives with the remainder of the *Pandora*'s crew, the court-martial is to take place. I shall certainly attend, and we must have an able counsellor to assist, for I will not deceive you, my dear Nessy, however favourable circumstances may appear, our martial law is severe; by the tenor of it, the man who stands neuter is equally guilty with him who lifts

---

Batavia (*previous page*)
Batavia, now Jakarta, was one of the most unhealthy places on earth for European visitors. The death rate was in excess of 50,000 a year in the eighteenth century and one of the prime causes was the network of canals which the Dutch had incorporated in the town's layout. They were stagnant, full of filth and a breeding ground for disease. Cook lost thirty men as a result of his stay there. Bligh took his boat party to Batavia in order to find passage back to Britain, but disease took away Elphinstone (Master's Mate), Peter Linkletter (seaman) and John Lamb (butcher). Thomas Hall (cook) also died here from an illness contracted at Timor.

Adventure Bay, Van Dieman's Land
Bligh visited Adventure Bay three times, in 1777, 1788 and 1792. His journals and charts show that he was the first to explore and make discoveries of several important places in the vicinity of the bay. The crude hut shown in the foreground was constructed by the aborigines and was one of many found around the bay. Bligh described them as being eight feet wide and about four feet high, constructed of small branches, the larger ends of which were fixed into the ground while the upper ends were tied with 'a kind of tough grass'. Sheets of bark were laid over the branches 'in the manner of tiles'.

'Village' of Matavai
Matavai Bay provided an excellent anchorage for visiting ships because of the fresh-water Vaipopoo river that flowed along behind the beach to the point. In places the river was more than thirty feet in width.

his arm against his captain in such cases. His extreme youth and his delivering himself up, are the strong points of his defence. Adieu! my dearest Nessy; present my love to your mother and sisters, and rest assured of my utmost exertions to extricate your brother. – Your affectionate uncle,

T. PASLEY.'

This excellent man did not stop here: knowing that sea-officers have a great aversion from counsel, he writes [to Peter Heywood] to say, 'A friend of mine, Mr. Graham, who has been secretary to the different Admirals on the Newfoundland station for these twelve years, and consequently has acted as judge-advocate at courts-martial all that time, has offered me to attend you; he has a thorough knowledge of the service, uncommon abilities, and is a very good lawyer. He has already had most of the evidences with him. Adieu! my young friend; keep up your spirits, and rest assured I shall be watchful for your good. My heart will be more at ease, if I can get my friend Graham to go down, than if you were attended by the first counsel in England.' Mr. Graham accordingly attended, and was of the greatest service at the trial. . . .

Nessy Heywood had expressed a strong desire to see her brother, but was told the rules of the service would not allow it; also, that it would agitate him, when he ought to be cool and collected, to meet his approaching trial. This was quite enough :– 'But as for myself,' she says, 'no danger, no fatigue, no difficulties, would deter me. If I were not allowed to see you, yet being in the same place which contains you, would be joy inexpressible! I will not, however, any longer desire it, but will learn to imitate your fortitude and patience.'

Mr. Heywood of Maristow, and his daughter, Mrs. Bertie, had intimated the same thing. These excellent people, from the moment of young Heywood's arrival, had shown him every kindness, supplied him with money, and what was better, with friends, who could give him the best advice. To Mrs. Bertie, Miss Nessy Heywood thus addresses herself.

'Overwhelmed with sensations of gratitude and pleasure which she is too much agitated to express, permit me, dearest Madam, at my mamma's request, to offer you hers and our most sincere acknowledgements for your invaluable letter, which, from the detention of the packet, she did not receive till yesterday. My beloved brother speaks with every expression a grateful heart can dictate of your excellent father's goodness in providing for all his wants, even before he could have received any letters from us to that purpose.

'Ah! my dear Madam, how truly characteristic is this of the kind friendship with which he has ever honoured our family! But my beloved Peter does not know that Mr. Heywood has a daughter, whose generosity is equal to his own, and whose amiable compassion for his sufferings it will be as impossible for us to forget, as it is to express the admiration and gratitude it has inspired. . . .

'In one of my brother's letters, he hints that he shall not be permitted to see any of his relations till his trial is over, and that he therefore does not expect us. I have, however, written to Mr. Heywood (without whose approbation I would by no means take any step) for permission to go to him. If it is absolutely impossible for me to see him (though in the presence of witnesses), yet even that prohibition, cruel as it is, I could bear with patience, provided I might be near him, to see the ship in which he at present exists – to breathe the same air which he breathes. . . . I earnestly hope Mr. Heywood will not judge it improper to comply with my request, and shall wait with eager impatience the arrival of his next letter. . . .

'I have the honour to be, with every sentiment of gratitude, &c., &c., &c.,
'NESSY HEYWOOD.'

Among the numerous friends that interested themselves in the fate of this unhappy youth, was his uncle, Colonel Holwell. The testimony he bears to his excellent character is corroborated by all who knew him while a boy at home. About a fortnight before the trial he writes to him thus:—

'*21st August*, 1792.

'MY VERY DEAR PETER, – I have this day received yours of the 18th, and am happy to find by its contents that, notwithstanding your long and cruel confinement, you still preserve your health, and write in good spirits. Preserve it, my dear boy, awful as the approaching period must be, even to the most innocent, but from which all who know you have not a doubt of your rising as immaculate as a new-born infant. I have known you from your cradle, and have often marked with pleasure and surprise the many assiduous instances (far beyond your years) you have given of filial duty and paternal affection to the best of parents, and to brothers and sisters who doated on you. Your education has been the best; and from these considerations alone, without the very clear evidence of your own testimony, I would as soon believe the Archbishop of Canterbury would set fire to the city of London as suppose you could, directly or indirectly, join in such a d—d absurd piece of business. Six years in the navy myself, and twenty-eight years a soldier, I flatter myself my judgement will not prove erroneous.'

With similar testimonies and most favourable auguries from Commodore Pasley, the Rev. Dr. Scott, of the Isle of Man, and others, young Heywood went to his long and anxiously expected trial, which took place on the 12th September, and continued to the 18th of that month. Mrs. Heywood had been anxious that Erskine and Mingay should be employed as counsel, but Mr. Graham, whom Commodore Pasley had so highly recommended, gave his best assistance; as did also Mr. Const, who had been retained, for which the Commodore expresses his sorrow, as sea officers, he says, have a great aversion to lawyers. Mr. Peter Heywood assigns a better reason; in a letter to his sister Mary he says, that 'Counsel to a naval prisoner is of no effect, and as they are not allowed to speak, their eloquence is not of the least efficacy; I request, therefore, you will desire my dear mother to revoke the letter she has been so good to write to retain Mr. Erskine and Mr. Mingay, and to forbear putting herself to so great and needless an expense, from which no good can accrue. *I* alone must fight my own battle; and I think my telling the truth undisguised, in a plain, short, and concise manner, is as likely to be deserving the victory, as the most elaborate eloquence of a Cicero upon the same subject.' . . .

At a Court Martial assembled on board His Majesty's Ship Duke in Portsmouth Harbour on the twelfth Day of September and continued by Adjournment from Day to Day (Sunday excepted) until the eighteenth Day of the same Month, one thousand seven hundred and ninety two.

Present

The Right Honorable Lord Hood Vice Admiral of the Blue and Commander in Chief of His Majesty's Ships and Vessels at Portsmouth and Spithead, President.

Captain Sir Andrew Snape Hamond Bart. Captain John Colpoys
George Montagu Sir Roger Curtis Kn.
John Bazely Sir Andrew Snape Douglas
John Thomas Duckworth John Nicholson Inglefield
John Knight Albemarle Bertie
Richard Goodwin Keats

Pursuant to an Order from the Right Honorable Lords Commissioners of the Admiralty dated the 20th August last and directed to the President representing that by an Order from the late board of Admiralty dated the 16th August 1787 Lieutenant (now Captain) William Bligh was appointed to command His Majesty's armed Vessel

Facsimile: Minutes of the court-martial.
'If any person in or belonging to the fleet shall make or endeavour to make, any mutinous assembly, upon any pretence whatsoever, every person offending herein, and being convicted thereof by the sentence of the court martial, shall suffer death.' (*Articles of War*.)

CHAPTER SIX

The Court-martial

The Court assembled to try the prisoners on board his Majesty's ship *Duke*, on the 12th September, 1792, and continued by adjournment from day to day (Sunday excepted) until the 18th of the same month. [The minutes being very long, a brief abstract only, containing the principal points of evidence, is here given.]

PRESENT
Vice-Admiral Lord Hood, *President*
Capt. Sir Andrew Snape Hamond, Bart.,
       John Colpoys,
       Sir George Montague,
       Sir Roger Curtis,
       John Bazeley,
       Sir Andrew Snape Douglas,
       John Thomas Duckworth,
       John Nicholson Inglefield,
       John Knight,
       Albermarle Bertie,
       Richard Goodwin Keats.

The charges set forth that Fletcher Christian, who was mate of the *Bounty*, assisted by others of the inferior officers and men, armed with muskets and bayonets, had violently and forcibly taken that ship from her commander, Lieutenant Bligh; and that he, together with the master, boatswain, gunner, and carpenter, and other persons (being nineteen in number), were forced into the launch and cast adrift. That Peter Heywood, James Morrison, Charles Norman, Joseph Coleman, Thomas Ellison, Thomas M'Intosh, Thomas Burkitt, John Millward, William Muspratt, and Michael Byrne, had been brought to England, &c., and were now put on their trial.

Mr. Fryer, the master of the *Bounty*, being first sworn, deposed—

That he had the first watch; that between ten and eleven o'clock Mr. Bligh came on deck, according to custom, and after a short conversation, and having given his orders for the night, left the deck; that at twelve he was relieved by the gunner, and retired, leaving all quiet; that at dawn of day he was greatly alarmed by an unusual noise; and that, on attempting to jump up, John Sumner and Matthew Quintal laid their hands upon his breast and desired him to lie still, saying he was their prisoner; that on expostulating with them, he was told, 'Hold your tongue, or you are a dead man, but if you remain quiet there is none on board will hurt a hair of your head'; he further deposes, that on raising himself on the locker, he saw on the ladder, going upon deck, Mr. Bligh in his shirt, with his hands tied

Lord Hood
Nelson had a very high opinion of Hood. He fought in the West Indies and at the crucial battle of the Chesapeake in 1781. According to Heywood, Lord Hood offered him a place in his flag-ship *Victory* immediately after he had received his Royal Pardon.

Sir Andrew Snape Hammond
Sir Andrew Hammond became Comptroller (Navy Board) in 1794, and had a running battle with Earl St Vincent, First Lord of the Admiralty, over the building of more 74-gun ships. The relationship got so bad that the Navy Board complained, in 1804, of 'the indignities, the unjust reproofs and reprimands, [and] the harsh and severe language which have been exercised towards us during the last two years.'

Admiral Sir John Colpoys
Colpoys was a severe disciplinarian who gained an unenviable reputation below decks. During the Spithead mutiny in 1797 he ordered the marines to open fire on unarmed mutineers. In the peace settlement negotiated between Lord Howe and the mutineers' leaders, Colpoys headed the list of officers the seamen insisted were to be sent ashore if they were to return to duty. The Admiralty agreed and Colpoys lost his command.

Sir Roger Curtis
In the mutiny of 1797, Sir Roger Curtis was made prisoner and the ships in his squadron were sailed by the men to join the mutineers at Spithead. Of the 101 officers, warrant officers and midshipmen sent ashore under the agreement that ended the mutiny, more than half came from the eight ships in Curtis's squadron. He was to become a 'warm and sincere' friend of Peter Heywood.

Captain John Thomas Duckworth
Another of the captains overthrown by the mutineers in 1797. He told his men, 'Captain Duckworth has resolved never to command such a set of villains till he has proved to the world through a court-martial your baseness and his innocence.' Next day the Royal Pardon arrived and he resumed command. Nobody was court-martialled.

Captain John Nicholson Inglefield
Inglefield distinguished himself by capturing the *Cesar* (a '74') in 1782 with the loss of only eight of his men. But a 'rascal of a marine corporal,' searching for rum with the aid of a candle, set the ship alight and thirty more men perished in the fire.

Captain John Knight
During the Nore mutiny in 1979 Captain Knight acted as a go-between, having won the respect and confidence of the leading mutineer Richard Parker. Knight was later called as a defence witness at Parker's trial.

Captain Albemarle Bertie
Captain Bertie was related, by marriage, to Peter Heywood's family. He provided Heywood with money while he was held prisoner in the *Hector* and his wife corresponded with Heywood's mother during the trial, assuring her that her son's life was more safe at that time than it had been before his arrest. It was also from Captain Bertie's ship *Triumph* that Bligh, in 1787, managed to get Thomas Ledward as an assistant surgeon to replace the drunken Huggan on the *Bounty*.

Sir Richard Goodwin Keats
Captain Keats was among those officers put ashore during the Plymouth mutiny of 1797 from the *Galatea* – the ship having returned to port expressly for that purpose.

Lord Hood

Sir Andrew Snape Hammond

Admiral Sir John Colpoys

Sir Roger Curtis

Captain John Thomas Duckworth

Captain John Nicholson Inglefield

Captain John Knight

Captain Albemarle Bertie

Sir Richard Goodwin Keats

behind him, and Christian holding him by the cord; that the master-at-arms, Churchill, then came to his cabin and took a brace of pistols and a hanger, saying, 'I will take care of these, Mr. Fryer'; that he asked, on seeing Mr. Bligh bound, what they were going to do with the captain; that Sumner replied, 'D—n his eyes, put him into the boat, and let the —— see if he can live upon three-fourths of a pound of yams a day'; that he remonstrated with such conduct, but in vain. They said he must go in the small cutter. 'The small cutter!' Mr. Fryer exclaimed; 'why her bottom is almost out, and very much eaten by the worms!' to which Sumner and Quintal both said, 'D—n his eyes, the boat is too good for him'; that after much entreaty he prevailed on them to ask Christian if he might be allowed to go on deck, which, after some hesitation, was granted. When I came on deck, says Mr. Fryer, Mr. Bligh was standing by the mizen-mast, with his hands tied behind him, and Christian holding the cord with one hand, and a bayonet in the other, I said, 'Christian, consider what you are about.' 'Hold your tongue, Sir,' he said; 'I have been in hell for weeks past; Captain Bligh has brought all this on himself.' I told him that Mr. Bligh and he not agreeing was no reason for taking the ship. 'Hold your tongue, Sir,' he said. I said, – Mr. Christian, you and I have been on friendly terms during the voyage, there-fore give me leave to speak, – let Mr. Bligh go down to his cabin, and I make no doubt we shall all be friends again; – he then repeated, 'Hold your tongue, Sir; it is too late'; and threatening me if I said anything more. Mr. Fryer then asked him to give a better boat that the cutter; he said, 'No, that boat is good enough.' Bligh now said to the master, that the man behind the hen-coops (Isaac Martin) was his friend, and desired him (the master) to knock Christian down, which Christian must have heard, but took no notice; that Fryer then attempted to get past Christian to speak to Martin, but he put his bayonet to his breast saying, 'Sir, if you advance an inch farther, I will run you through,' and ordered two armed men to take him down to his cabin. Shortly afterwards he was desired to go on deck, when Christian ordered him into the boat: he said, 'I will stay with you, if you will give me leave.' No, Sir,' he replied, 'go directly into the boat.' Bligh, then on the gangway, said, 'Mr. Fryer, stay in the ship.' 'No, by G—d, Sir,' Christian said, 'go into the boat, or I will run you through.' Mr. Fryer states, that during this time very bad language was used by the people towards Mr. Bligh; that with great difficulty they prevailed on Christian to suffer a few articles to be put into the boat; that after the persons were ordered into the boat to the number of nineteen, opprobrious language continued to be used, several of the men calling out 'Shoot the ——,' that Cole, the boatswain, advised they should cast off and take their chance, as the mutineers would certainly do them a mischief if they stayed much longer. Mr. Fryer then states the names of those who were under arms; and that Joseph Coleman, Thomas M'Intosh, Charles Norman, and Michael Byrne (prisoners) wished to come into the boat, declaring they had nothing to do in the business; that he did not perceive Mr. Peter Heywood on deck at the seizure of the ship.

On being asked what he supposed Christian meant when he said he had been in hell for a fortnight? he said, from the frequent quarrels that they had, and the abuse he had received from Mr. Bligh, and that the day before the mutiny Mr. Bligh had challenged all the young gentlemen and people with stealing his cocoa-nuts.

Mr. Cole, the boatswain, deposes, – that he had the middle watch; was awakened out of his sleep in the morning, and heard a man calling out to the carpenter, that they had mutinied and taken the ship; that Christian had the command, and that the captain was a prisoner on the quarter-deck; that he went up the hatchway, having seen Mr. Heywood and Mr. Young in the opposite berth; that coming on deck he saw the captain with his hands tied behind him, and four sentinels standing over him, two of which were Ellison and Burkitt, the prisoners; that he asked Mr. Christian what he meant to do, and was answered by his ordering him to hoist the boat out, and shook the bayonet, threatening him and damning him if he did not take care; that when he found the captain was to be sent out of the ship, he again went aft with the carpenter to ask for the long-boat; that they asked three or four times before he granted it; that he saw Mr. Peter Heywood, one of the prisoners, lending a hand to get the fore-stayfall along, and when the boat was hooked on, spoke something to him, but what it was does not know, as Christian was threatening him at the time; that Heywood then went below, and does not remember seeing him afterwards; that after the few things were got into the boat, and most of the people in her, they were trying for the carpenter's tool-chest, when Quintal said, 'D—n them, if we let them have these things they will build a vessel in a month'; but when all were in the boat she was veered astern, when Coleman, Norman, and M'Intosh, prisoners, were crying at the gangway, wishing to go in the boat; and Byrne in the cutter alongside was also crying; that he advised Mr. Bligh to cast off, as he feared they would fire into the boat.

The Court asked if he had any reason to believe that any other of the prisoners than those named were detained contrary to their inclinations? Answer – 'I believe Mr. Heywood was; I thought all along he was intending to come away; he had no arms, and he assisted to get the boat out, and then went below; I heard Churchill call out, 'Keep them below.' *The Court* – 'Do you think he meant Heywood?' 'I have no reason to think any other.'

Mr. Peckover the gunner's evidence is similar to that of Mr. Cole's and need not be detailed.

Mr. Purcell, the carpenter, corroborated, generally, the testimony of the three who had been examined. *The Court* asked, 'Did you see Mr. Heywood standing upon the booms?' 'Yes; he was leaning the flat part of his hand on a cutlass, when I exclaimed, In the name of God, Peter, what do you with that? when he instantly dropped it, and assisted in hoisting the launch out, and handing the things into the boat, and then went down below, when I heard Churchill call to Thompson to keep them below, but could not tell whom he meant; I did not see Mr. Heywood after that.' *The Court* – 'In what light did you look upon Mr. Heywood, at the time you say he dropped the cutlass on your speaking to him?' *Witness* – 'I looked upon him as a person confused, and that he did not know he had the weapon in his hand, or his hand being on it, for it was not in his hand; I considered him to be confused, by his instantly dropping it, and assisting in hoisting the boat out, which convinced me in my own mind that he had no hand in the conspiracy; that after this he went below, as I think, on his own account, in order to collect some of his things to put into the boat.' *The Court* – 'Do you, upon the solemn oath you have taken, believe that Mr. Heywood, by being armed with a cutlass at the time you have mentioned, by anything that you could collect from his gestures or speeches, had any intention of opposing, or joining others that might oppose, to stop the progress of the mutiny?' *Witness* – 'No.' *The Court* – 'In the time that Mr. Heywood was assisting you to get the things into the boat, did he, in any degree whatever, manifest a disposition to assist in the mutiny?' *Witness* – 'No.' *The Court* – 'Was he, during that time, deliberate or frightened, and in what manner did he behave himself?' *Witness* – 'I had not an opportunity of observing his every action, being myself at that time engaged in getting several things into the boat, so that I cannot tell.' *The Court* – 'Putting every circumstance together, declare to this court, upon the oath you have taken, how you considered his behaviour, whether as a person joined in the mutiny, or as a person wishing well to Captain Bligh?' *Witness* – 'I by no means considered him as a person concerned in the mutiny or conspiracy.'

Lieutenant Thomas Hayward, late third lieutenant of the *Pandora*, and formerly midshipman of the *Bounty*, deposes, – that he had the morning watch; that at four o'clock Fletcher Christian relieved the watch as usual; that at five he ordered him, as master's mate of his watch, to look out, while he went down to lash his hammock up; that while looking at a shark astern of the ship, to his unutterable surprise, he saw Fletcher Christian, Charles Churchill, Thomas Burkitt (the prisoner), John Sumner, Matthew Quintal, William M'Koy, Isaac Martin, Henry Hillbrant, and Alexander Smith, coming aft, armed with muskets and bayonets; that on going forward, he asked Christian the cause of such an act, who told him to hold his tongue instantly; and leaving Isaac Martin as a sentinel on deck, he proceeded with the rest of his party below to Lieutenant Bligh's cabin; that the people on deck were Mr. John Hallet, myself, Robert Lamb, Butcher, Thomas Ellison (prisoner) at the helm, and John Mills at the conn; that he asked Mills if he knew any thing of the matter, who pleaded total ignorance, and Thomas Ellison quitted the helm and armed himself with a bayonet; that the decks now became thronged with armed men; that Peter Heywood, James Morrison (two of the prisoners), and George Stewart, were unarmed on the booms; that Fletcher Christian and his gang had not been down long before he heard the cry of murder from Lieutenant Bligh, and Churchill calling out for a rope, on which Mills, contrary to all orders and entreaties, cut the deep-sea line and carried a piece of it to their assistance; that soon after

Lieutenant Bligh was brought upon the quarter-deck with his hands bound behind him, and was surrounded by most of those who came last on deck.

This witness then states, that on the arrival of the *Pandora* at Matavai Bay, Joseph Coleman was the first that came on board; that he was upset in a canoe and assisted by the natives; that as soon as the ship was at anchor, George Stewart and Peter Heywood came on board; that they made themselves known to Captain Edwards, and expressed their happiness that he was arrived; that he asked them how they came to go away with his Majesty's ship the *Bounty*, when George Stewart said, when called upon hereafter, he would answer all particulars; that he was prevented by Captain Edwards from answering further questions, and they were sent out of the cabin to be confined. He then describes the manner in which the rest of the mutineers were taken on the island. Having stated that when he went below to get some things he saw Peter Heywood in his berth, and told him to go into the boat, he was asked by *the Court* if Heywood was prevented by any force from going upon deck, he answered, 'No.' *The Court* – 'Did you, from his behaviour, consider him as a person attached to his duty, or to the party of the mutineers?' *Witness* – 'I should rather suppose, after my having told him to go into the boat, and he not joining us, to be on the side of the mutineers; but that must be understood only as an opinion, as he was not in the least employed during the active part of it.' *The Court* – 'Did you observe any marks of joy or sorrow on his countenance or behaviour?' *Witness* – 'Sorrow.'

Lieutenant Hallet, late midshipman of the *Bounty*, states, – that he had the morning-watch; that he heard Lieutenant Bligh call out murder, and presently after saw him brought upon deck naked, excepting his shirt, with his hands tied behind him, and Christian holding the end of the cord which tied them in one hand, and either a bayonet or a cutlass in the other; that the cutter was hoisted out, and Mr. Samuel, Mr. Hayward, and myself ordered to go into her; but the boatswain and carpenter going aft, and telling Christian they wished to go with the captain rather than stay in the ship, and asking to have the launch, it was granted. On being asked if he saw Peter Heywood on that day, he replied, once, on the platform, standing still and looking attentively towards Captain Bligh; never saw him under arms nor spoke to him; does not know if he offered to go in the boat, nor did he hear any one propose to him to go in the boat; that when standing on the platform, Captain Bligh said something to him, but what he did not hear, upon which Heywood laughed, turned round, and walked away.

Captain Edwards being then called and sworn, was desired by the Court to state the conversation that passed between him and Coleman, Peter Heywood, and George Stewart, when they came on board the *Pandora*.

Edwards – 'Joseph Coleman attempted to come on board before the ship came to an anchor at Otaheite; he was soon afterwards taken up by canoes and came on board before the ship came to an anchor; I began to make inquiries of him after the *Bounty* and her people. The next who came on

Portsmouth: View from the Saluting Platform.
This was such a busy and important naval port that the arrival and departure of His
Majesty's ships necessitated the permanent manning of the signalling guns in order to
satisfy the demands of naval protocol.

board were Stewart and Peter Heywood; they came after the ship was at
anchor, but before any boat was on shore. I did not see them come alongside.
I desired Lieutenant Larkin to bring them down to the cabin. I asked them
what news; Peter Heywood, I think, said he supposed I had heard of the
affair of the *Bounty*. I don't recollect all the conversation that passed between
us; he sometimes interrupted me by asking for Mr. Hayward, the lieutenant
of the *Pandora*, whether he was on board or not – he had heard that he was;
at last I acknowledged that he was, and I desired him to come out of my
state-room, where I had desired him to go into, as he happened to be with
me at the time. Lieutenant Hayward treated him with a sort of contemptuous
look, and began to enter into conversation with him respecting the *Bounty*,

but I called the sentinel in to take them into custody, and ordered Lieutenant Hayward to desist, and I ordered them to be put into irons; some words passed, and Peter Heywood said he should be able to vindicate his conduct.

Lieutenant Corner, of the *Pandora*, merely states his being sent to bring the rest of the mutineers on board, who were at some distance from Matavai Bay.

The prisoners being called on for their defence, the witnesses were again separately called and examined on the part of the prisoners.

Mr. Fryer, the master, called in and examined by Mr. Heywood. – 'If you had been permitted, would you have stayed in the ship in preference to going into the boat?' *Witness* – 'Yes.' *Prisoner* – 'Had you stayed in the ship in expectation of retaking her, was my conduct such as would have induced you to intrust me with your design; and do you believe I would have favoured it, and given you all the assistance in my power?' *Witness* – 'I believe he would: I should not have hesitated a moment in asking of him when I had had an opportunity of opening my mind to him.'

The same question being put to *Mr. Cole*, the boatswain, *Mr. Peckover*, the gunner, and *Mr. Purcell*, the carpenter, they all answered in the affirmative.

Mr. Heywood asked, 'What was my general conduct, temper, and disposition on board the ship?' *Witness* – 'Beloved by everybody, to the best of my recollection.' To the same question, *Mr. Cole* answers, 'Always a very good character.' *Mr. Peckover* – 'The most amiable, and deserving of every one's esteem.' *Mr. Purcell* – 'In every respect becoming the character of a gentleman, and such as merited the esteem of everybody.'

Mr. Cole being examined, gave his testimony, – that he never saw Mr. Heywood armed; that he did not consider him of the mutineers' party; that he saw nothing of levity or apparent merriment in his conduct; that when he was below with Stewart, he heard Churchill call out, 'Keep them below,' and that he believes Heywood was one of the persons meant – has no doubt of it at all; that Bligh could not have spoken to him, when on the booms, loud enough to be heard; that Hayward was alarmed, and Hallet alarmed; that he by no means considers Heywood or Morrison as mutineers.

Mr. Purcell being examined, states, – that, respecting the cutlass on which he saw Mr. Heywood's hand resting, he does not consider him as being an armed man; that he never thought him as of the mutineers' party; that he never heard Captain Bligh speak to him; that he thinks, from his situation, he could not have heard him; that he was by no means guilty of levity or apparent merriment; that he heard the master-at-arms call out to keep them below; that Mr. Hallet appeared to him to be very much confused; and that Mr. Hayward likewise appeared to be very much confused.

The Court asked, – 'As you say you did not look upon the prisoner as a person armed, to what did you allude when you exclaimed, "Good God, Peter, what do you do with that?"' *Witness* – 'I look upon it as an accidental thing.'

Captain Edwards, being asked by Heywood – 'Did I surrender myself to you upon the arrival of the *Pandora* at Otaheite?' *Witness* – 'Not to me, to the Lieutenant. I apprehend he put himself in my power. I always understood he came voluntarily; our boats were not in the water.' *Prisoner* – 'Did I give you such information respecting myself and the *Bounty* as afterwards proved true?' *Witness* – 'He gave me some information respecting the people on the island, that corroborated with Coleman's. I do not recollect the particular conversation, but in general it agreed with the account given by Coleman.'

Mr. Fryer again called in and examined by Mr. Morrison – Mr. Fryer states, he saw him assist in hoisting out the boats; that he said to him (Fryer), 'Go down below.' *The Court* asked, 'Whether it might not have been from a laudable motive, as supposing your assistance at that time might have prevented a more advantageous effort?' *Witness* – 'Probably it might: had I stayed in the ship, he would have been one of the first that I should have opened my mind to, from his good behaviour in the former part of the voyage': states his belief, that he addressed him as advice; and that, in hoisting out the boat, he was assisting Captain Bligh.

Mr. Cole, the boatswain, states, that he ordered Morrison to go and help them with the cutter; that he told him the boat was overloaded; that Captain Bligh had begged that no more people should go in her, and said he would take his chance in the ship; that he shook Morrison by the hand, and said he would do him justice in England; that he had no reason to suppose him concerned in the mutiny.

Lieutenant Thomas Hayward states, that Morrison appeared joyful, and supposed him to be one of the mutineers; on being asked by Morrison if he could declare before God and the Court that what he stated was not the result of a private pique? *Witness* – 'Not the result of any private pique, but an opinion formed after quitting the ship, from his not coming with us, there being more boats than one; cannot say they might have had the cutter.' This witness was pleased to remember nothing that was in favour of the prisoner.

Lieutenant Hallet states, he saw Morrison under arms; being asked in what part of the ship, he says, 'I did not see him under arms till the boat was veered astern, and he was then looking over the taffrail, and called out, in a jeering manner, "If my friends inquire after me, tell them I am somewhere in the South Seas." '

Captain Edwards bore testimony that Morrison voluntarily surrendered himself.

Mr. Fryer did not see Morrison armed; he was in his watch, and he considered him a steady, sober, attentive, good man; and acknowledged, that if he had remained in the ship, with the view of retaking her, Morrison would have been one of the first he should have called to his assistance.

Mr. Cole gave testimony to his being a man of good character, attentive to his duty, and he never knew any harm of him.

Mr. Purcell bore witness to his good character, being always diligent and attentive; did not see him under arms on the taffrail; never heard him use any jeering speeches.

Respecting the prisoner *Muspratt*, *Mr. Cole*'s evidence proves that he had a musket in his hands, but not till the latter part of the business; it is also proved that he assisted in getting things into the launch. *Mr. Peckover* saw him standing on the forecastle doing nothing – he was not armed.

Lieutenant Hayward saw Muspratt among the armed men: was asked, when Captain Bligh used the words, 'Don't let the boat be overloaded, my lads' – 'I'll do you justice'; do you understand the latter words, 'My lads, I'll do you justice,' to apply to clothes or to men, whom he apprehended might go into the boat? *Witness* – 'If Captain Bligh made use of the words "my lads," it was to the people already in the boat, and not to those in the ship.' *The Court* – 'To whom do you imagine Captain Bligh alluded: was it, in your opinion, to the men in the boat with him, or to any persons then remaining in the ship?' *Witness* – 'To persons remaining in the ship.'

Against the prisoners Ellison, Burkitt, and Millward, the evidence given by all the witnesses so clearly and distinctly proved they were under arms the whole time, and actively employed against Bligh, that it is unnecessary to go into any detail as far as they are concerned.

The Court having called on the prisoners, each separately, for his defence, Mr. Heywood delivered his as follows:–

'My lords and gentlemen of this honourable Court, – Your attention has already been sufficiently exercised in the painful narrative of this trial; it is therefore my duty to trespass further on it as little as possible.

'The crime of mutiny, for which I am now arraigned, is so seriously pregnant with every danger and mischief, that it makes the person so accused appear at once the object of unpardonable guilt and exemplary vengeance. In such a character it is my misfortune to appear before this tribunal.

'Appearances, probably, are against me, but they are appearances only; for unless I may be deemed guilty for feeling a repugnance at embracing death unnecessarily, I declare before this Court and the tribunal of Almighty God, I am innocent of the charge. . . .

'When first this sad event took place I was sleeping in my hammock; nor, till the very moment of being awakened from it, had I the least intimation of what was going on. The spectacle was as sudden to my eyes, as it was unknown to my heart; and both were convulsed at the scene.

'Matthew Thompson was the first that claimed my attention upon waking: he was sitting as a sentinel over the arm-chest, and my berth, and informed me that the captain was a prisoner, and Christian had taken the command of the ship. I entreated for permission to go upon deck; and soon after the boatswain and carpenter had seen me in my berth, as they were going up the fore-hatchway, I followed them, as is stated in their evidence. It is not in my power to describe my feelings upon seeing the captain as I did,

A Seaman.

So much has been written about the British seaman, some of it fact, much of it fiction, and always with a rich dose of romanticism, that it is almost impossible to generalize. Considering the conditions under which they were forced to live (but forgetting just how bad it was for their class ashore), it is surprising that ships' crews did not mutiny more often. The reason is probably that mutiny requires the presence of capable leaders, or at least one man of superior education. For the most part, British seamen did as they were ordered while on board ship – but deserted in droves at every available opportunity. During the American War of Independence, thousands of seamen deserted to join the rebels and fight against the British.

A Master and Commander.

The Master's duty was to manage the conduct of the ship under the Captain. He directed the sailing, the trimming and setting of sails, and the daily fixing of the ship's position. He did all the inshore surveying in foreign waters. He was also in charge of the ship's stores and checked the boatswain's and carpenter's accounts. Cook appointed Bligh, a midshipman, to be Master of the *Resolution* at the age of twenty-three. He died an Admiral. John Fryer, the Master of the *Bounty*, was thirty-seven years old and never advanced in rank. Up to the 1800s it was still possible to break into the senior ranks from a Master's warrant, but in the nineteenth century this became an increasingly remote possibility.

A Lieutenant.

A ship of the line carried several lieutenants while a small ship might have only one, doubling as Captain. The Lieutenant's Commission was the most sought-after prize of the young midshipman. Date of seniority could influence promotion to the all-important rank of Post Captain, which, once achieved, assured its holder – barring death, infirmity, disgrace or exceedingly bad luck – his Admiral's flag. First Lieutenants generally did most of the work while the Captain would take all the credit, or sometimes blame. He managed the men through the mates and midshipmen and generally set the disciplinary tone of the ship. He was responsible to the Captain (or to the Admiralty if he commanded a small

A SEAMAN
with a Man of War's Barge.

A MASTER and COMMANDER
with a Sloop of War

ship) for *everything* that happened on, and to, the ship: and as his career rested on that
responsibility, he would react passionately against anything that posed a threat to his record.

A Midshipman.

Young Gentlemen (some not so young and some not so gentle), entered the naval service
intending to become midshipmen. After several years service and the examination for the
rank of Lieutenant, they could aim to be on the first rung of the promotion ladder. The
Master watched over their navigational training; the Mates over their seamanship. They
stood watches and commanded men – sometimes abusing their powers. The *Bounty*
mutineers, for example, prefered Heywood to Stewart as a midshipman because of the
latter's petty tyranny. Barrow had a rather romantic notion of life in a midshipmen's
mess. For the most part it could be a vulgarizing, if not brutalizing, experience, particularly
prior to 1800. The *Bounty* carried five Young Gentlemen – Young, Hayward, Hallet,
Heywood and Tinkler.

A Post Captain.

The Captain was held to be totally responsible for everything connected with his ship
and its mission. Post Captain was the name of the rank of Captain. The captain of a ship
did not necessarily hold this rank: he could be a lieutenant, as was Cook when he commanded the *Endeavour*, and Bligh the *Bounty*. In a ship of the line the Captain was a
remote figure, held in awe or fear depending on his style of command. Even in the late
eighteenth century the volume of paperwork he handled was formidable – as the archives
of the Public Record Office show. He had considerable, but not unlimited, powers of
discipline over the crew, but was responsible to the Admiralty under the Articles of War
and the customs of the service. He could not order physical punishment of lieutenants or
warrant officers, nor could he award more than a few dozen lashes without the backing of
a court-martial. A post captain could be dismissed for a variety of offences, and the
records show that several were. Morrison's charge of Bligh stealing cheeses from the ship's
stores would, if proven in court, have cost him his commission, as would the charge that he
falsified some of the ship's accounts.

A MIDSHIPMAN
with a Longing Boat

A POST CAPTAIN
with a Frigate and Ships of the Line

who, with his hands tied behind him, was standing on the quarter-deck, a little abaft the mizen-mast, and Christian by his side. My faculties were benumbed, and I did not recover the power of recollection until called to by somebody to take hold of the tackle-fall, and assist to get out the launch, which I found was to be given to the captain instead of the large cutter, already in the water alongside the ship. It were in vain to say what things I put into the boat, but many were handed in by me; and in doing this it was that my hand touched the cutlass (for I will not attempt to deny what the carpenter has deposed), though, on my conscience, I am persuaded it was of momentary duration, and innocent as to intention. The former is evident, from its being unobserved by every witness who saw me upon deck, some of whom must have noticed it had it continued a single minute; and the latter is proved by the only person who took notice of the circumstance, and has also deposed that, at the moment he beheld me, I was apparently in a state of absolute stupor. The poison, therefore, carries with it its antidote; and it seems needless to make any further comment on the subject. . . .

'The boat and ship, it is true, presented themselves to me without its once occurring that I was at liberty to choose, much less that the choice I should make would be afterwards deemed criminal; and I bitterly deplore that my extreme youth and inexperience concurred in torturing me with apprehensions, and prevented me from preferring the former; for as things have turned out, it would have saved me from the disgrace of appearing before you as I do at this day.

'Add to my youth and inexperience, that I was influenced in my conduct by the example of my messmates, Mr. Hallet and Mr. Hayward, the former of whom was very much agitated, and the latter, though he had been many years at sea, yet, when Christian ordered him into the boat, he was evidently alarmed at the perilous situation, and so much overcome by the harsh command, that he actually shed tears.

'My own apprehensions were far from being lessened at such a circumstance as this, and I fearfully beheld the preparations for the captain's departure as the preliminaries of inevitable destruction, which, although I did not think could be more certain, yet I feared would be more speedy, by the least addition to their number.

'To show that I have no disposition to impose upon this Court, by endeavouring to paint the situation of the boat to be worse than it really was, I need only refer to the captain's own narrative, wherein he says that she would have sunk with them on the evening of the 3rd May, had it not been for his timely caution of throwing out some of the stores, and all the clothes belonging to the people, excepting two suits for each.

'Now what clothes or stores could they have spared which in weight would have been equal to that of two men? (for if I had been in her, and the poor fellow, Norton, had not been murdered at Tofoa, she would have been encumbered with our additional weight), and if it be true that she was saved by those means, which the captain says she was, it must follow that if Norton and myself had been in her (to say nothing of Coleman, M'Intosh, Norman, and Byrne, who, 'tis confessed, were desirous of leaving the ship), she must either have gone down with us, or, to prevent it, we must have lightened her of the provisions and other necessary articles, and thereby have perished for want – dreadful alternative! . . .

'To be starved to death, or drowned, appeared to be inevitable if I went in the boat; and surely it is not to be wondered at, if, at the age of sixteen years, with no one to advise with, and so ignorant of the discipline of the service (having never been at sea before) as not to know or even suppose it was possible that what I should determine upon might afterwards be alleged against me as a crime – I say, under such circumstances, in so trying a situation, can it be wondered at, if I suffered the preservation of my life to be the first, and to supersede every other, consideration.

'Besides, through the medium of the master, the captain had directed the rest of the officers to remain on board, in hopes of re-taking the ship. Such is the master's assertion, and such the report on board, and as it accorded with my own wishes for the preservation of my life, I felt myself doubly justified in staying on board, not only as it appeared to be safer than going in the boat, but from a consideration also of being in the way to be useful in assisting to accomplish so desirable a wish of the captain. . . .

'If deliberate guilt be necessarily affixed to all who continued on board the ship, and that in consequence they must be numbered with Christian's party – in such a strict view of matters it must irrevocably impeach the armourer and two carpenter's mates, as well as Martin and Byrne, who certainly wished to quit the ship. And if Christian's first intention of sending away the captain, with a few persons only, in the small cutter, had not been given up, or if even the large cutter had not been exchanged for the launch, more than half of those who did go with him would have been obliged to stay with me. Forgetful for a moment of my own misfortunes, I cannot help being agitated at the bare thought of their narrow escape.

'Every body must, and I am sure that this Court will, allow that my case is a peculiarly hard one, inasmuch as the running away with the ship is a proof of the mutiny having been committed. The innocent and the guilty are upon exactly the same footing – had the former been confined by sickness, without a leg to stand on, or an arm to assist them in opposing the mutineers, they must have been put upon their trial, and instead of the captain being obliged to prove their guilt, it would have been incumbent upon them to have proved themselves innocent. How can this be done but negatively? If all who wished it could not accompany the captain, they were necessarily compelled to stay with Christian; and being with him, were dependent on him, subject to his orders, however disinclined to obey them, for force in such a state is paramount to every thing. But when, on the contrary, instead of being in arms, or obeying any orders of the mutineers, I did every thing in my power to assist the captain, and those who went with him, and by all my actions (except in neglecting to do what, if I had done, must have endangered the lives of those who were so fortunate as to quit the ship) I showed myself faithful to the last moment of the captain's stay, what is there to leave a doubt in the minds of impartial and dispassionate men of my being perfectly innocent? Happy indeed should I have been if the master had stayed on board, which he probably would have done, if his reasons for wishing to do so had not been overheard by the man who was in the bread-room.

'Captain Bligh in his narrative acknowledges that he had left some friends on board the *Bounty*, and no part of my conduct could have induced him to believe that I ought not to be reckoned of the number. Indeed from his attention to and very kind treatment of me personally, I should have been a monster of depravity to have betrayed him. And yet Mr. Hallet has said that he saw me laugh at a time when, Heaven knows, the conflict in my own mind, independent of the captain's situation, rendered such a want of decency impossible. The charge in its nature is dreadful, but I boldly declare, notwithstanding an internal conviction of my innocence has enabled me to endure my sufferings for the last sixteen months, could I have laid to my heart so heavy an accusation, I should not have lived to defend myself from it. And this brings to my recollection another part of Captain Bligh's narrative, in which he says, "I was kept apart from every one, and all I could do was by speaking to them in general, but my endeavours were of no avail, for I was kept securely bound, and no one but the guard was suffered to come near me."

'If the captain, whose narrative we may suppose to have been a detail of every thing which happened, could only recollect that he had spoken generally to the people, I trust it will hardly be believed that Mr. Hallet, without notes, at so distant a period as this, should be capable of recollecting that he heard him speak to any one in particular. At the time to which I allude, Mr. Hallet (if I am rightly informed) could not have been more than fifteen years of age. I think if circumstances be considered, and an adequate idea of the confused state of the ship can be formed by this Court, it will not appear probable that this young gentleman should have been so perfectly unembarrassed as to have been able to particularize the muscles of a man's countenance, even at a considerable distance from him; and what is still more extraordinary is, that he heard the captain call to me from abaft the mizen to the platform where I was standing, which required an exertion of voice, and must have been heard and noticed by all who were present; yet he who was standing between us, and noticing the transactions of us both, could not hear what was said.

'If, in the ordinary course of life, it is not an easy matter precisely to account for our own actions, how much more difficult and hazardous must it be, in new and momentous scenes, when the mind is hurried and distressed by conflicting passions, to judge of another's conduct; and yet here are two young men, who, after a lapse of near four years (in which period one of them, like myself, has grown from a boy to be a man), without hesitation, in a matter on which my life is depending, undertake to account for some of my actions, at a time, too, when some of the most experienced officers in the ship are not ashamed to acknowledge they were overcome by the confusion which the mutiny occasioned, and are incapable of recollecting a number of their own transactions on that day. . . .

'May they not both be mistaken? Let it be remembered that their long intimacy with Captain Bligh, in whose distresses they were partakers, and whose sufferings were severely felt by them, naturally begot an abhorrence towards those whom they thought the authors of their misery, – might they not forget that the story had been told to them, and by first of all believing, then constantly thinking of it, be persuaded at last it was a fact within the compass of their own knowledge.

'It is the more natural to believe it is so, from Mr. Hallet's forgetting what the captain said upon the occasion, which, had he been so collected as he pretends to have been, he certainly must have heard. Mr. Hayward, also, it is evident, has made a mistake in point of time as to the seeing me with Morrison and Millward upon the booms; for the boatswain and carpenter in their evidence have said, and the concurring testimony of every one supports the fact, that the mutiny had taken place, and the captain was on deck, before they came up, and it was not till after that time that the boatswain called Morrison and Millward out of their hammocks; therefore to have seen me at all upon the booms with those two men, it must have been long after the time that Mr. Hayward has said it was. Again Mr. Hayward has said that he could not recollect the day nor even the month when the *Pandora* arrived at Otaheite. Neither did Captain Edwards recollect when, on his return, he wrote to the Admiralty, that Michael Byrne had surrendered himself as one of the *Bounty*'s people, but in that letter he reported him as having been apprehended, which plainly shows that the memory is fallible to a very great degree; and it is a fair conclusion to draw that, if when the mind is at rest, which must have been the case with Mr. Hayward in the *Pandora* and things of a few months' date are difficult to be remembered, it is next to impossible, in the state which every body was on board the *Bounty*, to remember their particular actions at the distance of three years and a half after they were observed.

'As to the advice he says he gave me, to go into the boat, I can only say, I have a faint recollection of a short conversation with somebody – I thought it was Mr. Stewart – but be that as it may, I think I may take upon me to say it was on deck and not below, for on hearing it suggested that I should be deemed guilty if I stayed in the ship, I went down directly, and in passing Mr. Cole, told him, in a low tone of voice, that I would fetch a few necessaries in a bag and follow him into the boat, which at that time I meant to do, but was afterwards prevented.

'Surely I shall not be deemed criminal that I hesitated at getting into a boat whose gunnel, when she left the ship, was not quite eight inches above the surface of the water. And if, in the moment of unexpected trial, fear and confusion assailed my untaught judgement, and that by remaining in the ship I appeared to deny my commander, it was in appearance only – it was the sin of my head – for I solemnly assure you before God, that it was not the vileness of my heart.

'I was surprised into my error by a mixture of ignorance, apprehension, and the prevalence of example; and, alarmed as I was from my sleep, there was little opportunity and less time for better recollection. The captain, I am persuaded, did not see me during the mutiny, for I retired, as it were, in sorrowful suspense, alternately agitated between hope and fear, not knowing what to do. The dread of being asked by him, or of being ordered by Christian to go into the boat, – or, which appeared to me worse than either, of being desired by the latter to join his party, induced me to keep out of the sight of both, until I was a second time confined in my berth by Thompson, when the determination I had made was too late to be useful.

'One instance of my conduct I had nearly forgot, which, with much anxiety and great astonishment, I have heard observed upon and considered as a fault, though I had imagined it blameless, if not laudable – I mean the assistance I gave in hoisting out the launch, which, by a mode of expression of the boatswain's, who says I did it voluntarily (meaning that I did not refuse my assistance when he asked me to give it), the Court, I am afraid has considered it as giving assistance to the mutineers, and not done with a view to help the captain; of which, however, I have no doubt of being able to give a satisfactory explanation in evidence.

'Mr. Hayward, although he says he rather considered me as a friend to Christian's party, states that his last words to me were, "Peter, go into the boat," which words could not have been addressed to one who was of the party of the mutineers.

'It were trespassing unnecessarily upon the patience of the Court, to be giving a tedious history of what happened in consequence of the mutiny, and how, through one very imprudent step, I was unavoidably led into others.

'But, amidst all this pilgrimage of distress, I had a conscience, thank heaven, which lulled away the pain of personal difficulties, dangers, and distress. It was this conscious principle which determined me not to hide myself as if guilty. No – I welcomed the arrival of the *Pandora* at Otaheite, and embraced the earliest opportunity of freely surrendering myself to the captain of that ship. . . .

'Believe me, again I entreat you will believe me, when, in the name of the tremendous judge of heaven and earth (before whose vindictive Majesty I may be destined soon to appear), I now assert my innocence of plotting, abetting, or assisting, either by word or deed, the mutiny for which I am tried – for, young as I am, I am still younger in the school of art and such matured infamy. . . .

'If I am found worthy of life, it shall be improved by past experience, and especially taught from the serious lesson of what has lately happened; but if nothing but death itself can atone for my pitiable indiscretion, I bow with submission and all due respect to your impartial decision. . . .

'P. HEYWOOD.'

Mr. Morrison's Defence

Sets out by stating that he was waked at daylight by Mr. Cole the boatswain, who told him that the ship was taken by Christian; that he assisted in clearing out the boat at Mr. Cole's desire, and says, 'While I was thus employed Mr. Fryer came to me and asked if I had any hand in the mutiny; I told him No. He then desired me to see who I could find to assist me, and try to rescue the ship; I told him I feared it was then too late, but would do my endeavour; when John Millward, who stood by me, and heard what Mr. Fryer said, swore he would stand by me if an opportunity offered. Mr. Fryer was about to speak again, but was prevented by Matthew Quintal, who, with a pistol in one hand, collared him with the other, saying, "Come, Mr. Fryer, you must go down into your cabin"; and hauled him away. Churchill then came, and shaking his cutlass at me, demanded what Mr. Fryer said. I told him that he only asked me if they were going to have the longboat, upon which Alexander Smith (Adams), who stood on the opposite side of the boat, said, "It's a d—d lie, Charley, for I saw him and Millward shake hands when the master spoke to them." Churchill then said to me, "I would have you mind how you come on, for I have an eye upon you." Smith at the same time called out, "Stand to your arms, for they intend to make a rush." This, as it was intended, put the mutineers on their guard, and I found it necessary to be very cautious how I acted; and I heard Captain Bligh say to Smith, "I did not expect you would be against me, Smith"; but I could not hear what answer he made.'

He says that, while clearing the boat, he heard Christian order Churchill to see that no arms were put into her; to keep Norman, M'Intosh, and Coleman in the ship, and get the officers into the boat as fast as possible; that Mr. Fryer begged permission to stay, but to no purpose. 'On seeing Mr. Fryer and most of the officers going into the boat, without the least appearance of an effort to rescue the ship, I began to reflect on my own situation; and seeing the situation of the boat, and considering that she was at least a thousand leagues from any friendly settlement, and judging, from what I had seen of the Friendly Islanders but a few days before, that nothing could be expected from them but to be plundered or killed, and seeing no choice but of one evil, I chose, as I thought the least, to stay in the ship, especially as I considered it as obeying Captain Bligh's orders, and depending on his promise to do justice to those who remained. I informed Mr. Cole of my intention, who made me the like promise, taking me by the hand and saying, "God bless you, my boy; I will do you justice if ever I reach England."

'I also informed Mr. Hayward of my intention; and on his dropping a hint to me that he intended to knock Churchill down, I told him I would second him, pointing to some of the Friendly Island clubs which were sticking in the booms, and saying, "There were tools enough": but (he adds) I was suddenly damped to find that he went into the boat without making the attempt he had proposed.'

He then appeals to the members of the Court, as to the alternative they would themselves have taken:– 'A boat alongside, already crowded; those who were in her crying out she would sink; and Captain Bligh desiring no more might go in – with a slender stock of provisions, – what hope could there be to reach any friendly shore, or withstand the hostile attacks of the boisterous elements? The perils those underwent who reached the island of Timor, and whom nothing but the apparent interference of Divine Providence could have saved, fully justify my fears, and prove beyond a doubt that they rested on a solid foundation; for by staying in the ship, an opportunity might offer of escaping, but by going in the boat nothing but death appeared, either from the lingering torments of hunger and thirst, or from the murderous weapons of cruel savages, or being swallowed up by the deep.

'I have endeavoured,' he says, 'to recall to Mr. Hayward's remembrance a proposal he at one time made, by words, of attacking the mutineers, and of my encouraging him to the attempt, promising to back him. He says he has but a faint recollection of the business – so faint indeed that he cannot recall to his memory the particulars, but owns there was something passed to that effect. Faint, however, as his remembrance is (which for me is the more unfortunate), ought it not to do away all doubt with respect to the motives by which I was then influenced?' And, in conclusion, he says, 'I beg leave most humbly to remind the members of this honourable Court, that I did freely, and of my own accord, deliver myself up to Lieutenant Robert Corner, of H.M.S. *Pandora*, on the first certain notice of her arrival.'

William Muspratt's Defence

Declares his innocence of any participation in the mutiny; admits he assisted in hoisting out the boat; and in putting several articles into her; after which he sat down on the booms, when Millward came and mentioned to him Mr. Fryer's intention to rescue the ship, when he said he would stand by Mr. Fryer as far as he could; and with that intention, and for that purpose only, he took up a musket which one of the people had laid down, and which he quitted the moment he saw Bligh's people get into the boat. Solemnly denies the charge of Mr. Purcell against him, of handing liquor to the ship's company. Mr. Hayward's evidence, he trusts, must stand so impeached before the Court, as not to receive the least attention, when the lives of so many men are to be affected by it – for, he observes, he swears that Morrison was a mutineer, because he assisted in hoisting out the boats; and that M'Intosh was not a mutineer, notwithstanding he was precisely employed on the same business – that he criminated Morrison from the appearance of his countenance – that he had only a faint remembrance of that material and striking circumstance of Morrison offering to join him to retake the ship – that, in answer to his (Muspratt's) question respecting Captain Bligh's words, 'My lads, I'll do you justice' he considered them applied to the people in the boat, and not to those in the ship – to the same question put by the Court, he said they applied to persons remaining in the ship. And he notices some other instances which he thinks most materially affect Mr. Hayward's credit; and says, that if he had been under arms when Hayward swore he

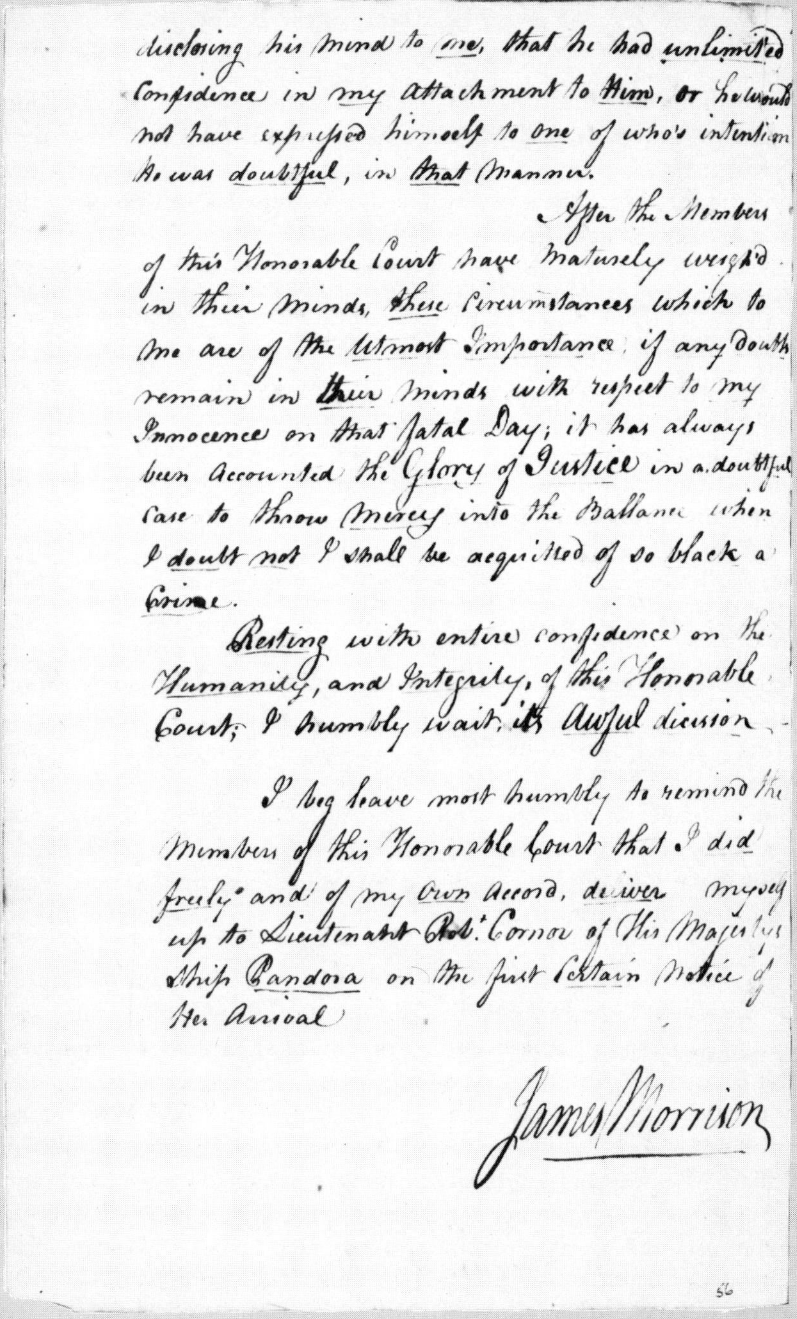

disclosing his mind to me, that he had unlimited
Confidence in my Attachment to Him, or he would
not have expressed himself to one of who's intention
he was doubtful, in that Manner.

After the Members
of this Honorable Court have maturely weigh'd
in their minds, these Circumstances which to
me are of the utmost Importance; if any doubt
remain in their minds with respect to my
Innocence on that fatal Day; it has always
been Accounted the Glory of Justice in a doubtful
Case to throw Mercy into the Ballance when
I doubt not I shall be acquitted of so black a
Crime.

Resting with entire confidence on the
Humanity, and Integrity, of this Honorable
Court; I humbly wait its Awful dicision —

I beg leave most humbly to remind the
Members of this Honorable Court that I did
freely and of my own Accord, deliver myself
up to Lieutenant Robt. Corner of His Majestys
Ship Pandora on the first Certain Notice of
Her Arrival

James Morrison

56

Minutes of the court-martial – Morrison's defence.
Contrary to Morrison's concluding statement that he delivered himself freely and of his
own accord to Lieutenant Corner of the *Pandora*, 'On the first Certain Notice of her
Arrival,' the evidence suggests that this was not the case. The *Pandora*'s boats chased the
mutineers' tender but could not catch it. Morrison sailed it *away* from the *Pandora* and
not towards her. Morrison was captured by Tahitians and handed over to Lieutenant
Corner the next day. His conduct, to say the least, made Captain Edwards highly
suspicious of his intentions. The court apparently agreed, and found him guilty – but for
some reason recommended mercy.

was, he humbly submits Mr. Hallet must have seen him. And he concludes with asserting (what indeed was a very general opinion), 'that the great misfortune attending this unhappy business is, that no one ever attempted to rescue the ship; that it might have been done, Thompson being the only sentinel over the arm-chest.'

Michael Byrne's Defence

was very short. He says, 'It has pleased the Almighty, among the events of His unsearchable providence, nearly to deprive me of sight, which often puts it out of my power to carry the intentions of my mind into execution.

'I make no doubt but it appears to this honourable Court, that on the 28th of April, 1789, my intention was to quit his Majesty's ship *Bounty* with the officers and men who went away, and that the sorrow I expressed at being detained was real and unfeigned.

'I do not know whether I may be able to repeat the exact words that were spoken on the occasion, but some said, "We must not part with our fiddler"; and Charles Churchill threatened to send me to the shades if I attempted to quit the cutter, into which I had gone for the purpose of attending Lieutenant Bligh'; and, without further trespassing on the time of the Court, he submits his case to its judgement and mercy.

It is not necessary to notice any parts of the defence made by Coleman, Norman, and M'Intosh, as it is clear, from the whole evidence and from Bligh's certificates, that those men were anxious to go in the boat, but were kept in the ship by force.

It is equally clear, that Ellison, Millward, and Burkitt, were concerned in every stage of the mutiny, and had little to offer in their defence in exculpation of the crime of which they were accused.

On the sixth day, namely, on the 18th of September, 1792, the Court met, – the prisoners were brought in, audience admitted, when the president, having asked the prisoners if they or any of them had anything more to offer in their defence, the Court was cleared, and agreed, –

'That the charges had been proved against the said Peter Heywood, James Morrison, Thomas Ellison, Thomas Burkitt, John Millward, and William Muspratt; and did adjudge them, and each of them, to suffer death, by being hanged by the neck, on board such of his Majesty's ship or ships of war, and at such time or times, and at such place or places, as the commissioners for executing the office of Lord High Admiral of Great Britain and Ireland, etc., or any three of them, for the time being, should, in writing, under their hands, direct; but the Court, in consideration of various circumstances, did humbly and most earnestly recommend the said Peter Heywood and James Morrison to his Majesty's mercy; and the Court further agreed, that the charges had not been proved against the said Charles Norman, Joseph Coleman, Thomas M'Intosh, and Michael Byrne, and did adjudge them, and each of them, to be acquitted.'

The Court was then opened and audience admitted, and sentence passed accordingly.

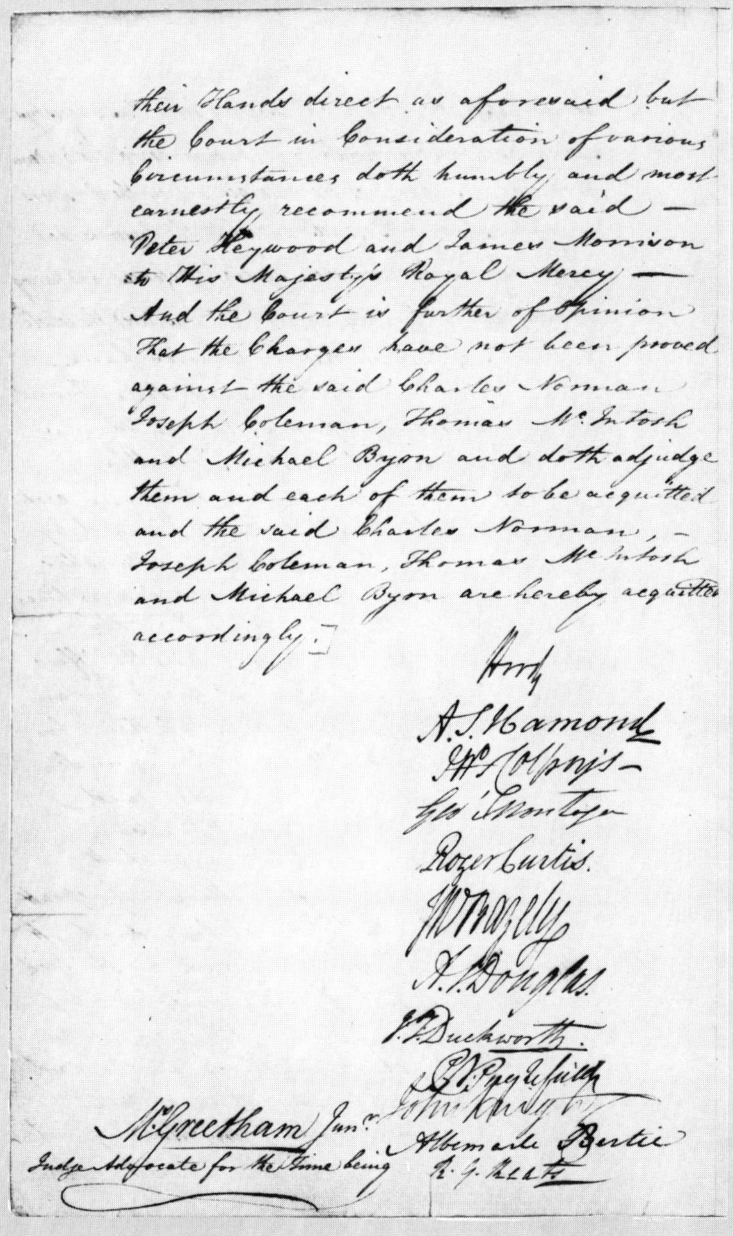

their Hands direct as aforesaid but
the Court in Consideration of various
Circumstances doth humbly and most
earnestly recommend the said —
Peter Heywood and James Morrison
to His Majesty's Royal Mercy —
And the Court is further of Opinion
That the Charges have not been proved
against the said Charles Norman
Joseph Coleman, Thomas McIntosh
and Michael Byrn and doth adjudge
them and each of them to be acquitted
and the said Charles Norman, —
Joseph Coleman, Thomas McIntosh
and Michael Byrn are hereby acquitted
accordingly.

Hood
A. S. Hamond
Jno. Colpoys
Geo. Montagu
Roger Curtis
J. Bazely
A. J. Douglas
J. T. Duckworth
J. N. Inglefield
John Knight
Albemarle Bertie
R. G. Keats

M. Greetham Junr.
Judge Advocate for the time being

Facsimile: the sentence of the court-martial.
Barrow suggests that Muspratt escaped execution because his conviction rested on the testimony of Lieutenant Hayward only. This is not the case. Immediately the court passed sentence, Muspratt presented an appeal on a legal technicality spotted by his astute lawyer. He had wanted to call in his defence the evidence of Byrne and Norman, but was prevented from doing so by the court's decision to try those men who were certain to be acquitted (on Bligh's written testimony) at the same time as those whose cases were open to doubt. Unable to call his witnesses, Muspratt claimed he had been denied a fair trial. His respite was due entirely to this technicality and not to any view the court may have had about Hayward. Both Cole and Fryer also testified against Muspratt. There is little doubt that on the evidence Muspratt was guilty of mutiny and desertion and that the court only allowed his appeal while legal opinion was consulted.

King George III

Britain's king, the third George from the German province of Hanover-Braunschweig, came to the throne when his grandfather died in 1760 – the crown prince having been killed in 1751 by a cricket ball. George III reigned throughout some of the most challenging years faced by Britain, particularly in her foreign affairs. The wars in Europe, maritime conflicts in many parts of the world, the loss of the American colonies and the great age of exploration, all coincided with his reign – as did the beginnings of the great industrial transformation that was to revolutionize the world even more profoundly than the constitutional changes in America and France.

CHAPTER SEVEN

The King's Warrant

It was a very common feeling that Heywood and Morrison, the former in particular, had been hardly dealt with by the Court in passing upon them a sentence of death, tempered as it was with the recommendation to the king's mercy. It should, however, have been recollected, that the Court had no discretional power to pass any other sentence but that, or a full acquittal. It is not enough in cases of mutiny (and this case was aggravated by the piratical seizure of a king's ship) that the officers and men in his Majesty's naval service should take no active part; – to be neutral or passive is considered as tantamount to aiding and abetting. Besides, in the present case, the remaining in the ship along with the mutineers, without having recourse to such means as offered of leaving her, presumes a voluntary adhesion to the criminal party. The only fault of Heywood, and a pardonable one on account of his youth, and inexperience, was his not asking Christian to be allowed to go with his captain, – his not *trying* to go in time. M'Intosh, Norman, Byrne, and Coleman were acquitted because they expressed a strong desire to go, but were forced to remain. This was not only clearly proved, but they were in possession of written testimonies from Bligh to that effect; and so would Heywood have had, but for some prejudice Bligh had taken against him, in the course of the boat-voyage home, for it will be shown that Bligh knew he was confined to his berth below.

In favour of three of the four men condemned without a recommendation, there were unhappily no palliating circumstances. Millward, Burkitt, and Ellison were under arms from first to last; and Ellison not only left the helm to take up arms, but, rushing aft towards Bligh, called out, 'D—n him, I'll be sentry over him.' The fourth man, Muspratt, was condemned on the evidence of Lieutenant Hayward. This, however, appears to have been duly appreciated by the Lords Commissioners of the Admiralty, and in consequence the poor man escaped an ignominious death. [Muspratt survived thanks to the skill of his lawyer, who spotted, and successfully exploited, a legal loophole created by the court's conduct of the trial. Muspratt entered a plea of wrongful conviction and gained a stay of execution: by the time the King's Bench sat, and ruled in his favour, Millward, Burkitt and Ellison had all been hanged.]

The family of young Heywood in the Isle of Man had been buoyed up, from various quarters, with the almost certainty of his full acquittal. From the 12th September, when the court-martial first sat, till the 24th of that month, they were prevented, by the strong and contrary winds which cut off all communication with England, from receiving any tidings whatever. But while Mrs. Heywood and her daughters were fondly flattering themselves

NEW INN AND ARDGLASS PACKET
OFFICE, PEEL.

with everything being most happily concluded, one evening, as they were indulging these pleasing hopes, a little boy, the son of one of their particular friends, ran into the room and told them, in the most abrupt manner, that the trial was over and all the prisoners condemned, but that Peter Heywood was recommended to mercy; he added that a man whose name he mentioned had told him this. The man was sent for, questioned, and replied he had seen it in a newspaper at Liverpool, from which place he was just arrived in a small fishing-boat, but had forgotten to bring the paper with him. In this state of doubtful uncertainty this wretched family remained another whole week, harassed by the most cruel agony of mind, which no language can express. The affectionate Nessy determined at once to proceed to Liverpool, and so on to London. She urges her brother James at Liverpool to hasten to Portsmouth: 'Don't wait for me, I can go alone; fear and even despair will support me through the journey; think only of our poor unfortunate and adored boy.' And she adds, 'yet, if I could listen to reason (which is indeed difficult), it is not likely that anything serious has taken place, or will do so, as we should then certainly have had an express.' She had a tempestuous passage of forty-nine hours, and to save two hours got into an open fishing-boat at the mouth of the Mersey, the sea running high and washing over her every moment. From Liverpool she set off the same night in the mail for London; and arrived at Mr. Graham's on the 5th October, who received her with the greatest kindness, and desired her to make his house her home.

The suspense into which the afflicted family in the Isle of Man had been thrown, by the delay of the packet, was painfully relieved on its arrival in the night of the 29th September, by the following letter from Mr. Graham to the Rev. Dr. Scott, which the latter carried to Mrs. Heywood's family the following morning.

New Inn and Ardglass Packet. (*left*)
The short but stormy passage from Douglas, Isle of Man, to Liverpool took Heywood's sister Nessy forty-nine hours in October 1792 when news of the trial's conclusion reached her on the island. Her indefatigable lobbying on Heywood's behalf continued until the Royal Pardon was issued. Her loyalty was extraordinary, her determination boundless, but of her letters and poems perhaps the least said the better.

View of Liverpool from across the River Mersey. (*below*)
Nessy arrived at Liverpool on 3 October and went on by the mail coach to London, where she arrived on the 5th. She stayed at Aaron Graham's house in Great Russell Street and it was from there that Peter Heywood wrote his 'anonymous' attack on Bligh within a few days of receiving the Royal Pardon for his part in the mutiny.

Captain Peter Heywood, painted in about 1820. (*overleaf*)
Heywood's defence at his court-martial rested on his youth, the innocence of himself and his messmate George Stewart, and the absence of any direct charges by Bligh against him in Bligh's written accounts. The evidence strongly indicates that Stewart played a far more culpable role than Heywood would ever admit to. Tom Ellison, only seventeen years old, was executed. He had no relatives among the judges: nor did he inherit £30,000 during the trial. Heywood's family connections managed to get the trial moved forward – so that the hearing would take place while Bligh was away in the *Providence* – knowing that Bligh's personal testimony would certainly hang him.

'*Portsmouth, Tuesday, 18th September*
'SIR, – Although a stranger, I make no apology in writing to you. I have attended and given my assistance at Mr. Heywood's trial, which was finished and the sentence passed about half an hour ago. Before I tell you what that sentence is, I must inform you that his life is safe, notwithstanding it is at present at the mercy of the king, to which he is in the strongest terms recommended by the Court. That any unnecessary fears may not be productive of misery to the family, I must add, that the king's attorney-general (who with Judge Ashurst attended the trial) desired me to make myself perfectly easy, for that my friend was as safe as if he had not been condemned. I would have avoided making use of this dreadful word, but it must have come to your knowledge, and perhaps unaccompanied by many others of a pleasing kind. To prevent its being improperly communicated to Mrs. or the Misses Heywood, whose distresses first engaged me in the business, and could not fail to call forth my best exertions upon the occasion, I send you this by express. The mode of communication I must leave to your discretion; and shall only add that, although from a combination of circumstances, ill-nature, and mistaken friendship, the sentence is in itself terrible, yet it is incumbent on me to assure you that, from the same combination of circumstances, everybody who attended the trial is perfectly satisfied in his own mind that he was *hardly guilty in appearance, in intention he was perfectly innocent.* I shall of course write to Commodore Pasley, whose mind, from my letter to him of yesterday, must be dreadfully agitated, and take his advice about what is to be done when Mr. Heywood is released. I shall stay here till then, and my intention is afterwards to take him to my house in town, where I think he had better stay till one of the family calls for him: for he will require a great deal of tender management after all his sufferings; and it would perhaps be a necessary preparation for seeing his mother, that one or both his sisters should be previously prepared to support her on so trying an occasion.'

On the following day Mr. Graham again writes to Dr. Scott, and among other things observes, 'It will be a great satisfaction to his family to learn, that the declarations of some of the other prisoners, since the trial, put it past all doubt that the evidence upon which he was convicted must have been (to say nothing worse of it) an unfortunate belief, on the part of the witness [presumably Hallet] of circumstances which either never had existence, or were applicable to one of the other gentlemen who remained in the ship, and not to Mr. Heywood.'

On the 20th September Mr. Heywood addresses the first letter he wrote, after his conviction, to Dr. Scott.

'HONOURED AND DEAR SIR, – On Wednesday the 12th instant the awful trial commenced, and on *that* day, *when in Court*, I had the pleasure of receiving your most kind and parental letter, in answer to which I now communicate to you the melancholy issue of it, which, as I desired my friend Mr. Graham to inform you of immediately, will be no dreadful news to you. On Tuesday morning the 18th the dreadful sentence of death was pronounced upon me, to which (being the just decree of that Divine Providence who first gave me breath) I bow my devoted head, with that fortitude, cheerfulness, and resignation, which is the duty of every member of the church of our blessed Saviour and Redeemer Christ Jesus.

'I have not been found guilty of the slightest act connected with that detestable crime of mutiny, but am doomed to die for not being active in my endeavours to suppress it. Could the witnesses who appeared on the Court-martial be themselves tried, *they* would also suffer for the very same and only crime of which I have been found guilty. But I am to be the victim. So far from repining at my fate, I receive it with a dreadful kind of joy, composure, and serenity of mind; well assured that it has pleased God to point me out as a subject through which some greatly useful (though at present unsearchable) intention of the divine attributes may be carried into execution for the future benefit of my country. Why should I be sorry to leave a world in which I have met with nothing but misfortunes and all their concomitant evils? I shall on the contrary endeavour to divest myself of all wishes for the futile and sublunary enjoyments of it, and prepare my soul for its reception into the bosom of its Redeemer. For though the very strong recommendation I have had to his Majesty's mercy by all the members of the Court may meet with his approbation, yet that is but the balance of a straw, a mere uncertainty, upon which no hope can be built; the other is a certainty that must one day happen to every mortal, and therefore the salvation of my soul requires my most prompt and powerful exertions during the short time I may have to remain on earth.

'As this is too tender a subject for me to inform my unhappy and distressed mother and sisters of, I trust, dear Sir, you will either show them this letter, or make known to them the truly dreadful intelligence in such a manner as (assisted by your wholesome and paternal advice) may enable them to bear it with Christian fortitude. . . .

'PETER HEYWOOD.'

His next letter is to his dearly beloved Nessy.

'Had I not a strong idea that, ere this mournful epistle from your ill-fated brother can reach the trembling hand of my ever dear and much afflicted Nessy, she must have been informed of the final issue of my trial on Wednesday morning, by my honoured friend Dr. Scott, I would not now add trouble to the afflicted by a confirmation of it. Though I have indeed fallen an early victim to the rigid rules of the service, and though the jaws of death are once more opened upon me, yet do I not now nor ever will bow to the tyranny of base-born fear.

'If earthly Majesty, to whose mercy I have been recommended by the Court, should refuse to put forth its lenient hand and rescue me from what is *fancifully* called an ignominious death, there is a heavenly King and Redeemer ready to receive the righteous penitent, on whose gracious mercy alone I, as we all should, depend, with that pious resignation which is the duty of every Christian.

'Oh! my sister, my heart yearns when I picture to myself the indescribable affliction which this melancholy intelligence must have caused in the mind of my much honoured mother. But let it be your peculiar endeavour to watch over her grief and mitigate her pain.

'I have had all my dear Nessy's letters; the one of the 17th this morning, but alas! what do they now avail? The contrast between last week's correspondence and this is great indeed; but why? we had only hope then; and have we not the same now? certainly. Endeavour then, my love, to cherish that hope, and with faith rely upon the mercy of that God who does as to Him seems best and most conducive to the general good of His miserable creatures.

'Bear it then with Christian patience, and instil into the mind of my dear and now sorrowful sisters, by your advice, the same disposition; and, for heaven's sake, let not despair touch the soul of my dear mother.'

In another letter to his dearest Nessy, who encourages him to take hope, he says, 'Alas! it is but a broken stick which *I* have leaned on, and it has pierced my soul in such a manner that I will never more trust to it, but wait with a contented mind and patience for the final accomplishment of the Divine will. . . . *Mrs. Hope* is a faithless and ungrateful acquaintance, with whom I have now broken off all connexions, and in her stead have endeavoured to cultivate a more sure friendship with *Resignation*, in full trust of finding her more constant.' . . .

To her sister Mary in the Isle of Man Nessy Heywood says, 'With respect to that little wretch Hallet, his intrepidity in court was astonishing; and after every evidence had spoken highly in Peter's favour, and given testimony of his innocence, so strong that not a doubt was entertained of his acquittal *he* declared, unasked, that while Bligh was upon deck, he (Hallet) saw him look at and speak to Peter. What he said to him Hallet could not hear, (being at the distance of twenty feet from Bligh, and Peter was twenty feet farther off, consequently a distance of forty feet separated Mr. Bligh and my brother); but he added that Peter, on *hearing* what Mr. Bligh said to him, *laughed* and turned contemptuously away. No other witness saw Peter laugh but Hallet; on the contrary, all agreed he wore a countenance on that day remarkably sorrowful; yet the effect of this cruel evidence was wonderful upon the minds of the Court, and they concluded by pronouncing the dreadful sentence, though at the same time accompanied by the strongest recommendation to mercy. Assure yourselves (I have it from Mr. Graham's own mouth), that Peter's honour is and will be as secure as his own; that every professional man, as well as every man of sense, of whatever denomination, does and will esteem him highly.'

From this time a daily correspondence passed between Peter Heywood and his sister Nessy, the latter indulging hope, even to a certainty, that she will not be deceived, – the other preaching up patience and resignation, with a full reliance on his innocence and integrity. 'Cheer up then,' says he, 'my dear Nessy; cherish *your hope*, and I will exercise *my patience*.' Indeed so perfectly calm was this young man under his dreadful calamity, that in a very few days after condemnation his brother says, 'While I write this, Peter is sitting by me making an Otaheitan vocabulary, and so happy and intent upon it, that I have scarcely an opportunity of saying a word to him; he is in excellent spirits, and I am convinced they are better and better every day.'

This vocabulary is a very extraordinary performance; it consists of one hundred full-written folio pages, the words alphabetically arranged, and all the syllables accented. It appears, from a passage in the *Voyage of the Duff*, that a copy of this vocabulary was of great use to the missionaries who were first sent to Otaheite in this ship.

During the delay which took place in carrying the sentence into execution, Commodore Pasley, Mr. Graham, and others, were indefatigable in their inquiries and exertions to ascertain what progress had been made in bringing to a happy issue the recommendation to the fountain of mercy: not less so was Nessy Heywood: from Mr. Graham she learnt what this excellent man considered to be the principal parts of the evidence that led to the conviction of her unhappy brother, which, having understood to be the following, she transmitted to her brother:–

First. That he assisted in hoisting out the launch.

Second. That he was seen by the carpenter resting his hand upon a cutlass.

Third. That on being called to by Lieutenant Bligh, he laughed.

Fourth. That he remained in the Bounty, instead of accompanying Bligh in the launch.

On these points of the evidence, Mr. Heywood made the following comments, which he sent from Portsmouth [on board the *Duke*] to his sister in town.

'*First. That I assisted in hoisting out the launch.* – This boat was asked for by the captain and his officers, and whoever assisted in hoisting her out were their friends; for if the captain had been sent away in the cutter (which was Christian's first intention), he could not have taken with him more than nine or ten men, whereas the launch carried nineteen.

'*Second. That I was seen by the carpenter resting my hand on a cutlass.* – I was seen in this position by no other person than the carpenter – no other person therefore could be intimidated by my appearance. Was the carpenter intimidated by it? – No. So far from being afraid of me, he did not even look upon me in the light of a person armed, but pointed out to me the danger there was of my being thought so, and I immediately took away my hand from the cutlass, upon which I had very innocently put it when I was in a state of stupor. . . .

'*Third. That, upon being called to by the captain, I laughed.* – If this was believed by the Court, it must have had, I am afraid, a very great effect upon its judgement; for, if viewed in too serious a light, it would seem to bring together and combine a number of trifling circumstances, which by themselves could only be treated merely as matters of suspicion. It was no doubt, therefore, received with caution, and considered with the utmost candour. The different ways of expressing our various passions are, with many, as variable as the features they wear. Tears have often been, nay generally are, the relief of excessive joy, while misery and dejection have, many a time, disguised themselves in a smile; and convulsive laughs have betrayed the anguish of an almost broken heart. To judge, therefore, the principles of the heart, by the barometer of the face, is as erroneous as it would be absurd and unjust. This matter may likewise be considered in another point of view. Mr. Hallet says I laughed in consequence of being called to by the captain, who was abaft the mizen-mast, while I was upon the platform near

The Tough old Commodore (Thomas Pasley).
Five years after the *Bounty* mutineers were tried, Vice-Admiral Thomas Pasley sat as
President of the Court at the court-martial of Richard Parker, leader of the Nore mutiny.
Pasley was a large, square-set man with a long bony nose and a face generally out of
symmetry – all of which is neatly captured in this cartoon by Thomas Rowlandson. (*c.*1790)

the fore-hatchway, a distance of more than thirty feet: if the captain intended I should hear him, and there can be no doubt that he wished it – if he really called to me, he must have exerted his voice, and very considerably too; and yet Mr. Hallet himself, who, by being on the quarter-deck, could not have been half the distance from the captain that I was, even he, I say, could not hear what was said to me: how then, in the name of God, was it possible that I should have heard the captain at all, situated, as I must have been, in the midst of noisy confusion? And if I did not hear him, which I most solemnly aver to be the truth, even granting that I laughed (which, however, in my present awful situation I declare I believe I did not), it could not have been at what the captain said. Upon this ground, then, I hope I shall stand acquitted of this charge, for if the crime derives its guilt from the knowledge I had of the captain's speaking to me, it follows, of course, that if I did not hear him speak, there could be no crime in my laughing.

[Later, while serving on the *Penelope*, Hallet is reliably reported to have frequently expressed deep contrition for having given evidence which he subsequently became convinced was incorrect. He claimed to have been confused when under examination in court and that during the alarm and confusion of the mutiny he must have 'confounded Heywood with some other person'.]

'*Fourth. That I remained on board the ship, instead of going in the boat with the captain.* – That I was at first alarmed and afraid of going into the boat I will not pretend to deny; but that afterwards I wished to accompany the captain, and should have done it, if I had not been prevented by Thompson, who confined me below by the order of Churchill, is clearly proved by the evidence of several of the witnesses. The boatswain says, that just before he left the ship I went below, and in passing him said something about a bag – (it was, that I would put a few things into a bag and follow him); the carpenter says he saw me go below at this time; and both those witnesses say that they heard the master-at-arms call to Thompson "*to keep them below.*" The point, therefore, will be to prove to whom this order, "*keeep them below,*" would apply. The boatswain and carpenter say they have no doubt of its meaning me as one; and that it must have been so, I shall have very little difficulty in showing, by the following statement:–

'There remained on board the ship after the boat put off, twenty-five men. Messrs. Hayward and Hallet have proved that the following were under arms:– Christian, Hillbrant, Millward, Burkitt, Muspratt, Ellison, Sumner, Smith, Young, Skinner, Churchill, M'Koy, Quintal, Morrison, Williams, Thompson, Mills, and Brown, in all eighteen. The master (and upon this occasion I may be allowed to quote from the captain's printed narrative) mentions Martin as one, which makes the number of armed men nineteen, none of whom, we may reasonably suppose, were ordered to be kept below. Indeed, Mr. Hayward says, that there were at the least eighteen of them upon deck, when he went into the boat; and if Thompson, the sentinel over the arm-chest, be added to them, it exactly agrees with the number above-named; there remains then six, to whom Churchill's order, "*keep them below*," might apply, namely, Heywood, Stewart, Coleman, Norman, M'Intosh and Byrne.

'Could Byrne have been one of them? *No*, for he was in the cutter alongside. Could Coleman have been one of them? *No*, for he was at the gangway when the captain and officers went into the launch, and aft upon the taffrail when the boat was veered astern. Could Norman have been one of them? *No*, for he was speaking to the officers. Could M'Intosh have been one of them? *No*, for he was with Coleman and Norman, desiring the captain and officers to take notice that they were not concerned in the mutiny. It could then have applied to nobody but to Mr. Stewart and myself; and by this order of Churchill, therefore, was I prevented from going with the captain in the boat.

'The foregoing appear to me the most material points of evidence on the part of the prosecution. My defence being very full, and the body of evidence in my favour too great to admit of observation in this concise manner, I shall refer for an opinion thereon to the minutes of the court-martial.

(signed) 'P. HEYWOOD.'

There is a note in Marshall's *Naval Biography*, furnished by Captain Heywood, which shows one motive for keeping him and Stewart in the ship. It is as follows:– 'Mr. Stewart was no sooner released than he demanded of Christian the reason of his detention; upon which the latter denied having given any directions to that effect; and his assertion was corroborated by Churchill, who declared that he had kept both him and Mr. Heywood below, knowing it was their intention to go away with Bligh; "in which case," added he, "what would become of us, if any thing should happen to you; who is there but yourself and them to depend upon in navigating the ship?"' It may be suspected, however, that neither Christian nor Churchill told the exact truth, and that Mr. Heywood's case is, in point of fact, much stronger than he ever could have imagined; and that if Bligh had not acted the part of a prejudiced and unfair man towards him, he would have been acquitted by the Court on the same ground that Coleman, Norman, M'Intosh, and Byrne were, – namely, that they were detained in the ship against their will, as stated by Bligh in the narrative on which they were tried, and also in his printed report. Many things are set down in Bligh's original manuscript journal, that have not appeared in any published document; and on this part of the subject there is, in the former, the following very important admission. 'As for the officers, whose cabins were in the cockpit, there was no relief for them; *they endeavoured to come to my assistance, but were not allowed to put their heads above the hatchway*.' To say, therefore, that in the suppression of this passage Bligh acted with prejudice and unfairness, is to make use of mild terms; it has more the appearance of a deliberate act of malice, by which two innocent men might have been condemned to suffer an ignominious death, one of whom was actually brought into this predicament; – the other only escaped it by a premature death. It may be asked, how did Bligh know that Stewart and Heywood endeavoured, but were not allowed, to come to his assistance? Confined as he was on the quarter-deck, how could he know what was going on below? The answer is, he must have known it from Christian himself; Churchill, no doubt, acted entirely by his leader's orders, and the latter could give no orders that were not heard by Bligh, whom he never left, but held the cord by which his hands were fettered, till he was forced into the boat. Churchill was quite right as to the motive of keeping these young officers; but Christian had no doubt another and a stronger motive: he knew how necessary it was to interpose a sort of barrier between himself and his mutinous gang; he was too good an adept not to know that seamen will always pay a more ready and cheerful obedience to officers who are *gentlemen,* than to those who may have risen to command from among themselves. It is indeed a common observation in the service, that officers who have risen from *before the mast* are generally the greatest tyrants. It was Bligh's misfortune not to have been educated in the cockpit of a man of war, among young gentlemen, which is to the navy what a public school is to those who are to move in civil society. What painful sufferings to the individual, and how much misery to an affectionate family might have been spared, had Bligh, instead of suppressing, only suffered the passage to stand as originally written in his journal!

The remarks of young Heywood above recited, were received and transmitted by his sister Nessy in a letter to the Earl of Chatham, then first Lord of the Admiralty, in which she says:–

'MY LORD, – To a nobleman of your lordship's known humanity and excellence of heart, I dare hope that the unfortunate cannot plead in vain. Deeply impressed as I therefore am, with sentiments of the most profound respect for a character which I have been ever taught to revere, and alas! nearly interested as I must be in the subject of these lines, may I request your lordship will generously pardon a sorrowful and mourning sister, for presuming to offer the enclosed (remarks) for your candid perusal. It contains a few observations made by my most unfortunate and tenderly beloved brother, Peter Heywood, endeavouring to elucidate some parts of the evidence given at the court-martial lately held at Portsmouth upon himself and other prisoners of his Majesty's ship *Bounty.* When I assure you, my lord, that he is dearer and more precious to me than any object on earth, I am persuaded you will not wonder, nor be offended, that I am thus bold in conjuring your lordship will consider, with your usual candour and benevolence, the "Observations" I now offer you.'

Whether this letter and its enclosure produced any effect on the mind of Lord Chatham does not appear; but no immediate steps were taken, nor was any answer given; and this amiable young lady and her friends were suffered to remain in the most painful state of suspense for another fortnight. A day or two before the warrant was despatched, that excellent man, Mr. Graham, writes to Mrs. Heywood:–

... 'The business, though not publicly known, is most certainly finished, and what I had my doubts about yesterday, I am satisfied of today. Happy, happy, happy family! accept of my congratulations – not for what it is in the power of words to express – but for what I know you will feel, upon being told that your beloved Peter will soon be restored to your bosom, with every virtue that can adorn a man, and ensure to him an affectionate, a tender, and truly welcome reception.' ...

View of the Admiralty, 1775.
The Old Admiralty, built by Thomas Ripley in 1722–1725, was surrounded by a high brick wall to prevent angry seamen breaking the windows in protest at arrears in their pay. The New Admiralty was added in 1786 as a residence for the First Lord and the First Secretary. The Adam screen facing Whitehall was built in 1760. In the Board Room with its beautiful dark oak panelling and high white ceiling the members of the Board of Admiralty conducted their business round a long mahogany table. The semaphore signalling system installed on the roof in 1796 enabled the Admiralty to communicate with Portsmouth and Chatham in about ten minutes.

On the 24th October, the king's warrant was despatched from the Admiralty, granting a full and free pardon to Heywood and Morrison, a respite for Muspratt, which was followed by a pardon; and for carrying the sentence of Ellison, Burkitt, and Millward into execution, which was done on the 29th, on board his Majesty's ship *Brunswick*, in Portsmouth harbour. On this melancholy occasion, Captain Hamond reports that 'the criminals behaved with great penitence and decorum, acknowledged the justice of their sentence for the crime of which they had been found guilty, and exhorted their fellow-sailors to take warning by their untimely fate, and whatever might be their hardships, never to forget their obedience to their officers, as a duty they owed to their king and country.' The captain adds, 'A party from each ship in the harbour, and at Spithead, attended the execution, and from the reports I have received, the example seems to have made a great impression upon the minds of all the ships' companies present.'

The same warrant that carried with it affliction to the friends of these unfortunate men, was the harbinger of joy to the family and friends of young Heywood. The happy intelligence was communicated to his affectionate Nessy on the 26th, who instantly despatched the joyful tidings to her anxious mother in the following characteristic note:–

'*Friday, 26th October, four o'clock.*

'Oh, blessed hour! – little did I think, my beloved friends, when I closed my letter this morning, that before night I should be out of my senses with joy! – this moment, this ecstatic moment, brought the enclosed [Information that the pardon was gone down to Portsmouth]. I cannot speak my happiness; let it be sufficient to say, that in a very few hours our angel Peter will be FREE! Mr. Graham goes this night to Portsmouth, and to-morrow, or next day at farthest, I shall be – oh, heavens! what shall I be? I am already transported, even to pain: then how shall I bear to clasp him to the bosom of your happy, ah! how very happy, and affectionate

'NESSY HEYWOOD.'

Nessy Heywood did not long survive her brother's liberty. This impassioned and most affectionate of sisters, with an excess of sensibility, which acted too powerfully on her bodily frame, sunk, as is often the case with such susceptible minds, on the first attack of consumption. She died within the year of her brother's liberation. On this occasion the following note from her afflicted mother appears among the papers from which the letters are taken. 'My dearest Nessy was seized, while on a visit at Major Yorke's, at Bishop's Grove near Tonbridge Wells, with a violent cold, and not taking proper care of herself, it soon turned to inflammation on her lungs, which carried her off at Hastings, to which place she was taken on the 5th September, to try if the change of air, and being near the sea, would recover her; but alas! it was too late for her to receive the wished for benefit, and she died there on the 25th of the same month 1793, and has left her only surviving parent a disconsolate mother, to lament, while ever she lives, with the most sincere and deep affliction, the irreparable loss of her most valuable, affectionate, and darling daughter.'

George John, 2nd Earl Spencer: First Lord of the Admiralty.
Spencer held the office of First Lord from 1794 to 1801, the year in which this painting by
J. S. Copley was made. His appointment was largely political but he developed into a very
successful First Lord. He presided over the Admiralty during the mutinies of 1797, and was
one of those in favor of making concessions to the seamen. In 1817 he became the 5th
Duke of Marlborough – the great-great-grandfather of Sir Winston Churchill (1874–1965).

But to return to Mr. Heywood. When the king's full and free pardon had been read to this young officer by Captain Montagu, with a suitable admonition and congratulation, he addressed that officer in the following terms:—

'SIR, – When the sentence of the law was passed upon me, I received it, I trust, as became a man; and if it had been carried into execution, I should have met my fate, I hope, in a manner becoming a Christian. Your admonition cannot fail to make a lasting impression on my mind. I receive with gratitude my sovereign's mercy, for which my future life shall be faithfully devoted to his service.' . . .

And well did his future conduct fulfil that promise. Notwithstanding the inauspicious manner in which the first five years of his servitude in the navy had been passed, two of which were spent among mutineers and savages, and eighteen months as a close prisoner in irons, in which condition he was shipwrecked, and within an ace of perishing, – notwithstanding this unpromising commencement, he re-entered the naval service under the auspices of his uncle, Commodore Pasley, and Lord Hood, who presided at his trial, and who earnestly recommended him to embark again as a midshipman without delay, offering to take him into the *Victory*, under his own immediate patronage. In the course of his service, to qualify for the commission of lieutenant, he was under the respective commands of three or four distinguished officers, who had sat on his trial, from all of whom he received the most flattering proofs of esteem and approbation. To the application of Sir Thomas Pasley to Lord Spencer for his promotion, that nobleman gave the following reply:—

'*Admiralty, Jan. 13th,* 1797.
'SIR, – I should have returned an earlier answer to your letter of the 6th instant, if I had not been desirous, before I answered it, to look over, with as much attention as was in my power, the proceedings on the Court-Martial held in the year 1792, by which Court Mr. Peter Heywood was condemned for being concerned in the mutiny on board the *Bounty*. I felt this to be necessary, from having entertained a very strong opinion that it might be detrimental to the interests of his Majesty's service, if a person under such a predicament should be afterwards advanced to the higher and more conspicuous situations of the navy; but having, with great attention, perused the minutes of that Court-Martial, as far as they relate to Mr. Peter Heywood, I have now the satisfaction of being able to inform you, that I think his case was such an one, as, under all its circumstances (though I do not mean to say that the Court were not justified in their sentence), ought not to be considered as a bar to his further progress in his profession; more especially when the gallantry and propriety of his conduct, in his subsequent service, are taken into consideration. I shall, therefore, have no difficulty in mentioning him to the commander-in-chief on the station to which he belongs, as a person from whose promotion, on a proper opportunity, I shall derive much satisfaction, more particularly from his being so nearly connected with you. – I have the honour to be, etc.
(Signed) 'SPENCER.'

It is not here intended to follow Mr. Heywood through his honourable career of service, during the long and arduous contest with France, and in the several commands with which he was entrusted. In a note of his own writing it is stated, that on paying off the *Montague*, in July, 1816, he came on shore, after having been actively employed *at sea* twenty-seven years, six months, one week, and five days, out of a servitude in the navy of twenty-nine years, seven months, and one day. Having reached nearly the top of the list of captains, he died in this present year [1831], leaving behind him a high and unblemished character in that service, of which he was a most honourable, intelligent, and distinguished member.

Peter Heywood
On 17 September 1792, when Heywood was on trial for his life, the following statement was read out to the court as part of his defense. 'Captain Bligh in his 'Narrative' acknowledges that he left some friends on board the 'Bounty', and no part of my Conduct could have induced him to believe that I ought not to be reckoned of that Number. Indeed, from his attention to and very kind treatment of me personally, I should have been a monster of depravity to have betray'd him. The Idea alone is sufficient to disturb a mind where humanity and gratitude have, I hope, ever been noticed as its Characteristic features . . .' (Minutes of the Court). On 5 November 1792, just one week after his Royal Pardon, this same man wrote to Edward Christian, Fletcher's brother, 'Sir, if it would not be disagreeable to you, I will myself have the pleasure of waiting on you, and endeavour to prove that your brother was not the vile wretch void of all gratitude, which the world had the unkindness to think of him: but, on the contrary, a most worthy character; ruined by having the misfortune, if it can be so called, of being a young man of strict honour, adorned with every virtue, and beloved by all (except one, whose ill report is his greatest praise) who had the pleasure of his acquaintance.' Taken together, the two statements shed a good deal of light on Heywood's character – and a shadow over his supposed innocence.

Captain Mayhew Folger
The Folgers were a prominent New England whaling and seafaring family and Captain
Mayhew Folger and his close friend Captain Amaso Delano discussed the fate of the
Bounty mutineers over many years, little knowing that Folger would himself solve the
mystery almost twenty years after Christian sailed away from Tahiti for the last time.
Adams presented Folger with the *Bounty*'s azimuth compass, which he passed on to the
Royal Navy in 1813. Folger's own grandson rose to the rank of Rear-Admiral in the
United States Navy.

CHAPTER EIGHT

The Last of the Mutineers

Twenty years had passed away, and the Bounty, and Fletcher Christian, and the piratical crew that he had carried off with him in that ship, had long ceased to occupy a thought in the public mind. Throughout the whole of that eventful period, the attention of all Europe had been absorbed in the contemplation of the revolutions of empires – the bustle and business of warlike preparations – the movements of hostile armies – battles by sea and land, and of all 'the pomp and circumstance of glorious war'. If the subject of the *Bounty* was accidentally mentioned, it was merely to express an opinion that this vessel, and those within her, had gone down to the bottom, or that some savage islanders had inflicted on the mutineers that measure of retribution so justly due to their crime. It happened, however, some years before the conclusion of this war of unexampled duration, that an interesting discovery was brought to light, in consequence of an American trading vessel having by mere chance approached one of those numerous islands in the Pacific, against whose steep and iron-bound shores the surf rolls with such tremendous violence, as to bid defiance to any attempt of boats to land, except at particular times and in very few places.

The first intimation of this extraordinary discovery was transmitted by Sir Sydney Smith from Rio de Janeiro, and received at the Admiralty, 14th May, 1809. It was conveyed to him from Valparaiso by Lieutenant Fitzmaurice, and was as follows:–

'Captain Folger, of the American ship *Topaz*, of Boston, relates that upon landing on Pitcairn's Island, in lat. 25° 2′ S., long. 130° W., he found there an Englishman of the name of Alexander Smith, the only person remaining of nine that escaped in his Majesty's late ship *Bounty*, Captain W. Bligh. Smith relates that, after putting Captain Bligh in the boat, Christian, the leader of the mutiny, took command of the ship and went to Otaheite, where the great part of the crew left her, except Christian, Smith, and seven others, who each took wives and six Otaheitan menservants, and shortly after arrived at the said island (Pitcairn), where they ran the ship on shore, and broke her up; this event took place in the year 1790.

'About four years after their arrival (a great jealousy existing), the Otaheitans secretly revolted, and killed every Englishman except himself whom they severely wounded in the neck with a pistol ball. The same night, the widows of the deceased Englishmen arose and put to death the whole of the Otaheitans, leaving Smith, the only man alive upon the island, with eight or nine women and several small children. On his recovery, he applied himself to tilling the ground, so that it now produces plenty of yams, cocoa-nuts, bananas, and plantains; hogs and poultry in abundance. There are now some grown-up men and women, children of the mutineers, on the island, the whole population amounting to about thirty-five, who acknowledge Smith as father and commander of them all; they all speak English, and have been educated by him (as Captain Folger represents) in a religious and moral way.

'The second mate of the *Topaz* asserts that Christian, the ringleader, became insane shortly after their arrival on the island, and threw himself off the rocks into the sea; another died of a fever before the massacre of the remaining six took place. The island is badly supplied with water, sufficient only for the present inhabitants, and no anchorage.

'Smith gave to Captain Folger a chronometer made by Kendall, which was taken from him by the Governor of Juan Fernandez.
'Extracted from the log-book of the *Topaz*, 29th Sept. 1808.
(Signed) 'WM. FITZMAURICE, Lieut.
'*Valparaiso, Oct. 10th, 1808.*'

This narrative stated two facts that established its general authenticity – the name of Alexander Smith, who was one of the mutineers, and the name of the maker of the chronometer, with which the *Bounty* was actually supplied. Interesting as this discovery was considered to be, it does not appear that any steps were taken in consequence, the government being at that time probably too much engaged in the events of the war; nor was anything further heard of this interesting little society, until the latter part of 1814, when a letter was transmitted by Rear Admiral Hotham, then cruising

---

Kendal's K2 Marine Timekeeper.
Larcum Kendal (1721–1795) made this timekeeper for the Board of Longitude in 1771 at a price of £200. In 1773 it was used by Phipps in the Polar expedition and for some years it was used by the Royal Navy on the North American station. Bligh took it with him in 1787: Christian took it to Pitcairn, and Adams gave it to Folger in 1808. Subsequently it was stolen by the Governor of Juan Fernandez. It next appeared in Concepcion, Chile, where it was sold for three doubloons to one Sr Castillo, whose family sold it to Captain (later Rear-Admiral Sir Thomas) Herbert of the *Calliope* for fifty guineas in 1840.

Facsimile: Log of the *Topaz*, 6 February 1808.
The *Topaz* left Boston on 5 April 1807 on a sealing voyage, touching at the Cape Verde Islands, Trinidad, Kerguelen and Adventure Bay, Tasmania. William Bligh was by this time Governor of New South Wales and about to be ousted, again, by the so-called Rum Corps in a coup engineered by John Macarthur. The *Topaz* left Tasmania for the Pacific in November 1807, and after calling at the Chatham and Pitt Islands arrived off Pitcairn Island in February. It was not the first ship to pass the island: the first had been seen as early as December 1795. Others had also passed by and one had even landed a boat party, but prior to the arrival of the *Topaz* no contact had been made with the fugitives hiding on the island.

On a Sealing Voyage to the South Pacific Ocean 1823

off the coast of America, from Mr. Folger himself, to the same effect as the preceding extract from his log, but dated March, 1813.

In the first-mentioned year (1814) we had two frigates cruising in the Pacific, – the *Briton*, commanded by Sir Thomas Staines, and the *Tagus*, by Captain Pipon. The following letter from the former of these officers was received at the Admiralty early in the year 1815.

'*Briton, Valparaiso, 18th Oct.*, 1814.

'I have the honour to inform you that on my passage from the Marquesas islands to this port, on the morning of the 17th September, I fell in with an island where none is laid down in the Admiralty or other charts, according to the several chronometers of the *Briton* and *Tagus*. I therefore hove to, until day-light, and then closed to ascertain whether it was inhabited, which I soon discovered it to be, and, to my great astonishment, found that every individual on the island (forty in number), spoke very good English. They proved to be the descendants of the deluded crew of the *Bounty*, who, from Otaheite, proceeded to the above-mentioned island, where the ship was burnt.

'Christian appeared to have been the leader and sole cause of the mutiny in that ship. A venerable old man, named John Adams, is the only surviving Eng-lishman of those who last quitted Otaheite in her, and whose exemplary con-duct, and fatherly care of the whole of the little colony, could not but command admiration. The pious manner in which all those born on the island have been reared, the correct sense of religion which has been instilled into their young minds by this old man, has given him the pre-eminence over the whole of them, to whom they look up as the father of one and the whole family.

'A son of Christian was the first born on the island, now about twenty-five years of age, named Thursday October Christian; the elder Christian fell a sacrifice to the jealousy of an Otaheitan man, within three or four years after their arrival on the island. The mutineers were accompanied thither by six Otaheitan men and twelve women; the former were all swept away by desperate contentions between them and the Englishmen, and five of the latter died at different periods, leaving at present only one man (Adams) and seven women of the original settlers.

'The island must undoubtedly be that called Pitcairn, although erroneously laid down in the charts. We had the altitude of the meridian sun close to it, which gave us 25° 4′ S. latitude, and 130° 25′ W. longitude, by the chronometers of the *Briton* and *Tagus*.

'It produces in abundance yams, plantains, hogs, goats, and fowls; but the coast affords no shelter for a ship or vessel of any description; neither could a ship water there without great difficulty.

'I cannot, however, refrain from offering my opinion, that it is well worthy the attention of our laudable religious societies, particularly that for propaga-ting the Christian religion, the whole of the inhabitants speaking the Otaheitan tongue as well as the English.

'During the whole of the time they have been on the island, only one ship has ever communicated with them, which took place about six years since, and this was the American ship *Topaz*, of Boston, Mayhew Folger, master.

'The island is completely iron-bound with rocky shores, and the landing in boats must be at all times difficult, although the island may be safely approached within a short distance by a ship.

(Signed) 'T. STAINES.'

Such was the first official account received of this little colony. As some further particulars of a society so singular, in all respects, were highly desirable, Captain Pipon, on being applied to, had the kindness to draw up the following narrative, which has all the freshness and attraction of a first communication with a new people.

Captain Pipon observes, that when they first saw the island, the latitude, made by the *Tagus*, was 24° 40′ S. and longitude 130° 24′ W., the ships being then distant from it five or six leagues; and, as in none of the charts in their possession was any land laid down in or near this meridian, they were extremely puzzled to make out what island it could possibly be; for Pitcairn's Island, being the only one known in the neighbourhood, was represented to be in longitude 133° 24′ W. If this new discovery as they supposed it to be, awakened their curiosity, it was still more excited when they ran in for the land the next morning, on perceiving a few huts, neatly built, amidst plantations laid out apparently with something like order and regularity; and these appearances confirmed them more than ever that it could not be Pitcairn's Island, because that was described by navigators to be uninhabited. Presently they observed a few natives coming down a steep descent with their canoes on their shoulders; and in a few minutes perceived one of those little vessels darting through a heavy surf, and paddling off towards the ships; but their astonishment was extreme when, on coming alongside, they were hailed in the English language, with 'Won't you heave us a rope now?'

The first young man that sprang, with extraordinary alacrity, up the side, and stood before them on the deck, said, in reply to the question, 'Who are you?' – that his name was Thursday October Christian, son of the late Fletcher Christian, by an Otaheitan mother; that he was the first born on the island, and that he was so called because he was brought into the world on a Thursday in October. Singularly strange as all this was to Sir Thomas Staines and Captain Pipon, this youth soon satisfied them that he was no other than the person he represented himself to be, and that he was fully acquainted with the whole history of the *Bounty*; and, in short, that the island before them was the retreat of the mutineers of that ship. Young Christian was, at this time, about twenty-four years of age, a fine tall youth, full six feet high, with dark, almost black, hair, and a countenance open and extremely interesting. As he wore no clothes except a piece of cloth round his loins, and a straw hat, ornamented with black cocks'-feathers, his fine figure and well-shaped muscular limbs were displayed to great advantage, and attracted general admiration. His body was much tanned by exposure to the weather, and his countenance had a brownish cast, unmixed however with that tinge of red so common among the natives of the Pacific islands.

'Added to a great share of good humour, we were glad to trace,' says Captain Pipon, 'in his benevolent countenance, all the features of an honest English face.' He told them he was married to a woman much older than himself, one of those that accompanied his father from Otaheite. The ingenuous manner in which he answered all questions put to him, and his whole deportment, created a lively interest among the officers of the ship, who, while they admired, could not but regard him with feelings of tenderness and compassion; his manner, too, of speaking English was exceedingly pleasing, and correct both in grammar and pronunciation. His companion was a fine handsome youth of seventeen or eighteen years of age, of the name of George Young, son of Young the midshipman.

Great was the astonishment of the two captains when, on Sir Thomas Staines taking the two youths below, and setting before them something to eat, they both rose up, and one of them, placing his hands together in a posture of devotion, pronounced, distinctly and with emphasis, in a pleasing tone of voice, the words, 'For what we are going to receive the Lord make us truly thankful.'

The youths were themselves greatly surprised at the sight of so many novel objects – the size of the ship – of the guns, and everything around them. Observing a cow, they were at first somewhat alarmed, and expressed a doubt whether it was a huge goat or a horned hog, these being the only two species of quadrupeds they had ever seen. A little dog amused them much. 'Oh! what a pretty little thing it is!' exclaimed Young, 'I know it is a dog, for I have heard of such an animal.'

These young men informed the two captains of many singular events that had taken place among the first settlers, but referred them for further particulars to an old man on shore, whose name, they said, was John Adams, the only surviving Englishman that came away in the *Bounty*, at which time he was called Alexander Smith.

This information induced the two captains to go on shore, desirous of learning correctly from this old man the fate, not only of Christian, but of the rest of his deluded accomplices, who had adhered to his fortunes. With the assistance of their two able conductors, they passed the surf among many rocks, and reached the shore without any other inconvenience than a complete wetting. Old Adams, having ascertained that the two officers alone had landed, and without arms, concluded they had no intention to take him prisoner, and ventured to come down to the beach, from whence he conducted them to his house. He was accompanied by his wife, a very old woman, and nearly blind. It seems they were both at first considerably alarmed; the sight of the king's uniform, after so many years, having no doubt brought fresh to the recollection of Adams the scene that occurred in the *Bounty*, in which he bore so conspicuous a part. Sir Thomas Staines, however, to set his mind at ease, assured him, that so far from having come to the island with any intention to take him away, they were not even aware that such a person as himself existed. Captain Pipon observes, 'that although in the eye of the law they could only consider him in the light of a criminal of the deepest dye, yet that it would have been an act of the greatest cruelty and inhumanity to have taken him away from his little family, who, in such a case, would have been left to experience the greatest misery and

Friday October Christian

Fletcher Christian's son by his marriage to 'Isabella' (named after his aunt Isabella Curwen) or 'Mauatua' (her native name, meaning mainmast because of her height and posture), was about twenty-five years old when this sketch was made. He would have been about three years of age when the massacres took place in around 1793. He had a brother Charles and a sister Mary. Christian first named his son 'Thursday' but the young man later changed this to 'Friday' when the Pitcairners discovered they were a day out in their calendar.

John Adams

Adams was born in 1767 in the Parish of St John, Hackney, to John and Dinah Adams. His father appears to have come from Ulster, and certainly Ireland was familiar, at least as a name, to the children born on Pitcairn. The three boys who came out to meet Folger, on being told he was American, asked, 'Where is America? Is it in Ireland?' Of Adams's role in the bloody massacres on Pitcairn, much remains unexplained. Certainly he was not the innocent bystander he claimed to be to Captains Staines and Pipon. He lied about his role in the mutiny, changed his story of Christian's death at least three times, and admitted to at least one murder – that of Matthew Quintal in 1799. Nevertheless he convinced all visitors of his total redemption.

distress, and ultimately, in all probability, would have perished of want.'

Adams, however, pretended that he had no great share in the mutiny: said that he was sick in bed when it broke out, and was afterwards compelled to take a musket in his hand; and expressed his readiness to go in one of the ships to England, and seemed rather desirous to do so. On this being made known to the members of the little society, a scene of considerable distress was witnessed; his daughter, a fine young woman, threw her arms about his neck, entreating him not to think of leaving them and all his little children to perish. All the women burst into tears, and the young men stood motionless and absorbed in grief; but on their being assured that he should, on no account, be molested, 'it is impossible,' says Captain Pipon, 'to describe the universal joy that these poor people manifested, and the gratitude they expressed for the kindness and consideration shown to them.'

They now learned from Adams that Fletcher Christian, on finding no good anchorage close to the island, and the *Bounty* being too weakly manned again to entrust themselves in her at sea, determined to run her into a small creek against the cliff, in order the more conveniently to get out of her such articles as might be of use for forming an establishment on the island, and to land the hogs, goats, and poultry, which they had brought from Otaheite. He then ordered her to be set on fire, with the view, probably, of preventing any escape from the island, and also to remove an object that, if seen, might be the means of discovering his retreat. His plan succeeded, and by Adams's account, everything went on smoothly for a short time; but it was clear enough that this misguided and ill-fated young man was never happy after the rash and criminal step he had taken; that he was always sullen and morose; and committed so many acts of wanton oppression, as very soon incurred the hatred and detestation of his companions in crime, over whom he practised that same overbearing conduct, of which he accused his commander Bligh.

The fate of this misguided young man, brought on by his ill-treatment both of his associates and the Indians he had carried off with him, was such as might be expected – he was shot by an Otaheitan while digging in his field, about eleven months after they had settled on the island, and his death was only the commencement of feuds and assassinations, which ended in the total destruction of the whole party, except Adams and Young. By the account of the former, the settlers from this time became divided into two parties, and their grievances and quarrels proceeded to such a height, that each took every opportunity of putting the other to death. Old John Adams was himself shot through the neck, but the ball having entered the fleshy part only, he was enabled to make his escape, and avoid the fury of his assailants. The immediate cause of Christian's murder was his having forcibly seized on the wife of one of the Otaheite men, which so exasperated the rest, that they not only sought the life of the offender, but of others also, who might, as they thought, be disposed to pursue the same course.

This interesting little colony was now found to contain about forty-six persons, mostly grown-up young people, with a few infants. The young men all born on the island were finely formed, athletic and handsome – their countenances open and pleasing, indicating much benevolence and goodness of heart, but the young women particularly were objects of attraction, being tall, robust, and beautifully formed, their faces beaming with smiles, and indicating unruffled good humour; while their manners and demeanour would have done honour to the most enlightened people on earth.

But their personal qualifications, attractive as they were, excited less admiration than the account which Adams gave of their virtuous conduct. He assured his visitors that not one instance of debauchery or immoral conduct had occurred among these young people, since their settlement on the island; nor did he ever hear, or believe, that any one instance had occurred of a young woman having suffered indecent liberties to be taken with her. Their native modesty, assisted by the precepts of religion and morality, instilled into their young minds by John Adams, had hitherto preserved these interesting people from every kind of debauchery. The young women told Captain Pipon, with great simplicity, that they were not married, and that their father, as they called Adams, had told them it was right they should wait with patience till they had acquired sufficient property to bring up a young family, before they thought of marrying; and that they always followed his advice because they knew it to be good.

It appeared that, from the time when Adams was left the sole survivor of all the males that had landed from the *Bounty*, the greatest harmony had prevailed in their little society; they all declared that no serious quarrels ever occurred among them, though a few hasty words might now and then be uttered. Adams assured his visitors that they were all strictly honest in all their dealings, lending or exchanging their various articles of live-stock or produce with each other, in the most friendly manner; and if any little dispute occurred, he never found any difficulty to rectify the mistake or misunderstanding that might have caused it, to the satisfaction of both parties. In their general intercourse they speak the English language commonly; and even the old Otaheitan women have picked up a good deal of this language. The young people, both male and female, speak it with a pleasing accent, and their voices are extremely harmonious.

The little village of Pitcairn is described as forming a pretty square; the house of John Adams, with its out-houses, occupying the upper corner, near a large banyan tree, and that of Thursday October Christian the lower corner opposite to it. The centre space is a fine open lawn, where the poultry wander, and is fenced round so as to prevent the intrusion of the hogs and goats. It was obviously visible, from the manner in which the grounds were laid out, and the plantations formed, that the labour and ingenuity of European hands had been employed. In their houses they have a good deal of decent furniture, consisting of beds and bedsteads, with coverings. They have also tables and large chests for their clothing; and their linen is made from the bark of a certain tree, and the manufacture of it is the employment of the elderly portion of the women. The bark is first soaked, then beaten with square pieces of wood, of the breadth of one's hand, hollowed out into grooves, and the labour is continued until it is brought to the breadth required, in the same manner as the process is conducted in Otaheite.

The younger part of the females are obliged to attend, with old Adams and their brothers, to the culture of the land, and Captain Pipon thinks this may be one reason why this old director of the work does not countenance too early marriages, for, as he very properly observed, when once they become mothers, they are less capable of hard labour, being obliged to attend to their children; and, judging from appearance, 'one may conclude,' says the Captain, 'they would be prolific'; that 'he did not see how it could be otherwise, considering the regularity of their lives, their simple and excellent though abstemious mode of living, their meals consisting chiefly of a vegetable diet, with now and then good pork and occasionally fish.'

The young girls are modestly clothed, having generally a piece of cloth of their own manufacture, reaching from the waist to the knees, and a mantle, or something of that nature, thrown loosely over the shoulders, and hanging sometimes as low as the ankles: this mantle, however, is frequently thrown aside, being used rather as a shelter for their bodies from the heat of the sun, or the severity of the weather, than for the sake of attaching any idea of modesty to the upper part of the person being uncovered; and it is not possible, he says, to behold finer forms than are exhibited by this partial exposure. . . .

'But,' says Captain Pipon, 'what delighted us most, was the conviction which John Adams had impressed on the minds of these young people, of the propriety and necessity of returning thanks to the Almighty for the many

---

Landing in Bounty Bay.
The extreme difficulty of landing a boat safely at Pitcairn Island made it an ideal refuge for the mutineers. The *Bounty* was burned, and finally sank, in this little bay. In 1957 Luis Marden of *National Geographic* salvaged pieces of the ship and found one of the anchors. The *Bounty*'s boats were saved from the wreck and John Williams threatened to put to sea in one of them unless he was given someone else's wife. The women tried to build a boat of their own in 1794, but it sank in the bay and it was not until after 1795 that the first canoes were constructed for inshore fishing.

Interior of Pitcairn Island.
The group of figures in the foreground clearly shows John Adams in his sailor's dress, which by 1825 was thirty-five years old. After the death of Young on Christmas Day 1800, Adams was the sole surviving adult male on the island and for a number of years afterwards he lived promiscuously with the eight Tahitian women. In the background of this sketch is the hill where Christian's cave was located and to which he often retreated for several days at a time.

blessings they enjoy. They never omit saying grace before and after meals, and the Lord's Prayer and the Creed they repeat morning and evening.'

The visitors having supplied these poor people with some tools, kettles, and other articles such as the high surf would allow them to land, took leave of these interesting people – satisfied that the island is so well fortified by nature, as to oppose an invincible barrier to an invading enemy; that there was no spot apparently where a boat could land with safety, and perhaps not more than one where it could land at all through the everlasting swell of the ocean.

It may here be remarked that, at the time when Folger visited the island, Alexander Smith went by his proper name, and that he had changed it to John Adams in the intermediate time between Folger's visit and that of Sir Thomas Staines; but it does not appear when or for what reason he assumed the latter name. It could not be with any view to concealment, for he freely communicated his history to Folger, and equally so to every subsequent visitor.

The interesting account of Captains Sir Thomas Staines and Pipon, in 1814, produced as little effect on the government as that of Folger; and nothing more was heard of Adams and his family for twelve years nearly, when, in 1825, Captain Beechey, in the *Blossom*, bound on a voyage of discovery, paid a visit to Pitcairn's Island. Some whale-fishing ship, however, had touched there in the intermediate time, and left on the island a person of the name of John Buffet. 'In this man,' says Captain Beechey, 'they have very fortunately found an able and willing schoolmaster; he had belonged to a ship which visited the island, and was so infatuated with the behaviour of the people that he resolved to remain among them; and, in addition to the instruction of the children, has taken upon himself the duty of clergyman, and is the oracle of the community.'

On the approach of the *Blossom* towards the island, a boat was observed, under all sail, hastening towards the ship. Her crew consisted of old Adams and many of the young men belonging to the island. They did not venture to lay hold of the ship till they had first inquired if they might come on board; and on permission being granted, they sprang up the side and shook every officer by the hand with undisguised feelings of gratification.

The activity of the young men, ten in number, outstripped that of old Adams, who was in his sixty-fifth year, and somewhat corpulent. He was dressed in a sailor's shirt and trousers, and a low-crowned hat, which he held in his hand until desired to put it on. He still retained his sailor's manners, doffing his hat and smoothing down his bald forehead whenever he was addressed by the officers of the *Blossom*. . . .

Captain Beechey procured from Adams a narrative of the whole transaction of the mutiny, which however is incorrect in many parts; and also a history of the broils and disputes which led to the violent death of all these misguided men (with the exception of Young and Adams), who accompanied Christian in the *Bounty* to Pitcairn's Island.

His Majesty's Ship *Blossom.*
The *Blossom* visited Pitcairn in 1825 and Lieutenant Peard's *Diary* of the visit reports
Adams as saying, 'A midshipman named Stewart, observed him preparing a raft and asked
him why he was doing so. Christian replied that he meant to quit the ship and hoped to
reach shore on his raft. Upon which Stewart exclaimed, "Why don't you try the people,
you know they are very much dissatisfied with the Captain." ' Both Beechey's narrative
and Peard's show Adams flatly contradicting the account given by Peter Heywood.

His Majesty's Ship BLOSSOM

It may be recollected that the *Bounty* was carried away from Otaheite by
nine of the mutineers:—

1.	FLETCHER CHRISTIAN	Acting Lieutenant.
2.	EDWARD YOUNG	Midshipman.
3.	ALEXANDER SMITH (*alias* JOHN ADAMS)	Seaman.
4.	WILLIAM M'KOY	⎫
5.	MATTHEW QUINTAL	
6.	JOHN WILLIAMS	⎬ Seamen.
7.	ISAAC MARTIN	⎭
8.	JOHN MILLS	Gunner's Mate.
9.	WILLIAM BROWN	Botanist's Assistant.

They brought with them six men and twelve women, natives of Tabouai
and Otaheite. The first step after their arrival was to divide the whole island

into nine equal portions, to the exclusion of those poor people whom they had seduced to accompany them, and some of whom are stated to have been carried off against their inclination. At first they were considered as the friends of the white men, but very soon became their slaves. They assisted in the cultivation of the soil, in building houses, and in fetching wood and water, without murmuring or complaining; and things went on peaceably and prosperously for about two years, when Williams, who had lost his wife about a month after their arrival, by a fall from a rock while collecting bird's eggs, became dissatisfied, and insisted on having another wife, or threatened to leave the island in one of the *Bounty*'s boats. Being useful as an armourer, the Europeans were unwilling to part with him, and he, still persisting in his unreasonable demand, had the injustice to compel one of the Otaheitans to give up his wife to him.

By this act of flagrant oppression his countrymen made common cause with their injured companion, and laid a plan for the extermination of the Europeans; but the women gave a hint of what was going forward in a song, the burden of which was, 'Why does black man sharpen axe?—to kill white man.' The plot being thus discovered, the husband who had his wife taken from him, another whom Christian had shot at (though, it is stated, with powder only), fled into the woods, and were treacherously murdered by their countrymen, on the promise of pardon for the perpetration of this foul deed.

Tranquillity being thus restored, matters went on tolerably well for a year or two longer; but the oppression and ill-treatment which the Otaheitans received, more particularly from Quintal and M'Koy, the most active and determined of the mutineers, drove them to the formation of another plot for the destruction of their oppressors, which but too successfully succeeded. A day was fixed for attacking and putting to death all the Englishmen while at work in their respective plantations. Williams was the first man that was shot. They next proceeded to Christian, who was working at his yam-plot, and shot him. Mills, confiding in the fidelity of his Otaheitan friend, stood his ground, and was murdered by him and another. Martin and Brown were separately attacked and slain, one with a maul, the other with a musket. Adams was wounded in the shoulder, but succeeded in making terms with the Otaheitans; and was conducted by them to Christian's house, where he was kindly treated. Young, who was a great favourite of the women, was secreted by them during the attack, and afterwards carried to Christian's house. M'Koy and Quintal, the worst of the gang, escaped to the mountains. 'Here,' says Captain Beechey, 'this day of bloodshed ended, leaving only four Englishmen alive out of nine. It was a day of emancipation to the blacks, who were now masters of the island, and of humiliation and retribution to the whites.'

The men of colour now began to quarrel about choosing the women whose European husbands had been murdered; the result of which was the destruction of the whole of the former, some falling by the hands of the women, and one of them by Young, who it would seem coolly and deliberately shot him. Adams now proceeded into the mountains to communicate the fatal intelligence to the two Europeans, M'Koy and Quintal, and to solicit their return to the village. All these events are stated to have happened so early as October, 1793.

From this time to 1798, the remnant of the colonists would appear to have gone on quietly with the exception of some quarrels these four men had with the women, and the latter among themselves; ten of them were still remaining, who lived promiscuously with the men, frequently changing their abode from one house to another. Young, being a man of some education, kept a kind of journal, but it is a document of very little interest, containing scarcely anything more than the ordinary occupations of the settlers, the loan or exchange of provisions, the dates when the sows farrowed, the number of fish caught, etc., and it begins only at the time when Adams and he were sole masters of the island; and the truth, therefore, of all that has been told rests solely on the degree of credit that is due to Adams.

M'Koy, it appears, had formerly been employed in a Scotch distillery, and being much addicted to ardent spirits, set about making experiments on the tee-root (*Dracaena terminalis*), and at length unfortunately succeeded in producing an intoxicating liquor. This success induced his companion Quintal to turn his kettle into a still. The consequence was, that these two men were in a constant state of drunkenness, particularly M'Koy, on whom, it seems, it had the effect of producing fits of delirium; and in one of these he threw himself from a cliff and was killed on the spot. Captain Beechey says, 'the melancholy fate of this man created so forcible an impression on the remaining few, that they resolved never again to touch spirits; and Adams has, I believe, to this day kept his vow.'

Some time in the following year, that is, about 1799, 'we learned from Adams,' says Captain Beechey, 'that Quintal lost his wife by a fall from the cliff, while in search of bird's eggs; that he grew discontented, and, though there were several disposable women on the island, and he had already experienced the fatal effects of a similar demand, nothing would satisfy him but the wife of one of his companions. Of course, neither of them felt inclined to accede to this unreasonable demand; and he sought an opportunity of putting them both to death. He was fortunately foiled in his first attempt, but swore openly he would speedily repeat it. Adams and Young having no doubt he would follow up his intention, and fearing he might be more successful in the next attempt, came to the resolution that, as their own lives were not safe while he was in existence, they were justified in putting him to death, which they did by felling him, as they would an ox, with a hatchet.

Such was the polluted source, thus stained with the guilt of mutiny, piracy, and murder, from which the present simple and innocent race of islanders has proceeded; and what is most of all extraordinary, the very man from whom they have received their moral and religious instruction is

Christian's house, Pitcairn Is.

Fletcher Christian, 1764–1794 (?), the leader of the mutiny, has left no known account of his version of what happened and why. If he did return to Cumberland, England, then his family have kept the secret well to date. Remarkably, no letters appear to have survived though he wrote some from Cape Town to his family in 1788. He took with him to Pitcairn his Tahitian woman, 'Isabella', and they had three children. According to Beechey, Christian found a cave on the mountain behind his house where he kept provisions and ammunition to defend himself if the navy arrived to arrest him. Adams claimed he was shot dead by the natives while working in his yam plot.

one who was among the first and foremost in the mutiny, and deeply im-plicated in all its deplorable consequences. This man and Young were now the sole survivors out of the fifteen males that had landed upon the island; and, as Beechey says, it would have been wonderful, after the many dreadful scenes at which they had assisted, if the solitude and tranquillity that ensued had not disposed them to repentance. They had a Bible and a Prayer Book, which were found in the *Bounty*, and they read the Church Service regularly every Sunday. They now resolved to have morning and evening family prayers, and to instruct the children, who amounted to nineteen, many of them between the ages of seven and nine years. Young, however, was not long suffered to survive his repentance. An asthmatic complaint terminated his existence about a year after the death of Quintal; and Adams was now left the sole survivor of the guilty and misguided mutineers of the *Bounty*. It is remarkable that the name of Young should never once occur in any shape as connected with the mutiny, except in the evidence of Lieutenant Hayward, who includes his name in a mass of others. He neither appears among the armed nor the unarmed; he is not stated to be among those who were on deck, and was probably therefore one of those who were confined below. Bligh, nevertheless, has not omitted to give him a character. 'Young was an able and stout seaman; he, however, always proved a worthless wretch.'

If the sincere repentance of Adams, and his most successful exertions to train up the rising generation in piety and virtue, can be considered as expiating in some degree his former offences, this survivor is fully entitled to every indulgence that frail humanity so often requires, and which indeed has been extended to him, by all the officers of the navy who have visited the island. They have all strongly felt that the merits and redeeming qualities of the latter years of his life have so far atoned for his former guilt, that he ought not to be molested, but rather encouraged, in his meritorious efforts, if not for his own sake, at least for that of the innocent young people dependent on him.

Still it ought never to be forgotten that he was one of the first and most daring in the atrocious act of mutiny and piracy, and that, had he remained in Otaheite, and been taken home in the *Pandora*, nothing could have saved him from an ignominious death.

Adams told two different stories with regard to the conduct of Christian. To Sir Thomas Staines and Captain Pipon, he represented this ill-fated young man as never happy, after the rash and criminal step he had taken, and that he committed so many acts of cruelty, as to incur the hatred and detestation of his associates in crime. Whereas he told Captain Beechey, that Christian was always cheerful; that his example was of the greatest service in exciting his companions to labour; that he was naturally of a happy, ingenuous disposition, and won the good opinion and respect of all who served under him. . . .

That Christian, so far from being cheerful, was, on the contrary, always uneasy in his mind about his own safety, is proved by his having selected a cave at the extremity of the high ridge of craggy hills that runs across the island, as his intended place of refuge, in the event of any ship of war discovering the retreat of the mutineers, in which cave he resolved to sell his life as dearly as he could. In this recess he always kept a store of provisions, and near it erected a small hut, well concealed by trees, which served the purpose of a watch-house. 'So difficult,' says Captain Beechey, 'was the approach to this cave, that even if a party were successful in crossing the ridge, he might have bid defiance, as long as his ammunition lasted, to any force.'

The truth is, as appears in Morrison's journal, that during the short time they remained at Tabouai, and till the separation of the mutineers at Otaheite, when sixteen forsook him, and eight only, of the very worst, accompanied him in quest of some retreat, he acted the part of a tyrant to a much greater extent than the man who, he says, drove him to the act of mutiny. After giving an account of the manner of his death, Captain Beechey says, 'Thus fell a man who, from being the reputed ringleader of the mutiny, has obtained an unenviable celebrity, and whose crime may perhaps be considered as in some degree palliated by the tyranny which led to its commission.' It is to be hoped, such an act as he was guilty of will never be so considered.

If mutiny could be supposed to admit of palliation, a fatal blow would be struck not only at the discipline, but at the very existence, of the navy. Whenever an act of tyranny, or an unnecessary degree of severity, is exercised by a commanding officer, let the fact only be proved, and he is certain to be visited with all the rigour that the degree of his oppressive conduct will warrant. Had Christian but waited patiently the arrival of the *Bounty* in England, and the alleged conduct of Bligh towards his officers and crew had been proved, he would, unquestionably, have been dismissed from his Majesty's service.

At this point in his narrative, Sir John Barrow adds the following intriguing footnote:–

[As the manner of Christian's death has been differently reported to each different visitor, by Adams, some singular circumstances may here be mentioned that happened at home, just at the time of Folger's visit, and which might render Christian's death on Pitcairn's Island almost a matter of doubt.

About the years 1808 and 1809, a very general opinion was prevalent in the neighbourhood of the lakes of Cumberland and Westmoreland, that Christian was in that part of the country, and made frequent private visits to an aunt who was living there. Being the near relative of Mr. Christian Curwen, long Member of Parliament for Carlisle, and himself a native, he was well known in the neighbourhood. This, however, might be passed over as mere gossip, had not another circumstance happened just about the same time, for the truth of which the Editor does not hesitate to avouch.

In Fore Street, Plymouth Dock, Captain Heywood found himself one day walking behind a man whose shape had so much the appearance of Christian's that he involuntarily quickened his pace. Both were walking very fast, and the rapid steps behind him having roused the stranger's attention, he suddenly turned his face, looked at Heywood, and immediately ran off. But the face was as much like Christian's as the back and Heywood, exceedingly excited, ran also. Both ran as fast as they were able, but the stranger had the advantage and, after making several short turns, disappeared.

That Christian should be in England, Heywood considered as highly improbable, though not out of the scope of possibility; for at this time no account of him whatsoever had been received since they parted at Otaheite; at any rate the resemblance, the agitation, and the efforts of the stranger to elude him, were circumstances too strong not to make a deep impression on his mind. At the moment his first thought was to set about making some further enquiries, but on recollection of the pain and trouble such a discovery must occasion him, he considered it more prudent to let the matter drop. But the circumstance was frequently called to his memory for the remainder of his life.]

With regard to Adams, though his subsequent conduct was highly meritorious, his crime like that of Christian can never be considered as wiped away. Sir Thomas Staines, the first British officer who called at the island, it may well be supposed, had to struggle, on this trying occasion, between duty and feeling. It was his imperative duty to have seized and brought him a prisoner to England, where he must have been tried, and would no doubt have been convicted, though he might, and probably would, from length of time and circumstances in his favour, have received the king's pardon. Perhaps, however, on the whole, it was fortunate, that in balancing, as it is known this gallant officer did, between the sense of duty and the sense of feeling, the latter prevailed, and justice yielded to mercy.

The *Blossom* was the first ship of war that John Adams had been on board of since the mutiny; and, as Captain Beechey observes, his mind would naturally revert to scenes that could not fail to produce a temporary embarrassment, but no apprehension for his safety appeared to form any part of his thoughts; and as every person endeavoured to set his mind at rest, he soon found himself at ease and at home.

On account of the rocks and formidable breakers, the party who went on shore were landed by the young men, two at a time, in their whale boat. 'The difficulty of landing,' says Captain Beechey, 'was more than repaid by the friendly reception we met with on the beach from Hannah Young, a very interesting young woman, the daughter of Adams. In her eagerness to greet her father, she had outrun her female companions, for whose delay she thought it necessary, in the first place, to apologise. . . . But her apology was rendered unnecessary by their appearance on the steep and circuitous path down the mountain; and, as they arrived on the beach, they successively welcomed us to their island, with a simplicity and sincerity which left no doubt of the truth of their professions.'

The whole group simultaneously expressed a wish that the visitors would stay with them several days; and on their signifying a desire to get to the village before dark and to pitch the observatory, every article and instrument found a bearer, along a steep path which led to the village, concealed by groups of cocoa-nut trees. The village consisted of five houses, on a cleared piece of ground sloping toward the sea. While the men assisted in pitching the tent, the women employed themselves in preparing the supper. The mode of cooking was precisely that of Otaheite, by heated stones in a hole made in the ground. At young Christian's the table was spread with plates, knives and forks. John Buffet said grace in an emphatic manner, and this is repeated every time a fresh guest sits down while the meal is going on.

It is remarkable enough, that although the female part of the society is highly respected, yet, in one instance, a distinction is kept up, which in civilized countries would be deemed degrading. It is that which is rigidly observed in all the South Sea Islands, that no woman shall eat in the presence of her husband; and though this distinction between man and wife is not carried quite so far in Pitcairn's Island, it is observed to the extent of excluding all women from table when there is a deficiency of seats.

The beds were next prepared. A mattress composed of palm-leaves was covered with native cloth made of the paper mulberry-tree, in the same manner as in Otaheite; the sheets were of the same material; and it appeared, from their crackling, that they were quite new from the loom, or rather the beater. The whole arrangement is stated to have been comfortable, and inviting to repose. One interruption only disturbed their first sleep. After the lights [torches made of *doodoe* nuts strung upon the fibres of a palm-leaf] were put out, the evening hymn was chanted by the whole family in the middle of the room. At early dawn they were also awaked by their morning hymn and the family devotion; after which the islanders all set out to their several occupations. Some of the women had taken the linen of their visitors to wash; others were preparing for the next meal; and others were employed in the manufacture of cloth.

The innocence and simplicity of these interesting young creatures are strongly exemplified in the following description. 'On looking round the apartment, though it contained several beds, we found no partition, curtain, or screen; they had not yet been considered necessary. So far, indeed, from concealment being thought of, when we were about to get up, the women, anxious to show their attention, assembled to wish us good morning, and to inquire in what way they could best contribute to our comforts. Many persons would have felt awkward at rising and dressing before so many pretty black-eyed damsels, assembled in the centre of a spacious room; but by a little habit we overcame this embarrassment.'

Their cottages are spacious, and strongly built of wood, in an oblong form, and thatched with the leaves of the palm-tree bent round the stem of a branch from the same, and laced horizontally to rafters, so placed as to give a proper pitch to the roof. An upper story is appropriated to sleeping, and has four beds, one in each angle of the room, and large enough for three or four persons to sleep on. The lower is the eating room, having a broad table with several stools placed round it. The lower room communicates with the upper, by a stout ladder in the centre. Immediately round the village are small enclosures for fattening pigs, goats, and poultry; and beyond them are the cultivated grounds producing the banana, plantain, melon, yam, taro, sweet potatoes, *tee*-tree, cloth-plant, with other useful roots, fruits, and a variety of shrubs. Every cottage has its out-house for making cloth, its baking-place, its pig-sty, and its poultry-house. . . .

The young children are punctual in their attendance at school, and are instructed by John Buffet in reading, writing, and arithmetic; to which are added, precepts of religion and morality, drawn chiefly from the Bible and Prayer Book. They possess no other books that might mystify and perplex their understandings on religious subjects. They seldom indulge in jokes or other kinds of levity; and Beechey says, they are so accustomed to take what is said in its literal meaning, that irony was always considered a falsehood in spite of explanation. The Sabbath is wholly devoted to the church service, to prayer, reading, and serious meditation; no work of any kind is done on that day, not even cooking, which is prepared on the preceding evening.

'I attended,' says Beechey, 'their church on this day, and found the service well conducted; the prayers were read by Adams, and the lessons by Buffet, the service being preceded by hymns. The greatest devotion was apparent in every individual; and in the children there was a seriousness unknown in the younger part of our communities at home. In the course of the Litany, they prayed for their sovereign and all the royal family, with much apparent loyalty and sincerity. A sermon followed, which was very well delivered by Buffet; and lest any part of it should be forgotten or escape attention, it was read three times. In about half an hour afterwards we again assembled to prayers, and at sunset service was repeated; so that, with their morning and evening prayers, they may be said to have church five times on a Sunday.'

Perhaps it will be thought by some that they carry their seriousness too far, and that the younger people are not allowed sufficient recreation. The exercise and amusement of dancing, once so much resorted to in most of the islands of the Pacific, is here almost excluded. . . .

They appeared to have little taste for music either instrumental or vocal. Adams, however, when on board the *Blossom* for two or three days, made no difficulty of joining in the dance and was remarkably cheerful, but on no occasion neglected his usual devotions. Captain Beechey has no doubt of the sincerity of his piety. He slept in the same cabin, but would never get into his cot until the captain was in bed and supposed to be asleep, when, in a retired corner of the cabin, he fell on his knees and performed his devotions.

This good old man told Beechey one day, that it would add much to his happiness if he would read the marriage ceremony to him and his wife, as he could not bear the idea of living with her without its being done, when a proper opportunity should offer, as was now the case. Though Adams was aged, and the old woman had been blind and bedridden for several years, Beechey says he made such a point of it, that it would have been cruel to refuse him. They were accordingly, the following day, duly united, and the event noted in a register by John Buffet. The marriages that take place among the young people are, however, performed by Adams, who makes use of a ring for such occasions, which has united every couple on the island since its first settlement; the regulated age under which no man is allowed to marry is twenty, and that of the woman eighteen. . . . Adams also officiates at christenings.

Captain Beechey has recently received a letter announcing the death of John Adams, which took place in March 1829. The demise of this old patriarch is the most serious loss that could have befallen this infant colony.

HMS *Seringapatam*
Captain Waldegrave brought clothing and agricultural tools to the Pitcairn Islanders as a
gift from the British Government in 1830. A year later Thursday October Christian died
when the Pitcairners were removed to Tahiti. The survivors returned again to Pitcairn a
few months later, much chastened by their experiences.

It is, therefore, gratifying to know, that five years after the visit of the *Blossom*,
and one year subsequent to Adams's death, it continued to enjoy the same
uninterrupted state of harmony and contentment as before.

In consequence of a representation, made by Captain Beechey when there,
of the distressed state of this little society, with regard to the want of certain
necessary articles, his Majesty's government sent out to Valparaiso, to be
conveyed from thence for their use, a proportion for sixty persons of the
following articles: sailor's blue jackets and trousers, flannel waistcoats,
pairs of stockings and shoes, women's dresses, spades, mattocks, shovels,
pickaxes, trowels, rakes; all of which were taken in his Majesty's ship
Seringapatam, commanded by Captain the Hon. William Waldegrave, who
arrived there in March 1830.

The ship had scarcely anchored when George Young was alongside in his
canoe, which he guided by a paddle; and soon after Thursday October
Christian, in a jolly-boat, with several others, who, having come on board,

were invited to breakfast, and one of them said grace as usual both before and after it. The captain, the chaplain, and some other officers accompanied these natives on shore, and having reached the summit of the first level or plain, which is surrounded by a grove or screen of cocoa-nut trees, they found the wives and mothers assembled to receive them. 'I have brought you a clergyman,' says the captain. 'God bless you,' issued from every mouth; 'but is he come to stay with us?' – 'No.' 'You bad man, why not?' – 'I cannot spare him, he is the chaplain of my ship; but I have brought you clothes and other articles, which King George has sent you.' 'But,' says Kitty Quintal, 'we want food for our souls.'

'Our reception,' says Captain Waldegrave, 'was most cordial, particularly that of Mr. Watson, the chaplain. The men sprang up to the trees, throwing down cocoa-nuts, the husks of which were torn off by others with their teeth, and offering us the milk. As soon as we had rested ourselves, they took us to their cottages, where we dined and slept.'

Captain Waldegrave says it was highly gratifying to observe their native simplicity of manners, apparently without guile: their hospitality was unbounded, their cottages being open to all, and all were welcome to such food as they possessed; pigs and fowls were immediately killed and dressed, and when the guests were seated, one of the islanders, in the attitude of prayer, repeated a simple grace for the present food they were about to partake of, beseeching, at the same time, spiritual nourishment; at the end of which each responded *amen*.

Captain Waldegrave, like all former visitors, bears testimony to the kind disposition and active benevolence of these simple islanders. The children, he says, are fond and obedient, the parents affectionate and kind towards their children. None of the party ever heard a harsh word made use of by one towards another. They never slander or speak ill of one another. If any question was asked as to the character or conduct of a particular individual, the answer would probably be something of this kind, 'If it could do any good, I would answer you; but as it cannot, it would be wrong to tell tales'; or if the question applied to one who had committed a fault, they would say, 'It would be wrong to tell my neighbour's shame.'

The women are clothed in white cloth made from the paper mulberry, the dress extending from the shoulders to the feet, in loose double folds. The mothers, while nursing, carry the infant within their dress; as the child advances in growth it sits across the hip of the parent with its little hands clinging to the shoulder, while the mother's arm passing round it keeps it in safety. The men and boys, except on Sunday, when they appear in English dresses, generally wear only the *mara*, or waist-cloth, which, passing over the hips, and between the legs, is knotted behind. The women, when working, use only a petticoat, with a jacket.

The men are stated to be from five feet eight inches to six feet high, of great muscular strength and excellent figures. 'We did not see,' says Captain Waldegrave, 'one cripple or defective person, except one boy, whom, in the most good-humoured way, and laughing heartily, they brought to me, observing, "You ought to be brothers, you have each lost the right eye." I acknowledged the connexion, and no doubt for the future he will be called the Captain.'

It is impossible not to feel a deep interest in the welfare of this little society, and at the same time an apprehension that something may happen to disturb that harmony and destroy that simplicity of manners which have hitherto characterised it. It is to be feared, indeed, that the seeds of discord are already sown. It appears from Captain Waldegrave's statement, that no less than three Englishmen have found their way into this happy society. One of them, John Buffet, mentioned by Beechey, is a harmless man, and of great use to the islanders in his capacity of clergyman and schoolmaster; he is also a clever and useful mechanic, as a shipwright and joiner, and is much beloved by the community. Two others have since been left on the island, one of them, by name John Evans, has married a daughter of John Adams, through whom he possesses and cultivates a certain portion of land. The third is George Hunn Nobbs, who calls himself pastor, registrar, and schoolmaster, thus infringing on the privileges of John Buffet; and being a person of superior talents, and of exceeding great impudence, has deprived Buffet of a great number of his scholars; and hence a sufficient cause exists of division and dissension among the members of the little society, which were never known before. Buffet and Evans support themselves by their industry, but Nobbs not only claims exemption from labour as being their pastor, but also exacts a maintenance at the expense of the community. He has married a daughter of Charles, and grand-daughter to the late Fletcher Christian, whose descendants, as captain of the gang, might be induced to claim superiority, and might be allowed it by general consent, had they but possessed a moderate share of talent; but it is stated that Thursday October and Charles Christian, the sons of the chief mutineer, are ignorant, uneducated men. The only chance for the continuance of peace is the general dislike in which this Nobbs is held, and the gradual intellectual improvement of the rising generation.

It seems that Adams on his death-bed called all the heads of families together, and urged them to appoint a chief; – this, however, they have not done, which makes it the more to be apprehended that Nobbs, by his superior talent or cunning, will force himself upon them into that situation. Captain Waldegrave thinks, however, that Edward Quintal, who possesses the best understanding of any on the island, will in time arrive at that honour; his only book is the Bible, but it is quite astonishing, he observes, what a fund of knowledge he has derived from it. His wife, too, is stated to be a woman of excellent understanding; and their eldest boy, William, has been so carefully educated, that he excels greatly all the others. The descendants of Young are also said to be persons generally of promising abilities. . . . [Meanwhile, it would seem] Nobbs has already thrust upon them what he calls a code of laws, in which he enumerates crimes, such as murder and

Facsimile: Frontispiece to Barrow's original account.
The frontispiece of the 1831 edition of Barrow's book on the *Bounty* mutiny depicts George Young and his wife Hannah Adams. The book appeared in several editions during the nineteenth century.

adultery, unknown and unheard of among these simple people since the time that Adams was sole legislator and patriarch. The punishment of adultery, to give a specimen of Nobbs's legislation, is whipping for the first offence to both parties, and marriage within three months; for the second, if the parties refuse to marry, the penalties are, forfeiture of lands, property, and banishment from the island. Offenders are to be tried before three elders who pronounce sentence.

As to the tenure of land, it is fortunately provided for previous to his arrival on the island. The whole island, it seems, was partitioned out by Adams among the families of the original settlers, so that a foreigner cannot obtain any, except by purchase or marriage. Captain Waldegrave reckons, that eleven-twelfths are uncultivated, and that population is increasing so rapidly, that in the course of a century the island will be fully peopled, and that the limit may be taken at one thousand souls. . . . [This assumption, however] is grounded on incorrect data; it does not follow, that because one-twelfth of the island will maintain eighty persons, the whole must support nine hundred and sixty persons, The island is not more than four square miles, or two thousand five hundred and sixty acres; and as a ridge of rocky hills runs from north to south, having two peaks exceeding one thousand feet in height, it is more than probable that not one half of it is capable of cultivation. . . .

It appears that Adams had contemplated the prospect of an increasing population with the limited means of supporting it, and requested that Beechey would communicate with the British Government upon the subject, which he says he did, and that, through the interference of the Admiralty and Colonial Office, means have been taken for removing them to any place they may choose for themselves. It is to be hoped, however, that no such interference will take place; for half a century, at least, there is no danger of any want of food. The attempt, however, was made through the means of a Mr. Nott, a missionary of Otaheite, who, being on a visit to this country, was authorised, on his return, to make arrangements for their removal to Otahaite, if they wished it, and if Pomarré, the king of the island, should not object to receive them; and he carried a letter to this chief from Lord Bathurst, acquainting him with the intention of the British Government, and expressing the hope that he would be induced to receive under his protection a people whose moral and religious character had created so lively an interest in their favour; but it fortunately happened that this missionary passed the island without stopping. A Mr. Joshua Hill subsequently proposed their removal to New South Wales, but his vessel was considered too small for the purpose.

Two years after this, as difficulties had occurred to prevent the above-mentioned intentions from being carried into effect, Sir George Murray deemed it desirable that no time should be lost in affording such assistance to these islanders as might, at all events, render their present abode as comfortable as circumstances would allow, *until* arrangements could be made for their future disposal, either in one of the Society Islands, as originally proposed, or at one of our settlements on New Holland. The assistance here alluded to has been afforded, as above mentioned, by his Majesty's ship *Seringapatam.*

It is sincerely to be hoped that removal will be no longer thought of. No complaint was made, no apprehension of want expressed to Captain Waldegrave, who left them contented and happy; and Captain Beechey, since his return, has received a letter from John Buffet, who informs him of a notification made by Nott the missionary at Otaheite, that the king was willing to receive them, and that measures would be taken for their removal; but, he adds, the people are so much attached to, and satisfied with, their native island, as not to have a wish to leave it. The breaking up of this happy, innocent, and simple-minded little society, by some summary process, would be a subject of deep regret to all who take an interest in their welfare; and to themselves it would be the inevitable loss of all those amiable qualities which have obtained for them the kind and generous sympathy of their countrymen at home.

The time must come when they will emigrate. When the hive is full, they will send out their swarms of their own accord. . . . [Meanwhile] there is no deficiency in the number and variety of plants, producing food and clothing [sufficient for the use of all.] . . .

Pomare, King of Tahiti.
Pomare, the former Otoo, or Tu, offered land to the people from Pitcairn Island if they should wish to settle in Tahiti instead of facing the hazards of life on the tiny island. But by the time the Pitcairners arrived, Pomare was dead and Tahiti was on the brink of civil war. Pomare's sister honored the offer he had made but the whole episode was a disastrous example of the best of intentions going terribly wrong. By 1831 Tahiti had lost for ever its former innocent charm.

Pomare, King of Tahiti. Engr. &c.

Happy, thrice happy people! May no improper intruders thrust themselves into your peaceful and contented society! May that Providence which has hitherto protected you, still continue to pour down those blessings upon you, of which you appear to be so truly sensible, and for which you are justly thankful! May it throw round the shores of your enviable little Eden, 'cherubim and a flaming sword,' to guard its approaches from those who would endanger your peace; and above all, shield you from those, who would perplex and confuse your unsophisticated minds, by mysterious doctrines which they do not themselves comprehend! Be assured that, so long as you shall adhere to the line of conduct you have hitherto pursued, and be contented with your present lot, your happiness is secure; but once admit ignorant or false teachers among you, and from that period you may date the commencement of misfortunes and misery!

Conclusion

Many useful and salutary lessons of conduct may be drawn from this eventful history, more especially by officers of the navy, both old and young, as well as by those subordinate to them. In the first place, it most strongly points out the dreadful consequences that are almost certain to ensue from a state of insubordination and mutiny on board a ship of war; and the equally certain fate that, at one time or other, awaits all those who have the misfortune to be concerned in a transaction of this revolting nature. In the present instance, the dreadful retribution which overtook them, and which was evinced in a most extraordinary manner, affords an awful and instructive lesson to seamen, by which they may learn, that although the guilty may be secured for a time in evading the punishment due to the offended laws of society, yet they must not hope to escape the pursuit of Divine vengeance. It will be recollected that the number of persons who remained in the *Bounty*, after her piratical seizure, and of course charged with the crime of mutiny, was twenty-five; that these subsequently separated into two parties, sixteen having landed at Otaheite, and afterwards taken from thence in the *Pandora*, as prisoners, and nine having gone with the *Bounty* to Pitcairn's Island.

Of the sixteen taken in the *Pandora*:–

1. Mr. Peter Heywood	midshipman	}	sentenced to death, but pardoned.
2. James Morrison	boatswain's mate		
3. William Muspratt	commander's steward		
4. Thos. Burkitt	seaman	}	condemned and executed.
5. John Millward	seaman		
6. Thos. Ellison	seaman		
7. Joseph Coleman	armourer	}	tried and acquitted.
8. Charles Norman	carpenter's mate		
9. Thos. M'Intosh	carpenter's crew		
10. Michael Byrne	seaman		
11. Mr. George Stewart	midshipman	}	drowned in irons when the *Pandora* was wrecked.
12. John Sumner	seaman		
13. Richard Skinner	seaman		
14. Henry Hillbrant	cooper		
15. Chas. Churchill	master-at-arms, murdered by Matthew Thompson.		
16. Matthew Thompson	seaman, murdered by Churchill's friends in Otaheite.		

Of the nine who landed on Pitcairn's Island :–

1. Mr. FLETCHER CHRISTIAN   acting-lieut. ⎫
2. JOHN WILLIAMS   seaman   ⎪ were murdered
3. ISAAC MARTIN   seaman   ⎬ by the
4. JOHN MILLS   gunner's mate   ⎪ Otaheitans.
5. WILLM. BROWN   botanist's assistant ⎭
6. MATTHEW QUINTAL   seaman, put to death by Young and Adams in self-defence.
7. WILLIAM M'KOY   seaman, became insane, and killed by throwing himself from a rock.
8. Mr. EDWARD YOUNG   midshipman, died of asthma.
9. ALEX. SMITH   seaman, died in 1829.
  alias John Adams

Young officers of the navy, as well as the common seamen, may also derive some useful lessons from the events of this history. They will see the melancholy results of affording the least encouragement for seamen to depart from their strict line of duty, and to relax in that obedience to the orders of superiors, by which alone the discipline of the service can be preserved; they will learn how dangerous it is to show themselves careless and indifferent in executing those orders, by thus setting a bad example to the men. It ought also to enforce on their minds, how necessary it is to avoid even the appearance of acting in any way that can be considered as repugnant to, or subversive of, the rules and regulations of the service; and most particularly to guard against any conduct that may have the appearance of lowering the authority of their superiors, either by their words or actions.

No doubt can remain on the minds of unprejudiced persons, or such as are capable of weighing evidence, that the two young midshipmen, Stewart and Heywood, were perfectly innocent of any share in the transaction in question; and yet, because they happened to be left in the ship, not only contrary to their wish and intention, but kept down below by force, the one lost his life, by being drowned in chains, and the other was condemned to die, and only escaped from suffering the last penalty of the law by a recommendation to the royal mercy. The only point in which these two officers failed, was, that they did not at once demand permission to accompany their commander, while they were allowed to remain on deck and had the opportunity of doing so. The manly conduct of young Heywood, throughout his long and unmerited sufferings, affords an example of firmness, fortitude, and resignation to the Divine will, that is above all praise; in fact, nothing short of conscious innocence could have supported him in the severe trials he had to undergo.

The melancholy effects which tyrannical conduct, harsh and opprobrious language, ungovernable passion, and a worrying and harassing temper, on the part of naval commanders, seldom fail to produce on the minds of those who are subject to their capricious and arbitrary command, are strongly exemplified in the cause and consequences of the mutiny in the *Bounty*, as described in the course of this history. Conduct of this kind, by making the inferior officers of a ship discontented and unhappy, has the dangerous tendency, as in the case of Christian, to incite the crew to partake in their discontent, and be ready to assist in any plan to get rid of the tyrant. We may see in it, also, how very little credit a commander is likely to gain, either with the service or the public at large, when the duties of a ship are carried on, as they would appear to have been in the *Pandora*, in a cold, phlegmatic, and unfeeling manner, and with an indifference to the comfort of all around him, – subjecting offenders of whatever description to unnecessary restraint, and a severity of punishment, which, though strictly within the letter of the law, contributes in no way to the ends of discipline or of justice.

The conduct of Bligh, however mistaken he may have been in his mode of carrying on the duties of the ship, was most exemplary throughout the long and perilous voyage he performed in an open boat, on the wide ocean, with the most scanty supply of provisions and water, and in the worst weather. The result of such meritorious conduct holds out every encouragement to both officers and men, by showing them that, by firmness and perseverance, and the adoption of well-digested measures, steadily pursued in spite of opposition, the most hopeless undertaking, to all appearance, may be successfully accomplished.

And lastly – The fate that has attended almost every one of those concerned in the mutiny and piracy of his Majesty's ship *Bounty* ought to operate as a warning to, and make a deep impression on the minds of, our brave seamen, not to suffer themselves to be led astray from the straightforward line of their duty, either by order or persuasion of some hot-brained, thoughtless, or designing person, whether their superior or equal, but to remain faithful, under all circumstances, to their commanding officer, as any mutinous proceedings or disobedience of his orders are sure to be visited upon them in the long run, either by loss of life, or by a forfeiture of that liberal provision which the British government has bestowed on its seamen for long and faithful services.

Articles of War

The following articles and orders were established from the 25th of December 1749; and are directed to be observed and put in execution, as well in time of peace as in time of war.

All commanders, captains, and officers, in or belonging to any of his Majesty's ships or vessels of war shall cause the public worship of Almighty God, according to the Liturgy of the Church of England established by law, to be solemnly, orderly, and reverently performed in their respective ships; and shall take care that prayers and preaching, by the chaplain in holy orders of the respective ships, be performed diligently; and that the Lord's day be observed according to law. — *Divine worship.*

II. All flag officers, and all persons in or belonging to his Majesty's ships or vessels of war, being guilty of profane oaths, cursings, execrations, drunkenness, uncleanness, or other scandalous actions, in derogation of God's honour, and corruption of good manners, shall incur such punishment as a court martial shall think fit to impose, and as the nature and degree of their offence shall deserve. — *Swearing, Drunkenness, scandalous actions, &c.*

III. If any officer, mariner, soldier, or other person of the fleet, shall give, hold, or entertain intelligence to or with any enemy or rebel, without leave from the king's Majesty, or the lord high admiral, or the commissioners for executing the office of lord high admiral, commander in chief, or his commanding officer, every such person so offending, and being thereof convicted by the sentence of a court martial, shall be punished with death. — *Holding intelligence with an enemy, or rebel.*

IV. If any letter or message from any enemy or rebel be conveyed to any officer, mariner, or soldier, or other in the fleet, and the said officer, mariner, soldier, or other as aforesaid, shall not, within twelve hours, having opportunity so to do, acquaint his superior officer, or the officer commanding in chief, with it; or if any superior officer, being acquainted therewith, shall not in convenient time reveal the same to the commander in chief of the squadron, every such person so offending, and being convicted thereof by the sentence of a court martial, shall be punished with death, or such other punishment as the nature and degree of the offence shall deserve, and the court martial shall impose. — *Letter or message from an enemy, or rebel.*

V. All spies, and all persons whatsoever who shall come, or be found, in the nature of spies, to bring or deliver any seducing letters or messages, from any enemy or rebel, or endeavour to corrupt any captain, officer, mariner, or other in the fleet to betray his trust, being convicted of any such offence, by the sentence of the court martial, shall be punished with death, or such other punishment as the nature and degree of the offence shall deserve, and the court martial shall impose. — *Spies, and all persons in the nature of spies.*

VI. No person in the fleet shall relieve an enemy or rebel with money, victuals, powder, shot, arms, ammunition, or any other supplies whatsoever, directly or indirectly, upon pain of death, or such other punishment as the court martial shall think fit to impose, and as the nature and degree of the crime shall deserve. — *Relieving an enemy or rebel.*

VII. All the papers, charter-parties, bills of lading, passports, and other writings whatsoever, that shall be taken, seized, or found a board any ship or ships, which shall be surprized or taken as a prize, shall be duly preserved, and the very original shall, by the commanding officer of the ship which shall take such prize, be sent entirely and without fraud to the court of admiralty, or such other court or commissioners as shall be authorized to determine whether such prize be a lawful capture, there to be viewed, made use of, and proceeded upon according to law, upon pain that every person offending herein shall forfeit and lose his share of the capture, and shall suffer such further punishment as the nature and degree of his offence shall be found to deserve, and the court martial shall impose. — *Papers, &c. found on board of prizes.*

VIII. No person in or belonging to the fleet, shall take out of any prize, or ship seized as a prize, any money, plate, or goods, unless it shall be necessary for the better securing thereof, or for the necessary use and service of any of his Majesty's ships or vessels of war, before the same be adjudged lawful prize in some admiralty court; but the full and entire account of the whole, without embezzlement, shall be brought in, and judgment passed entirely upon the — *Taking money or goods out of prizes.*

whole, without fraud; upon pain that every person offending herein shall forfeit and lose his share of the capture, and suffer such further punishment as shall be imposed by a court martial, or such court of admiralty, according to the nature and degree of the offence.

Stripping or ill treating prisoners.

IX. If any ship or vessel shall be taken as a prize, none of the officers, mariners, or other persons on board her, shall be stripped of their cloaths, or in any sort pillaged, beaten, or ill-treated, upon pain that the person or persons so offending, shall be liable to such punishments as a court martial shall think fit to inflict.

Preparation for fight.

X. Every flag officer, captain, and commander in the fleet, who upon signal or order of fight, or sight of any ship or ships which it may be his duty to engage, or who upon likelihood of engagement shall not make the necessary preparations for fight, and shall not in his own person, and according to his place encourage the inferior officers and men to fight courageously, shall suffer death, or such other punishment as from the nature and degree of the offence a court martial shall deem him to deserve; and if any person in the fleet shall treacherously or cowardly yield or cry for quarter, every person so offending, and being convicted thereof by sentence of a court martial, shall suffer death.

Yielding or crying for quarter.

Obedience to orders in battle.

XI. Every person in the fleet, who shall not duly observe the orders of the admiral, flag officer, commander of any squadron or division, or other his superior officer, for assailing, joining battle with, or making defence against any fleet, squadron, or ship; or shall not obey the orders of his superior officer as aforesaid, in time of action, to the best of his power, or shall not use all possible endeavours to put the same effectually into execution: every such person so offending, and being convicted thereof by the sentence of the court martial, shall suffer death, or such other punishment, as from the nature and degree of the offence a court martial shall deem him to deserve.

Withdrawing or keeping back from fight, &c.

XII. Every person in the fleet, who, through cowardice, negligence, or disaffection, shall in time of action withdraw or keep back, or not come into the fight or engagement, or shall not do his utmost to take or destroy every ship which it shall be his duty to engage; and to assist and relieve all and every of his Majesty's ships or those of his allies, which shall be his duty to assist and relieve; every such person so offending, and being convicted thereof by the sentence of a court martial, shall suffer death.

Forbearing to pursue an enemy, &c.

XIII. Every person in the fleet who through cowardice, negligence, or disaffection, shall forbear to pursue the chase of any enemy, pirate, or rebel, beaten or flying; or shall not relieve and assist a known friend in view to the utmost of his power, being convicted of any such offence by the sentence of a court martial, shall suffer death.

Delaying or discouraging any service.

XIV. If when action, or any service shall be commanded, any person in the fleet shall presume to delay or discourage the said action or service, upon pretence or arrears of wages, or upon any pretence whatsoever; every person so offending being convicted thereof by the sentence of the court martial, shall suffer death, or such other punishment, as from the nature and degree of the offence a court martial shall deem him to deserve.

Deserting to an enemy; running away with ships stores.

XV. Every person in or belonging to the fleet who shall desert to the enemy, pirate, or rebel; or run away with any of his Majesty's ships or vessels of war, or any ordnance, ammunition, stores, or provision, belonging thereto, to the weakening of the service, or yield up the same cowardly or treacherously to the enemy, pirate, or rebel, being convicted of any such offence by the sentence of the court martial, shall suffer death.

Desertion, and entertaining deserters.

XVI. Every person in or belonging to the fleet, who shall desert or entice others so to do, shall suffer death, or such other punishment as the circumstances of the offence shall deserve, and a court martial shall judge fit; and if any commanding officer of any of his Majesty's ships or vessels of war shall receive or entertain a deserter from any other of his Majesty's ships or vessels, after discovering him to be such deserter, and shall not with all convenient speed give notice to the captain of the ship or vessel to which such deserter belongs; or if the said ships or vessels are at any considerable distance from each other, to the secretary of the admiralty, or to the commander in chief, every person so offending, and being convicted thereof by the sentence of the court martial, shall be cashiered.

Convoys.

XVII. The officers and seamen of all ships appointed for convoys and guard of merchant ships, or of any other, shall diligently attend upon that charge, without delay, according to their instructions in that behalf; and whosoever shall be faulty therein, and shall not faithfully perform their duty, and defend the ships and goods in their convoy without either diverting to other parts or occasions, or refusing or neglecting to fight in their defence if they be assailed, or running away cowardly, and submitting the ships in their convoy to peril and hazard; or shall demand or exact any money or other reward from any merchant or master for convoying of any ships or vessels intrusted to their care, or shall misuse the masters of mariners thereof, shall be condemned to make reparation of the damage to the merchants, owners, and others, as the court of admiralty shall adjudge; and also be punished criminally according to the quality of their offences, be it by pains of death, or other punishment, according as shall be adjudged fit by the court martial.

XVIII. If any captain, commander, or other officer of any of his Majesty's ships or vessels, shall receive on board, or permit to be received on board such ship or vessel, any goods or merchandizes whatsoever, other than for the sole use of the ship of vessel, except gold, silver, or jewels, and except the goods and merchandizes belonging to any merchant, or other ship or vessel which may be shipwrecked, or in imminent danger of being shipwrecked, either on the high seas, or in any port, creek, or harbour, in order to the preserving them for their proper owners, and except such goods or merchandizes as he shall at any time be ordered to take or receive on board by order of the lord high admiral of Great Britain, or the commissioners for executing the office of lord high admiral for the time being; every person so offending, being convicted thereof by the sentence of the court martial, shall be cashiered, and be for ever afterwards rendered incapable to serve in any place or office in the naval service of his Majesty, his heirs and successors. *[margin: Receiving goods and merchandize on board.]*

XIX. If any person in or belonging to the fleet shall make, or endeavour to make, any mutinous assembly, upon any pretence whatsoever, every person offending herein, and being convicted thereof by the sentence of the court martial, shall suffer death. And if any person in or belonging to the fleet shall utter any words of sedition or mutiny, he shall suffer death, or such other punishment as a court martial shall deem him to deserve. And if any officer, mariner, or soldier, in or belonging to the fleet, shall behave himself with contempt to his superior officer, such superior officer being in the execution of his office, he shall be punished according to the nature of his offence, by the judgment of a court martial. *[margin: Mutinous assembly. Uttering words of sedition and mutiny. Contempt to superior officers.]*

XX. If any person in the fleet shall conceal any traiterous or mutinous practice, or design, being convicted thereof by the sentence of a court martial, he shall suffer death, or such other punishment as a court martial shall think fit; and if any person, in or belonging to the fleet, shall conceal any traiterous or mutinous words, spoken by any, to the prejudice of his Majesty or government, or any words, practice, or design, tending to the hindrance of the service, and shall not forthwith reveal the same to the commanding officer; or being present at any mutiny or sedition, shall not use his utmost endeavours to suppress the same, he shall be punished, as a court martial shall think he deserves. *[margin: Concealing traiterous or mutinous designs, &c.]*

XXI. If any person in the fleet shall find cause of complaint of the unwholesomeness of the victual, or upon other just grounds, he shall quietly make the same known to his superior, or captain, or commander in chief, as the occasion may deserve, that such present remedy may be had, as the matter may require; and the said superior, captain, or commander in chief, shall, as far as he is able, cause the same to be presently remedied; and no person in the fleet, upon any such or other pretence, shall attempt to stir up any disturbance, upon pain of such punishment as a court martial shall think fit to inflict, according to the degree of the offence. *[margin: No person upon any pretence to attempt to stir up disturbance.]*

XXII. If any officer, mariner, soldier, or other person in the fleet, shall strike any of his superior officers, or draw, or offer to draw, or lift up any weapon against him, being in the execution of his office, on any pretence whatsoever, every such person being convicted of any such offence, by the sentence of a court martial, shall suffer death; and if any officer, mariner, soldier, or other person in the fleet, shall presume to quarrel with any of his superior officers, being in the execution of his office, or shall disobey any lawful command of any of his superior officers; every such person being convicted of any such offence by the sentence of a court martial, shall suffer death, or such other punishment as shall, according to the nature and degree of the offence, be inflicted upon him, by the sentence of a court martial. *[margin: Striking a superior officer. Quarrelling. Disobedience.]*

XXIII. If any person in the fleet shall quarrel or fight with any other person in the fleet, or use reproachful or provoking speeches or gestures, tending to make any quarrel or disturbance, he shall, upon being convicted thereof, suffer such punishment as the offence shall deserve, and a court martial shall impose. *[margin: Fighting. Provoking speeches, &c.]*

Embezzlement of stores.

XXIV. There shall be no wasteful expence of any powder, shot, ammunition, or other stores in the fleet, nor any embezzlement thereof, but the stores and provisions shall be carefully preserved, upon pain of such punishment to be inflicted upon the offenders, abettors, buyers, and receivers (being persons subject to naval discipline), as shall be by a court martial found just in that behalf.

Burning a magazine, ship, &c.

XXV. Every person in the fleet, who shall unlawfully burn or set fire to any magazine or store of powder, or ship, boat, ketch, hoy, or vessel, or tackle, or furniture thereunto belonging, not then appertaining to an enemy, pirate, or rebel, being convicted of any such offence, by the sentence of a court martial, shall suffer death.

Steering and conducting ships, &c.

XXVI. Care shall be taken in the conducting and steering of any of his Majesty's ships, that through wilfulness, negligence, or other defaults, no ship be stranded, or run upon any rocks or sands, or split, or hazarded, upon pain, that such as shall be found guilty therein, be punished by death, or such other punishment as the offence by a court martial shall be judged to deserve.

Sleeping, negligence, and forsaking a station.

XXVII. No person in or belonging to the fleet shall sleep upon his watch, or negligently perform the duty inposed on him, or forsake his station, upon pain of death, or such other punishment as a court martial shall think fit to impose, and as the circumstance of the case shall require.

Murder.

XXVIII. All murders committed by any person in the fleet, shall be punished with death, by the sentence of a court martial.

Sodomy.

XXIX. If any person in the fleet, shall commit the unnatural and detestable sin of buggery or sodomy, with man or beast, he shall be punished with death, by the sentence of a court martial.

Robbery.

XXX. All robbery committed by any person in the fleet, shall be punished with death, or otherwise, as a court martial upon consideration of circumstances shall find meet.

False musters.

XXXI. Every officer or other person in the fleet, who shall knowingly make or sign a false muster or muster-book, or who shall command, counsel, or procure the making or signing thereof, or who shall aid or abet any other person in the making or signing thereof, shall, upon proof of any such offence being made before a court martial, be cashiered, and rendered incapable of further employment in his Majesty's naval service.

Apprehending and keeping criminals. Bringing offenders to punishment.

XXXII. No provost martial belonging to the fleet shall refuse to apprehend any criminal, whom he shall be authorized by legal warrant to apprehend; or to receive or keep any prisoner committed to his charge; or wilfully suffer him to escape, being once in his custody; or dismiss him without lawful order; upon pain of such punishment as a court martial shall deem him to deserve. And all captains, officers, and others in the fleet, shall do their endeavour to detect, apprehend, and bring to punishment all offenders, and shall assist the officers appointed for that purpose therein, upon pain of being proceeded against, and punished by a court martial, according to the nature and degree of the offence.

Behaving unbecoming an officer.

XXXIII. If any flag officer, captain, or commander, or lieutenant belonging to the fleet, shall be convicted before a court martial, of behaving in a scandalous, infamous, cruel, oppressive, or fraudulent manner, unbecoming the character of an officer, he shall be dismissed from his Majesty's service.

Mutiny, desertion, disobedience when on shore, in the king's dominions.

XXXIV. Every person being in actual service, and full pay, and part of the crew in or belonging to any of his Majesty's ships or vessels of war, who shall be guilty of mutiny, desertion, or disobedience to any lawful command, in any part of his Majesty's dominions on shore, when in actual service, relative to the fleet, shall be liable to be tried by a court martial, and suffer the like punishment for every such offence, as if the same had been committed at sea, on board any of his Majesty's ships or vessels of war.

Crimes committed on shore out of the king's dominions.

XXXV. If any person who shall be in actual service, and full pay, in his majesty's ships and vessels of war, shall commit upon the shore, in any place or places out of his majesty's dominions, any of the crimes punishable by these articles and orders, the person so offending shall be liable to be tried and punished for the same, in like manner to all intents and purposes, as if the said crimes had been committed at sea, on board any of his Majesty's ships or vessels of war.

Crimes not mentioned in this act.

XXXVI. All other crimes, not capital, committed by any person or persons in the fleet, which are not mentioned in this act, or for which no punishment is hereby directed to be inflicted, shall be punished according to the laws and customs in such cases used at sea.

Further Reading

A great deal has been written about the *Bounty* since Bligh brought home the news of the mutiny. A full bibliography would include several hundred titles of published books and articles and many more references to the manuscript material in various public libraries and private collections around the world. The following is a highly selective and brief guide to the more important items in *Bounty* literature.

MANUSCRIPTS

Captain Bligh's *Log of HMS Bounty* (used by Barrow) is in the Public Record Office, London (Adm 55/151). It was first published in 1937 by Golden Cockerel Press in two volumes (limited edition). A facsimile edition was published in 1976 by Genesis Publications (limited edition). A popular edition has been published by Bowker and Bertram, Sussex: *Mutiny!! Aboard H.M. Armed Transport 'Bounty' in 1789*, edited by R. M. Bowker. Bligh's private Log (one volume is missing) is in the Mitchell Library, Sydney (ML Safe 1/46).

The Journal manuscripts of James Morrison are in the Mitchell Library, Sydney: Manuscript 1 is titled: 'Memorandums and Particulars respecting the Bounty and her Crew' (ML Safe 1/33); Manuscript 2 is known as the *Journal* (ML Safe 1/42). Apart from the extracts in Barrow and those mentioned below, only the main journal has so far been published: *The Journal of James Morrison Boatswain's Mate of the Bounty describing the Mutiny & subsequent Misfortunes of the Mutineers together with an account of the Island of Tahiti*, edited by Owen Rutter, Golden Cockerel Press, London 1935.

A facsimile edition of both Morrison manuscripts and the manuscript notes of Bligh's 'Remarks on Morrison's Journal' (ML Safe 1/43) is to be published in 1980 by Genesis Publications, Guildford.

The correspondence between Captain Bligh and John and Francis Godolphin Bond, which George Mackaness published, is in a private collection and the National Maritime Museum, Greenwich. The material first appeared in a limited edition series (140 copies) but has recently been re-published by Review Publications of Dubbo, NSW, Australia, in their Australian Historical Monographs series as: 'Fresh Light on Bligh: Some Unpublished Correspondence', edited by George Mackaness, Vol. V (new series) 1976. Mackaness also edited extracts from Lieutenant Bond's Log Book on HMS *Providence* and they can be found in: *Journal and Proceedings of the Royal Australian Historical Society* 1960, Vol. XLVI, pp 24–66.

The minutes of the *Warrior* court-martial are in the Public Record Office, London (Adm 1/5367). These detail the charges against Bligh by Lieutenant Frazier. A copy of the 'Proceedings of a Court-Martial on Captain Joseph Short' is in the Mitchell Library (ML MS A85- Banks Papers, Brabourne Collection). The implications of this court-martial for Bligh is discussed in my *Bligh* (1978) Chapter 27. The court-martial of Lieutenant Kent is reported in *Naval Chronicle*, Vol 25, 1811, and in Marshall's *Royal Naval Biography*, Vol. 4, Part I, 1825. These courts-martial document the peculiarity of manner of Captain Bligh.

Extracts from Peter Heywood's manuscript Journal and George Stewart's manuscript Journal can be found among the private papers of Captain Edward Edwards, Admiralty Library, Fulham, London. Some of these extracts have been published in my *Bligh* (1978). They discuss the events in the *Bounty* after Christian took over and give a candid account of the breakdown of Christian's authority over some of the mutineers. This evidence should be set against the claims made in the *Appendix* (1794).

John Fryer (Master of the *Bounty*) wrote a 'Narrative' which has recently been published in facsimile by Genesis Publications (1979). Golden Cockerel Press published this manuscript, along with Bligh's voyage of the Bounty Launch, edited by Owen Rutter in 1934. Both these publications are limited editions. The original manuscript is in the United Service Institute, London.

BOOKS AND ARTICLES

Barney, Stephen, *Minutes of the Proceedings of the Court-Martial . . . on Ten Persons charged with Mutiny on Board His Majesty's Ship the Bounty with an Appendix containing A full Account of the real Causes and Circumstances of that unhappy Transaction, the most material of which have hitherto been withheld from the Public*, London, 1794. This was republished by J. M. Dent (London) and E. P. Dutton (New York) in the Everyman's Library Series in 1938: *A Book of the 'Bounty' and Selections from Bligh's Writings*, edited by George Mackaness. Edward Christian's *Appendix* is one of the key documents of the *Bounty* story: it states the case against Bligh as a commander. Barney's minutes only cover the evidence for the prosecution.

Bartrum, Mr, *Proceedings of A General Court-Martial . . . for the Trial of Lieut.-Col. Geo. Johnston . . . on A Charge of Mutiny . . . for Deposing . . . William Bligh, Esq.*, London, 1811. This is a very rare item. It details the events of the 'Rum Rebellion' in New South Wales in 1808 when Bligh was the Governor.

Beaglehole, John C., *Captain Cook and Captain Bligh*, D. E. Collins Lecture, University of Wellington, New Zealand, 1967. A brief comparative study of these two famous seamen by the world's authority on Captain Cook. It does not flatter Bligh.

Belcher, Lady (Diana), *The Mutineers of the Bounty and their Descendants in Pitcairn and Norfolk Islands,* London, 1870. Also published by Harper of New York in 1871. Diana Belcher was Captain Heywood's stepdaughter. She made some use of the Morrison manuscript and also provided a different view to Barrow's criticism of the pastoral stewardship of the Reverend Nobbs.

Bligh, William, *A Narrative of the Mutiny on board His Majesty's Ship Bounty; and the subsequent voyage of a part of the crew in the ship's boat, from Tofoa, one of the Friendly Islands, to Timor, a Dutch Settlement in the East Indies,* London, 1790. Barrow quotes from this account, written immediately after Bligh returned to Britain. It has been reproduced in the Everyman's Library edition, edited by George Mackaness, mentioned above.

Bligh, William (and Burney, James), *A Voyage to the South Sea, undertaken by command of His Majesty, for the purpose of Conveying the Bread-Fruit Tree to the West Indies, in His Majesty's Ship the Bounty, commanded by Lieutenant William Bligh* . . . London, 1792. This gives Bligh's full account of the *Bounty* voyage as prepared for press by Captain James Burney and Sir Joseph Banks. It has been republished several times: in the Everyman's edition, 1938; edited by Laurence Irving (Methuen & Co), London, 1936; edited by Milton Rugoff (Signet Classics) New York, 1962; edited by Nathan R. Teitel (Airmont Classics) New York, 1965.

Bligh, William, *An Answer to Certain Assertions contained in the Appendix to a Pamphlet,* London, 1794. This was Bligh's answer to Edward Christian (which provoked: *A Short Reply to Capt. William Bligh's Answer,* London, 1795). Bligh's *Answer* is in the Everyman's Library edition, 1938. The *Short Reply* was reproduced in facsimile by the Australiana Society in 1952 in a limited edition (Georgian House, Melbourne).

Darby, Madge, *Who Caused the Mutiny on the 'Bounty'?* Angus and Robertson, Sydney, 1965. The first book to explore the comment in Barrow about the strange lack of commitment of Midshipman Edward Young during the mutiny. She also was the first to raise the spectre of homosexuality as a possible cause of the mutiny.

Danielsson, Bengt, *What Happened on the Bounty,* Allen & Unwin, London, 1962. Excellent value, particularly for its details of the Tahitian social and political structure at the time of the *Bounty*'s visit.

David, Andrew C. F., 'Broughton's schooner and the *Bounty* mutineers', *Mariner's Mirror,* Vol. 63, pp 207–13. Refutes Barrow's account of the fate of Morrison's schooner.

Du Rietz, Rolf, *The Causes of the Bounty Mutiny: some comments on a book by Madge Darby,* Uppsala, 1965, in *Studia Bountyana,* Vol. 1. This and its companion volume: *The Causes of the Bounty Mutiny: a short reply to Mr. Rolf Du Rietz's comments,* Uppsala 1966, *Studia Bountyana,* Vol. 2., were published as Limited Editions and are among the most important of the post-war books on the *Bounty.* Du Rietz has been most emphatic about the importance of the Bond correspondence published by Mackaness.

Du Rietz, Rolf, *Note sur L'Histoire des Manuscrits de James Morrison* (in French), introduction to *Journal de James Morrison: second maitre a bord de la 'Bounty',* Musee de l'Homme, Paris, 1966. An authoritative study of the origins of the Morrison manuscripts.

Du Reitz, Rolf, *Thoughts on the Present State of Bligh Scholarship,* Uppsala, *Banksia,* (Vol. 1 (limited edition).

Edward, Edwards and Hamilton, George, *Voyage of HMS 'Pandora', despatched to arrest the mutineers of the 'Bounty' in the South Seas, 1790–91, being the narratives of Captain Edward Edwards RN, the commander, and George Hamilton, the surgeon; with introduction and notes by Basil Thomson,* London, 1915. This is an account of the *Pandora*'s voyage.

Gould, R. T., 'Bligh's Notes on Cook's Voyage' *Mariners' Mirror,* Vol. 14, 1928

Kennedy, Gavin, *Bligh,* Duckworth, London, 1978. A full length biography of Bligh, using the manuscript sources and the literature. Contains a detailed bibliography of over 300 items.

Knight, C., 'H.M. Armed Vessel *Bounty*', *Mariner's Mirror,* Vol. 22, no. 2. April, 1936, pp 183–99. The most authoritative study of the *Bounty* as a ship.

Lee, Ida, *Captain Bligh's Second Voyage to the South Sea,* Longman's London, 1920. The standard work on Bligh's voyage in the *Providence,* immediately after the *Bounty* voyage. Bligh's *Log of the Providence* was published in facsimile in 1976 by Genesis Publications, Guildford, in a limited edition.

Lloyd, Christopher, *Mr. Barrow of the Admiralty: A Life of Sir John Barrow 1764–1848,* Collins, London, 1970. An excellent biography of this talented man.

Mackaness, George, *The Life of Vice-Admiral William Bligh, RN, FRS,* Angus and Robertson, Sydney, 1931, in two volumes; an American single volume edition was published by Farrar & Rinehart, New York, n.d., and a slightly revised edition appeared in 1951 (Angus & Robertson). The first scholarly biography of Bligh.

McKee, Alexander, *The Truth About the Mutiny on the Bounty,* Mayflower, London, 1961. One of the most hostile accounts of Bligh as a commander.

Marshall, John, *Royal Naval Biography, or, Memories of the Services of all the Flag-Officers, Superannuated Rear-Admirals, Retired-Captains, Post-Captains and Commanders . . .* Longman, London, 1825, Vol. II, Part II, pp 747–97. The entry for Peter Heywood contains his version of the events leading to the mutiny and takes many extracts from Morrison's manuscript though his text differs from those in the Mitchell Library.

Maude, H. E., 'In Search of a Home: From the mutiny to Pitcairn Island', *The Journal of the Polynesian Society*, Vol. 68, no. 2, June, 1958, pp 106–16.

Montgomerie, H. S. *William Bligh of the 'Bounty' in Fact and Fable*, Williams & Norgate, London, 1937. Perhaps the most pro-Bligh biography published.

Murray, Thomas Boyles, *Pitcairn: the Island, the People, and the Pastor; with a short account of the mutiny of the Bounty*, Society for Promoting Christian Knowledge, London, 1853. Probably the most often published of all books on the *Bounty*.

Rutter, Owen, *The Court-Martial of the 'Bounty' Mutineers*, edited with an introduction and notes, William Hodge, Edinburgh, 1931, Notable British Trials Series. A transcription of the minutes of the court-martial (Public Record Office, Adm 1/5330) which gives both defence and prosecution evidence; compare with Barney, above.

Rutter, Owen, *Turbulent Journey: a life of William Bligh, Vice-Admiral of the Blue*, Nicholson and Watson, London, 1936. One of the best biographies of Bligh. Rutter had a thorough knowledge of the manuscript source material from his editorial work for Golden Cockerel Press in the 1930s.

Silverman, David, *Pitcairn Island*, World Publishing, Cleveland, Ohio, 1967. A first-class history of the island.

Smith, D. Bonner, 'Some Remarks about the Mutiny of the Bounty', *Mariner's Mirror*, Vol. 22, no. 2, 1936, April, pp 200–37, and 'More Light on Bligh and the Bounty', *Mariner's Mirror*, Vol. 23, no. 2, 1937, April, pp 210–28. Two excellent articles on aspects of the mutiny.

Smyth, W. H., 'Letter to Editor', *United Service Journal*, 1829, II, pp 366–67; 'Sketch of the career of the late Captain Peter Heywood', Ibid, 1831, I, pp 468–81; 'The Bounty Again!', Ibid, 1831, III, pp 305–14. Smyth was violently anti-Bligh. His hostility is unrestrained.

Walters, Stephen, 'The Literature of Bligh', *Sea Breezes*, Vol. 50, October, 1976, pp 608–11.

Wilkinson, C. S., *The Wake of the Bounty*, Cassel, London, 1953. Discusses the return of Fletcher Christian to Cumberland and the role of William Wordsworth and Samuel Coleridge in the 'cover up'.

Illustrations Acknowledgments

Please note that the following abbreviations have been adopted for the major sources of illustration. National Maritime Museum, London (NMM); National Portrait Gallery, London (NPG); Mitchell Library, Sydney, Australia (ML); Public Records Office, London (PRO).

Maps drawn by Eugene Fleury.

Index

Index references to the main narrative are given in roman type (123). References to people, places and events mentioned in captions are given in italic type (*123*).

THE MUTINY OF THE BOUNTY

has been set in Sabon by Tameside Filmsetting Limited, Ashton-under-Lyne, England. In 1960, Jan Tschichold was commissioned by a group of German master printers to create a typeface suitable for offset and letterpress printing, which could be adapted to both metal and photocomposition. Named after the Lyons typefounder, Sabon was the result. Its roots lie in the classic sixteenth-century faces of Claude Garamond, but Tschichold skillfully reworked the lighter designs making them suitable for modern printing techniques.

The book was printed on Hopper Sunray Vellum Natural and bound by Halliday Lithograph, West Hanover, Massachusetts, with jackets and color inserts by Rae Lithographers, Cedar Grove, New Jersey. The illustrations were selected and captioned by Gavin Kennedy, with picture research by Anne-Marie Ehrlich. Designed by Patrick Yapp, it was produced by Russel Sharp Limited, Horsham, West Sussex, England.

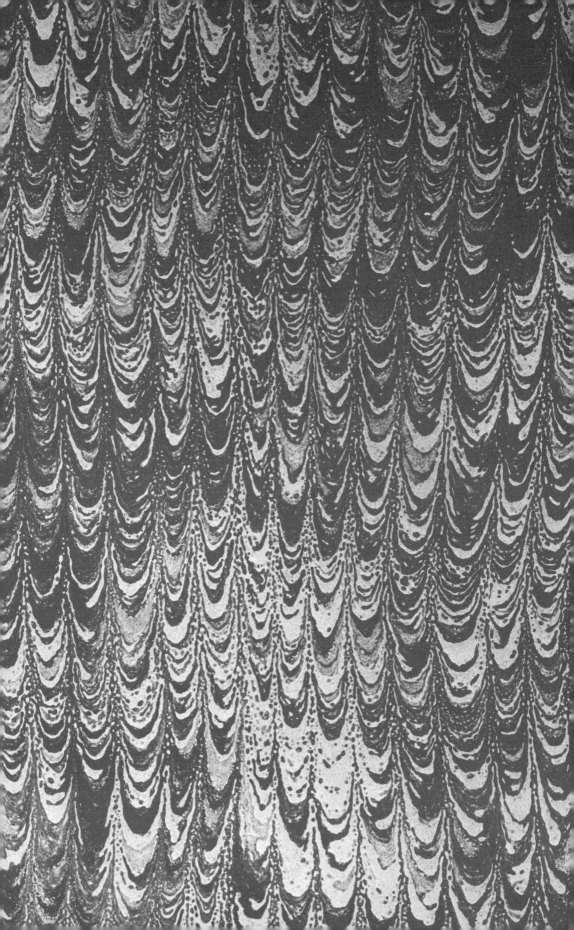